Welcome, Class of 2019!

As you begin this new and exciting chapter of your life at The Ohio State University, The Buckeye Book Community (BBC) is your first opportunity to engage with, contribute to and learn from the vibrant **community of learners** who will help make Ohio State your new home away from home.

This year's BBC selection, *The Good Food Revolution* by Will Allen, tells the true story of a pioneering urban farmer who strives to make his dream become a reality. All entering students are expected to read this book before returning to campus in August. When you return in the fall, you will discuss the book with your peers, advisors and professors, and engage with Mr. Allen when he visits the campus during your first semester.

First Year Experience is here to help you make the most of your first year, and the BBC is an important first step. This common reading program helps you **build strong connections** on campus and encourages you to **grapple with new ideas**. You'll share this experience with the entire first-year class as you're introduced to the expectation that Buckeyes cultivate the life of the mind, both in and out of the classroom.

We are excited for you to join our campus-wide conversation about *The Good Food Revolution*. Happy reading!

Sincerely,

Bernie Savarese

Director of Orientation
and First Year Experience

Check out
fye.osu.edu/bbc.html
for guiding questions
and details about BBC
activities this fall on the
Columbus campus.

#buckeyebook   #new2osu

THE
GOOD FOOD
REVOLUTION

∾

Growing Healthy Food,
People, and Communities

WILL ALLEN
with Charles Wilson

AVERY

an imprint of Penguin Random House

An imprint of Penguin Random House LLC
375 Hudson Street
New York, NY 10014

Previously published as a Gotham Books hardcover edition

First trade paperback printing, July 2013

Copyright © 2012 by William E. Allen

Most Avery books are available at special quantity discounts for bulk purchase for sales
promotions, premiums, fundraising, and educational needs. Special books or book excerpts also
can be created
to fit specific needs. For details, write SpecialMarkets@penguinrandomhouse.com.

The Library of Congress has cataloged the hardcover edition of this book as follows:
Allen, Will, 1949–
The good food revolution : growing healthy food, people, and communities / Will Allen with
Charles Wilson.
p. cm.
ISBN 978-1-59240-710-1 (HC) 978-1-59240-760-6 (PBK)
1. Urban agriculture—Social aspects. 2. Food supply—Social aspects.
3. Alternative agriculture. 4. Sustainable agriculture. 5. Community gardens.
I. Wilson, Charles, 1974– II. Title.
S494.5.U72A45 2012
631.5—dc23
2011045592
Special Markets 978-1-10198-400-0
Not for Resale

Printed in the United States of America

10 9 8 7 6 5 4 3 2 1

Set in Baskerville MT Std and Clarendon LT Std
Designed by Sabrina Bowers

To Cyndy, Erika, Jason, and Adrianna,
who braved this journey with me,
and to my parents, Willie Mae and O.W.,
whose wisdom helped guide the way.

In dirt is life.

GEORGE WASHINGTON CARVER

CONTENTS

PART 1 · ROOTS

PART 2 · SWEAT EQUITY

PART 3 · THE REVOLUTION

FOREWORD

By Eric Schlosser

Any discussion of race in American society seems, increasingly, to be taboo. The election of an African American president has led many to argue that the color of a person's skin has become irrelevant, discrimination is a thing of the past, and we now live amid a post-racial culture. In my view, that's wishful thinking. A long list of contrary arguments can be made—but the most useful, in this foreword, would be to mention how this country has, since its inception, produced its food. The history of agriculture in the United States is largely a history of racial exploitation. From the slavery that formed the rural economy of the South to the mistreatment of migrant farm workers that continues to this day, our food has too often been made possible by someone else's suffering. And that someone else tends not to be white.

Will Allen knows this history all too well. His family lived it. His parents escaped sharecropping, the form of servitude that replaced the plantation system after the Civil War, and like millions of other African Americans, they fled north. Their Great Migration was often an attempt not only to seek a better life in the city, but also to

leave behind the rural customs and trappings and mindset associated with centuries of hardship and pain. The great tragedy for
many African Americans, as Allen explains in this book, is that in
losing touch with the land and with traditions handed down for generations, they also lost an important set of skills: how to grow and
prepare healthy food. By heading north they frequently traded one
set of problems for another.

It's no coincidence that the epidemic of diet-related illnesses now
sweeping the country—obesity, diabetes, high blood pressure, heart
disease, strokes—are harming blacks the most. They are more likely
to be poor, to live in communities without supermarkets, farmers
markets, or produce stores. But their neighborhoods are crammed
with fast food restaurants, liquor stores, and convenience stores selling junk food. These are toxic environments when it comes to finding healthy food. Industry apologists like to argue that our decisions
about what to eat are the result of "personal responsibility" and
"freedom of choice." A recent study in Southern California contra-
dicts that sort of argument. It found that a person's life expectancy
can be predicted on the basis of his or her zip code. The wealthy in
Beverly Hills are likely to live ten years longer than the poor in
South Central Los Angeles. It's hard to place the blame solely on
your personal choices, when life expectancy can be determined in
large part by something that none of us can control: the neighborhood in which we were born.

Today the two leading causes of preventable death in the United
States are smoking and eating too much unhealthy food. When both
of those habits became unpopular among the white, well-educated,
upper-middle class, the companies that sell cigarettes and junk food
focused their marketing efforts on African Americans, people of
color, and the urban poor. Long after smoking was linked to cancer
and heart disease, the tobacco companies aggressively sought new
customers in minority communities. An internal marketing memo
by an executive at Brown & Williamson, the company that once sold
Kool cigarettes, explained the industry's thinking. "Clearly the sole
reason for B&W's interest in the black and Hispanic communities is

the actual and potential sales of B&W products," he wrote. "This relatively small and tightly knit minority community can work to B&W's marketing advantage, if exploited properly." Thanks to that sort of thinking, and the cigarette advertising that has flooded African American communities, the lung cancer rates among blacks are much higher than among whites. As the fast food chains pursue a similar strategy, disproportionately marketing their products to African Americans and fueling the obesity rate in low-income communities, the health disparity between blacks and whites continues to grow.

At Growing Power, the organization led by Will Allen, you will find a completely different sort of mentality. Instead of trying to earn profits by harming the poor, it hopes to create an alternative to the nation's centralized industrial food system. It's working to teach people how to grow food, cook food, and embrace a way of living that's sustainable. Allen has transformed a dilapidated set of greenhouses in downtown Milwaukee into the headquarters of an urban farming network that now operates in seven states. He has developed innovative methods of growing fruits and vegetables, of producing fish through aquaculture, and of using earthworms to transform waste products into fertilizer—all in the heart of a major city. To say that Allen's thinking is unconventional would be an understatement. But that's what has made him a pioneer of urban agriculture and a leader in today's food movement. He understood, long before most, that America's food system is profoundly broken—and that a new one, locally based and committed to social justice, must replace it.

The new farming techniques being perfected at Growing Power are not yet reliably profitable. This fact does not diminish their importance and must be viewed in a larger perspective. America's current agricultural system was hardly created by free market forces. Between 1995 and 2011, American farmers received about $277 billion in federal subsidies. And the wealthiest 10 percent of farmers received 75 percent of those subsidies. Almost two-thirds of American farmers didn't receive any subsidies at all. In addition to getting massive support from taxpayers, the current system is imposing enormous costs on society—costs that aren't included on the balance sheets of the major fast food and agribusiness companies. Last year the revenues of the fast food industry were about $168 billion, an impressive sum. But estimates of the cost of foodborne illnesses in the United States and of the nation's obesity epidemic, as calculated by researchers at Georgetown and Cornell universities, are even higher. Those two costs alone add up to about $320 billion. By any rational measure, this industrial food system isn't profitable or self-sufficient. Although Growing Power receives foundation grants, it's creating a system that will be sustainable. And the good that Growing Power's doing in the communities it serves—the heart attacks and strokes and hospital visits it helps people to avoid, the sense of empowerment it gives, the families it brings together—represent a form of social profit that's impossible to quantify.

This book tells Will Allen's story and lays out his farming philosophy. Instead of running from the past or trying to deny it, Allen has confronted the dark legacy of slavery and sharecropping. He has tried to reconcile the rural and urban experiences of African Americans, imagining a future that can combine the best elements of the two. He has spent years working among the poor, preaching a message of compassion and self-reliance. I admire what Will Allen has achieved. And I hope others, many others, will soon follow in his path.

THE
GOOD FOOD
REVOLUTION

Willie Mae Kenner

ESCAPE

She held a one-way ticket.

In December of 1934, my mother, Willie Mae Kenner, stood in the waiting room for colored people at the train station in Batesburg, South Carolina. She was twenty-five years old. Her two young boys, my older brothers, were at her side. She was heading to Union Station in Washington, D.C. She was trying to escape our family's long history in agriculture.

I imagine her on this day. Willie Mae was known to be beautiful and headstrong. Many local men had called her "fine"—she had strong legs, smooth skin, a round and lovely face, and thoughtful eyes. She also had dreams that were too big for her circumstances. She and her husband, and seven of her nine siblings, were share-croppers: tenant farmers who gave up half of the crop they planted and harvested each season in exchange for the right to pick it. It was the only life that she had known.

My mother held different hopes in her heart, both for herself and her children. She had fought to obtain a teaching degree from Schofield Normal and Industrial School, a two-year college initially set up after the Civil War by Quakers, to educate free slaves. She wanted to be a teacher. Her family noticed that when she was required to pick cotton or asparagus, she did the work without complaint. Yet she wore a long, flowing dress on top of her work shirt and pants while in the fields. It was as if she wanted to find a way to give grace and dignity to work that often provided neither.

From the train station in Batesburg, Willie Mae was trying to escape asparagus and cotton. At the time, the South was still in the thrall of "Jim Crow": the rigid set of laws set up after the Civil War to separate whites and blacks in almost every part of public life. The 1896 Supreme Court decision in *Plessy v. Ferguson*—allowing "separate but equal" facilities for black people—meant that my mother could not share the same train car with white passengers. She and her children could not even wait in the same area for the train to come. Her train car sat directly behind the coal car, where men shoveled the rocks into the roaring engine. The smoke of the engine blew through the car's windows and seeped into her clothes. She and her two boys would need to use a bathroom marked not "Men" or "Women" but "C," for "Colored."

Her journey was to take her to the nation's capital, where Willie Mae planned to reunite with her husband, James Kenner. His friends called him "Major," for reasons I never understood. He had left South Carolina after falling into debt. During the Great Depression, the price for cotton had dropped to only 5 cents a pound—down from 35 cents only a decade earlier. Major had found himself owing more to his landowner at the end of the planting season than when he began it. Sharecropping had begun to feel like slavery under another name.

"There's no money here," he told my mother shortly before leaving.

Major found a small place to live in Ken Gar, an all-black neighborhood on the edge of Kensington, Maryland, ten miles from the White House. He sent word to my mother to come. Major was now building houses instead of planting crops. Willie Mae had never seen the place she was going to call home.

My mother left the South before I was born. I know from relatives that she decided against boarding her departing train at the nearest station, in Ridge Spring, likely out of concern that local people would talk about her. When I was growing up, she rarely spoke of her Southern past, as if it were a secret that was best not talked about in polite company. She told my brothers and me that she liked the taste of every vegetable except asparagus—she simply had picked too much of it.

I have wondered what passed through her mind when the train pulled out of Batesburg. As the locomotive edged north out of South Carolina, she would have seen from the windows the life she had known. She would have seen the long-leaf pine trees, the sandy soil, and the fields that yielded cotton and parsnips and cabbage and watermelon. She would have seen other sharecroppers at work, their clothing heavy with sweat.

Willie Mae knew how to sustain her family in South Carolina. She had learned from her mother how to bed sweet potatoes and garden peas and cabbage and onions in the early spring. When the full heat of summer came, she had learned how to plant turnips and eggplants and cucumbers and hot peppers and okra and cantaloupes. She had learned how to take all the parts of a hog that the men slaughtered and turn it into souse (a pickled hog's head cheese), scrapple (a hog meatloaf), liver pudding, or a dish called "chitlin' strut"—fried pig intestines. She had learned in the late autumn how to can peaches and sauerkraut and pecans and yams for the cold season.

She was leaving for a city where it was uncertain if any of the skills she had—or any of the dreams she harbored—would matter.

All across the South, other sharecroppers were making the decision to uproot and go. My mother was only one of six million

African Americans in "The Great Migration," an exodus from the rural South to Northern cities. Of my mother's nine brothers and sisters who were born in Ridge Spring, South Carolina, seven left from the 1930s to 1950 for a new life in New York, New Jersey, or Maryland. Her family left farming in search of dignity. They left crop rows for sidewalks. Dirt roads for pavement. Woodstoves for gas ranges.

Half a century after Willie Mae left Ridge Spring, in an unlikely development, I returned to a profession that she and her family had tried so hard to leave behind.

Will Allen

RETURN

I am an urban farmer.

The poet Maya Angelou has said that you can never leave home. *It's in your hair follicles,* she said. *It's in the bend of your knees. The arch of your foot. You can't leave home. You can take it, and you can rearrange it.*

This was true for my mother. It is true for me. My family left the South, but it never entirely left us. In a matter of three decades in the twentieth century, the Great Migration transformed the African American experience from a rural to an urban one. The generation of African Americans born in the wake of that migration—my generation—would live in a world very different from that of our ancestors. In that transition, we lost the agricultural skills that had once been our birthright.

In 1920, there were more than 900,000 farms operated by African

Americans in the United States. Today, there are only 18,000 black people who name farming as their primary occupation. Black farmers cultivate less than half a percent of the country's farmland. The question is whether this should be called progress. Most black people who left agriculture in the twentieth century did so out of economic self-interest. My mother and Major Kenner were among tens of thousands of sharecroppers who saw no future in the rural South and who often talked about their past there with shame. They wished for a better life for their children.

Some black leaders encouraged my parents' generation to leave the land as a way of self-improvement. At the turn of the twentieth century, the great black intellectual W. E. B. DuBois had urged African Americans to find success through a liberal education.

"The Negro race," DuBois wrote, "is going to be saved by its exceptional men."

With this position, DuBois found himself in a long-standing argument with the educator and writer Booker T. Washington, who argued that black people would be better served by the development of practical abilities. He thought that African Americans should make an effort to improve their own position from within—by developing skills for self-sufficiency and by helping one another.

"Agriculture is, or has been, the basic industry of nearly every race or nation that has succeeded," Washington wrote. "Dignify and glorify common labor," he said elsewhere. "It is at the bottom that we must begin, not the top."

DuBois's ideas won. His vision helped give us a world where it was possible to have Martin Luther King, Jr., Jackie Robinson, Henry Louis Gates, Jr., Colin Powell, Ben Carson, John Lewis, and Barack Obama. African Americans proved their worth in corporate boardrooms, in Ivy League universities, on sports fields, in operating rooms, in the halls of Congress, and in the White House. This "Talented Tenth," as DuBois called top-performing African Americans, provided blacks with role models and reasons for pride.

Yet there never was a place among DuBois's Talented Tenth for farmers. And for all of the progress in civil rights in the past several decades, there is one area in which we have stepped backward. Great disparities have grown in the physical health of our people. This change has come directly in the wake of the departure of black farmers from their land.

Nearly half of African Americans born in the year 2000 are expected to develop type II diabetes. Four out of every ten African American men and women over the age of twenty have high blood pressure. Blacks are 30 percent more likely to die young from heart disease than whites. And while some suffer from the effects of too much unhealthy food, others go hungry. Almost one out of every six households in the United States will find themselves fearful sometime this year of not having enough food to eat.

These problems are not limited to one race, and they are not owing simply to faults of willpower or personal discipline. They are the symptoms of a broken food system. In inner-city communities throughout the United States, it is easier—and often less expensive—to buy a Twinkie or frosted cupcakes or a box of fried chicken than fresh vegetables or fruits. Our current generation of young people rarely eat fresh foods, don't know how to grow or prepare them, and in many cases, can't even identify them. They have become entirely dependent on a food system that is harming them.

I believe that equal access to healthy, affordable food should be a civil right—every bit as important as access to clean air, clean water, or the right to vote. While there are many reasons for the decline in number of black farmers, one of the most important is that they are almost always small farmers. They have suffered the same fate as other small farmers. Over the past fifty years, a new food system has helped push them off their land.

This system came to value quantity over quality, uniformity over diversity, and profit over stewardship. Farmers were encouraged to plant commodity crops like soybeans or corn from fencerow to fencerow, and to get big or get out. There was a relentless pursuit of cheapness over other values, and food came to be made by automated machines and chemical processes. Men in laboratories dreamed up foodstuffs that were calibrated with precise amounts of sugar and fat, and that were delivered to customers by airplanes and trucks in cardboard and plastic and cellophane. The farmer became less important than the food scientist, the distributor, the marketer, and the corporation. In 1974, farmers took home 36 cents of every dollar spent on food in the United States. Today, they get only 14 cents.

This is not the right path. It is endangering the health of our young people. It has brought us fewer jobs in agriculture, unhealthier diets, and a centralized control structure that has made people feel powerless over their food choices. It has stripped people of the dignity of knowing how to provide for themselves on the most basic level. It has given us two very different food systems—one for the rich and another for the poor. A large gap has opened between those who have access to nutritional education and cage-free eggs and organic mesclun greens and those whose easy options are fried chicken joints and tubs of ice cream and shrink-wrapped packages of cheap ground beef.

Food should be a cause for celebration, something that should bring people together. The work of my adult life has been to heal the rift in our food system and to create alternative ways of growing and distributing fresh food. My return to farming was a kind of homecoming. As a young man, I felt ashamed of my parents' sharecropping past. I didn't like the work of planting and harvesting that I was made to do as a child. I thought it was hard and offered little reward. I fought my family's history. Yet the desire to farm hid inside me.

It hid in my feet. They wanted the moist earth beneath them. It hid in my hands. They wanted to be callused and rough and caked with soil. It hid in my heart. I missed the rhythms of agriculture. I felt a desire for the quiet of the predawn and the feeling of physical self-worth and productivity that I only felt after a day when I had harvested a field or had sown one. For a long time, I had put my faith in different values. I had sought a life in professional basketball and then in the corporate world.

In my forties, I left that life behind. I opened my own city vegetable stand, five blocks from Milwaukee's largest public housing project. I recognized the potential I had to do much more, even as I struggled financially to keep my operation open. I wanted to try to heal the broken food system in the inner-city community where my market operated.

So I began to teach young people from the projects and the inner city how to grow food. I conveyed the life lessons that agriculture teaches. Through trial and error, my staff and I developed new models for growing food intensively and vertically in cities. We found ways to make fresh fruits and vegetables available to people with little income. We created full-time agricultural jobs for inner-city youth. We began to teach people—young and old, black and white—how to grow vegetables in small spaces and reclaim some small control over their food choices. We found ways to redirect organic waste from city landfills, and to use it instead to create fertile soil. We connected small farmers in Wisconsin to underserved markets in inner-city communities. We provided a space where corporate volunteers could work alongside black inner-city youth, hauling dirt, planting seeds, and harvesting together.

I did not anticipate how my work would grow, or how eager others would be to participate in it. Today, my urban farm produces forty tons of vegetables a year on three city acres. We provide fresh sprouts to thousands of students in the Milwaukee public school system, we distribute inexpensive market baskets of fresh fruits and vegetables to urban communities without grocery stores, and we raise one hundred thousand fish in indoor systems that resemble freshwater streams. We keep over five hundred egg-laying hens, and we have an apiary with fourteen beehives that provide urban honey. We maintain a retail store to sell fresh food to a community with few healthy options.

Our operation is far from perfect. But my staff and volunteers have become part of a hopeful revolution that is changing America's food system. This book is my story, and the story of our movement.

The back greenhouses of 5500 West Silver Spring Drive, 1993

PROMISES

In mid-life, I had arrived at that comfortable middle-class existence that so many in the Great Migration had wished for their children.

I was forty-three years old in January of 1993. I was driving in northwest Milwaukee in a company car on a frigid Wisconsin morning. I was on a sales run for the Procter & Gamble paper division. My job was to sell paper products: cases of Charmin toilet paper and Bounty paper towels and Puffs tissues. I wore a suit and tie. My long legs—I am six-foot-seven—were crammed up against the dashboard of a Chevrolet Malibu. The car seats were flecked with stray bits of fried chicken and donut residue. I had a good salary, a nice title, a generous retirement package.

I can't say, though, that I was happy. My adult working life had required several internal compromises. Before this job, I had worked a decade for the Marcus Corporation, managing half a dozen Kentucky Fried Chicken stores. Though I felt confident about my skills in business, my work had long felt like a project of my wallet rather than a project of my heart.

My chief competitors at Procter & Gamble were Kimberly-Clark and Scott Paper. My job required me to build good relationships with the managers of several dozen grocery stores in Milwaukee and Chicago. One of the expectations of my job was that I would maximize the "hip-to-eye" ratio of our products as compared to that of our competitors. Procter & Gamble wanted their products to sit on grocery shelves at the customers' hip-to-eye level, where they would be seen and most easily grabbed.

I needed Luvs to beat Huggies. I needed Puffs to beat Kleenex. Procter & Gamble's paper division kept track of how our products scored against our competition in each of my stores, and the company had several strategies to increase its market share. They asked me to try to obtain "movement numbers" from each grocery store manager. When analyzed, those numbers would allow us to see where products sold most briskly. Once I had those statistics in hand, young people in my corporate offices could go to their computers and craft a visual "planogram." This suggested where each product in a store could be stocked to increase sales. I presented our planograms to the grocery managers, and I offered Procter & Gamble's help resetting every item on their shelves—free of charge. I made the case in the manager's self-interest.

"You've got these products here that aren't selling," I'd say. "You're losing money. We'll restock them and get this thing fixed."

One of the essential things about the Procter & Gamble planogram was that it maximized the hip-to-eye ratio of Procter & Gamble's own products. So while I presented the planogram as being in the store's best interest, it was also always in my company's best interest. Kimberly-Clark and Scott sold their own planograms, so it was a very competitive business. My rivals often didn't like me because our company was powerful and I was often successful. One day, I heard a representative from Kimberly-Clark whisper under his breath as I passed by.

"There goes Procter & God," he said.

He thought that I was arrogant. I didn't care. I am a competitive man. I had stuffed myself into the shape of this job, and I was going to be true to my nature within its confines. I took some pride in the fact that I had won several sales awards. I had been responsible for one of the largest Pampers sales in the company's history—a single purchase to a grocery wholesaler of twenty-five thousand cases of diapers. I liked my colleagues and the man who hired me. Yet there was part of me that felt empty.

On this January day, as I was driving, I had a chance sighting that would allow me to consider the possibility of another life. I was traveling west on Silver Spring Drive in Milwaukee, on my way to speak to a manager at a grocery store. The avenue was an artery that connected the tony Milwaukee neighborhood of Whitefish Bay—sometimes called "White Folks' Bay"—with neighborhoods to its west, like Lincoln Park and Hampton Heights, that were poorer and black. The white and black communities were divided by the Milwaukee River.

I had never driven down this road before. I passed gas stations, an auto repair shop, churches, and a windowless convenience store offering cheap fried chicken. I drove past a gray Army Reserve training center. When I reached the intersection of West Silver Spring and Fifty-fourth Street, I saw a "For Sale" sign ahead of me on the right. It was painted on a four-by-four piece of plywood. The telephone number listed was a "286" number, which usually indicated a number for city government. The sign stood next to a row of greenhouses set back from the road. Those greenhouses really seemed out of place in this neighborhood. Attached to the one closest to the road was a small building—a shop?—with a concrete porch and an awning.

I tapped my brakes. I had only glimpsed the buildings for a few seconds as I passed. The sign intrigued me, though, because of an idea I had held quietly in my heart. I kept driving, slowly, and I didn't want to be late. Yet when I saw an opportunity ahead of me to make a U-turn, I returned quickly to the facility.

As I stepped out of the car, I saw five connected greenhouses stretched back away from the street. The glass in the front greenhouse was cracked in several places. I made out the shape of flowers through the humid windows. Outside hung a faded sign that read OLDE ENGLISH GREENHOUSE. At the back of a parking lot adjacent to the greenhouses there was a small red barn that looked like it belonged in the countryside. There was also vacant land in the rear of the property and a narrow yellow duplex on the other side of a parking lot.

I could not tell if anyone was inside the greenhouses or the shop, and I decided not to check. I took down the phone number on the sign. Later that afternoon, I called and got an answering machine on the Milwaukee city government's zoning and development committee. Through a friend who worked in real estate, I found out that the current tenants of the greenhouses and the shop were florists. They had fallen too far behind on their payments, and they were being evicted. When I finally reached someone with the city government, he asked me why I was calling.

"I am a farmer," I said. "I'm interested in the place as a market to sell my food."

∾

I was leading two lives. For several years, I had crammed a one-hundred-acre farm into the gaps of my corporate job. My farm had started small, as a hobby, but it had become outsized for a man whose salaried work was elsewhere. I grew on fifty acres owned by my wife's mother and on fifty acres that I leased in Oak Creek, Wisconsin, the town where I lived.

According to the 1990 census, I was one of only twenty-five black people in the entire state of Wisconsin to operate or manage a farm. From spring to fall, I often rose at 4 A.M. on weekdays to plant and harvest before changing clothes and heading to work. I returned home from work, changed clothes again, and watered or harvested late into the night. I was growing collard greens, curly-leaf mustard greens, slick-leaf mustard greens, turnip greens, corn, kale, Swiss chard, and tomatoes. I employed a few young people and some local Hmong farmers part-time as help.

The farm was kept alive by my own passion. I had learned the skills of planting and harvesting as a boy, from my parents. I was now growing more food than I knew how to sell. I gave much of it away to friends and family. I sold what I could out of the back of my pickup truck at weekend farmers markets. There was no significant money to be made from it. It was all I wanted to do.

When I saw the facility on West Silver Spring Drive, the place spoke to a dream I had. For the past year, I had been looking for a roadside stand to call my own.

A couple weeks after my telephone call to the Milwaukee zoning committee, a real-estate agent met me at the greenhouses. We parked our vehicles in a lot outside the red barn—the last remnant of an old farm that had once stood on that site. The agent began the tour by explaining that this two-acre plot sat in the middle of what used to be known as "Greenhouse Alley," a flower-growing district. The road directly north of West Silver Spring Drive was still called "Florist Avenue," though there were no longer any florists there.

As Milwaukee grew in the twentieth century, both north and west, the city absorbed the countryside. At one time, local farms had helped feed the residents of Milwaukee. Four blocks away, Wisconsin's largest public housing complex, called Westlawn, occupied seventy-five acres and contained more than three hundred housing units. That land had once been a single family farm. When the farmers were pushed out of the area, the agent explained, the floral industry had taken its place. Eventually, that industry was impacted by the growth of a global economy. Flowers began to be imported from South America, and local flower shops most often sold roses that had been flown in from Ecuador or Colombia. The florist who owned these greenhouses was the last to survive in Greenhouse Alley.

As I walked through the facility, I saw that the roofs of his greenhouses were linked together, forming one large structure that stretched back from the road. Rusting pin nails held in the glass panes. A ragged collection of flowers, cactuses, and bedding plants filled the greenhouses. There were holes in the glass and broken shards on the floor; many of the panes were slipping. Water from melted snow had dripped inside.

I was told that children across the street occasionally threw rocks at the glass roof and walls. The current tenant had tried without success to chase them away. The real estate agent said the city hoped that the new owner might cultivate a better relationship with the community.

We walked to the back of the property, behind the old red barn. Beside the barn was a slim yellow duplex that was included in the asking price. The shingled roof looked in need of repair. The lot outside included an acre of unused land bound by a chain-link fence. The land was overgrown with weeds and tall grass.

The whole place was a mess. But I could feel its potential. I knew from my drive through the neighborhood that I would not have any competition if I were to try to sell fresh fruits and vegetables there. The only other places I saw to buy food within a mile were a McDonald's, a Popeyes, and several convenience stores. I could provide parking on the street, and Silver Spring Drive seemed busy to me.

"I'm interested," I said.

The agent told me I had competition. A local congregation wanted to demolish the greenhouses and build a church on the site. If they were successful, the city would lose its last parcel of land zoned for agricultural use. I needed to convince the city's zoning and development committee that a produce stand would be better for the community than a church.

∾

A week later, I walked into city hall. I stood up before six committee members in a white conference room.

"My name is Will Allen," I began. "I am a farmer from Oak Creek."

I told the zoning and development committee that I wanted to create a farm stand. I said that a Kohl's grocery store had recently closed down the street from the greenhouses, and there was little access to healthy food in the area—despite the presence of the largest public housing project in Milwaukee. I said that it was my intention to hire local youth, as I had done in Oak Creek, where young people worked for me in the fields during the summer. I said that my three children had grown up on a farm with me and that it had taught them useful skills like hard work and self-discipline.

I continued, offering a vision of the role I hoped to play in a community I did not yet know. It was a hopeful presentation; it was also terribly naive. One of the aldermen listening on the committee was Don Richards. He had grown up on a farm in Sheboygan, a lakeside community north of Milwaukee. Don was rail thin with gray hair, and he sat silently as I gave my speech. After I finished, each committee member was allowed to ask questions. Don Richards spoke up.

"We have enough churches in our community," he said. "What you're planning to do is religion in itself."

Later that week, I received a call from the real estate agent who had given me my first tour of the greenhouses. He said that the board had approved my plan if I could come up with the financing. When I heard the news, I thought of Don Richards's faith in me. I thought his comment helped win the board's approval. He later told me what he was thinking.

"You made all of these outrageous promises," Don said. "I was taking a chance on you. But I didn't want you to make any more promises you couldn't keep."

ℳ

In 1993, my wife, Cyndy, and I had only a few savings from our nearly quarter of a century of marriage. We had paid for our son and two daughters to attend a private high school, and we were still paying for their college educations. Our daughter Adrianna, the youngest child, had recently left to attend New York University. To finance the purchase of the greenhouses, I would have to cash in my retirement savings and take out a mortgage. I knew it was a risk to abandon a secure income for something that had no guarantee of success. I felt confident, though, that I could make my business model work.

I left Procter & Gamble. From tapping out my 401(k) I obtained about $20,000 that I planned to use to cover some of my early operating costs. I would need an additional $70,000 to purchase the facility. The city recommended I turn to Firstar Bank, one of the few local banks that operated in low-income neighborhoods and communities of color. They had a branch not far from the greenhouses, at the corner of Fond du Lac and North Avenues. I had good credit at the time, and despite the novelty of the business I was proposing, I was approved without much difficulty.

Not long after I received the bank loan, I walked through the greenhouses again. The florists had trashed the place as they left—ripping out lighting fixtures and taking a generator that was supposed to have remained. There were holes in the glass that I had not seen before, and orange rust on the heating pipes.

I couldn't fix everything. My first priority was just to get the market open quickly to generate some revenue. Over the next few weeks, I made modest repairs. I swept and washed the concrete floors, which were cracked in places. I hired the last man in the Milwaukee area who knew how to repair greenhouses to fix the glass panes that were in most danger of falling. In the greenhouse nearest the road, I decided to paint the glass white to prevent the interior from getting too hot in the summer. I wanted this greenhouse to serve as my market. I didn't have the resources then to fix the other greenhouses, and I needed to focus on what was possible. To provide extra income, I also decided to lease out the facility's small shop to a florist friend for $1,000 a month. She wanted to service the funeral business and to work with FTD, the flowers-by-phone retailer. She hoped that with a low overhead, she could avoid the fate of the florist who preceded her.

I set my opening day for April 3, 1993. A friend painted me a sign on a piece of plywood: WILL'S ROADSIDE FARM MARKET. My brother-in-law had some T-shirts made up. They read: BIG WILL:

THE GUCCI OF GREENS. He called me the Gucci of Greens because he thought the spinach from my farm looked so luxurious, he said.

On the Saturday morning that I opened, I arrived with my son, Jason, and some friends before the sun came up. I had slept only a few hours that entire week, and I spent the night before we opened harvesting greens in the dark. I wanted my greens to be as fresh as possible. To supplement what I had grown, I ordered fruits and vegetables from other farmers. Many of those crops were Southern specialties: okra, butter beans, black-eyed peas (or "cowpeas," as I knew them as a boy, because they were colored like a Holstein). I barked directions to my son and friends who were helping me assemble the produce on tables.

"Stack 'em high and watch 'em fly!" I said.

I'd learned about the importance of good presentation in my years with Procter & Gamble. If you provided an image that evoked a bountiful harvest—a product spilling out of wicker baskets, for instance—people assumed it had to be good.

At Will's Roadside Farm Market, soon after it opened in 1993

When my friends and I finished readying the market, the sun was coming up. We prepared to open. Farming had taught me to have trust in the unseen. You plant for a harvest that you hope will arrive but that is never guaranteed. The opening of Will's Roadside Farm Market required a similar kind of faith. I hoped it would be rewarded.

Yet farming had also taught me to expect the unexpected. Two days of heavy rains could wash away a crop that you had worked on for weeks. A cruel drought could choke your plants, and they would come up stunted or withered. I didn't know yet what would become of my dream.

The back lot of Will's Roadside Farm Market, c. 1995

TRIAL BY FIRE

I started Will's Roadside Farm Market in 1993 for selfish reasons. In making the case for my business to the city's zoning committee, I said that I wanted to hire youth from the community. This was true. Yet if I were to be honest to myself, my greater desire was to be my own boss.

The experience of my first two years at the greenhouses, however, began to complicate these selfish wishes. I suffered financially in ways that I had not anticipated, and I was pushed to the brink of default on my loan. At the same time, I started to see a role I could play in the community where I had opened my shop.

Almost every small farmer I met was struggling in the 1990s. Most of them held down jobs outside of their farm work, to support their families. The state's agricultural economy was undergoing a great upheaval. Wisconsin would lose 200,000 acres of farmland in 1993 alone. Each year from 1978 to 1992, the state lost 1,000 to 1,500 individual farms. At the same time, the average farm in Wisconsin grew by seventy acres from the late 1950s to the early 1990s.

What I saw happening inside of Milwaukee helped me understand what was happening to small farmers in the countryside. The stretch of West Silver Spring Drive near my roadside stand had long been serviced by a Kohl's grocery store that closed in the late 1980s. At one time, there were roughly ten Kohl's grocers in Milwaukee—owned by a local family—and local farmers sold their produce directly to managers at these stores. When A&P bought Kohl's, however, local farmers no longer had these markets. Chain grocery stores almost always bought their produce from a handful of large regional wholesalers. The produce offered at wholesalers was almost always bought in bulk from large farms and flown in from a thousand or more miles away.

When A&P closed the former Kohl's supermarket along West Silver Spring Drive, it meant that McDonald's and a Popeyes fried chicken were the main food options for people in the community. During the 1970s and 1980s, hundreds of grocery stores closed in other African American neighborhoods throughout the United States as part of a tide of urban disinvestment. From 1978 to 1984 alone, Safeway closed more than six hundred stores located in inner cities, shifting its resources to suburban locations that could provide large parking lots and more affluent customers. Local farmers who wanted to reach urban communities were left without markets. A recent study of the food landscape in several states found that there were four times more grocery stores in neighborhoods with a majority white population than in neighborhoods that were primarily black.

I saw my farm stand's presence as an opportunity to fill an unmet demand. I wanted to help Wisconsin farmers reconnect with African American communities. Soon after my stand opened, I started something called the Rainbow Farmers Cooperative with a few farmer friends. African American farmers in the South have long established cooperatives as a way to support each other. During the civil rights era, for instance, black farmers near Memphis organized to share gasoline when fuel suppliers in the city discriminated against them. The idea of our cooperative was twofold. First, by banding together, we could have enough produce collectively to try to sell in bulk to the wholesalers. Secondly, I wanted to provide the farmers a chance to sell their produce at Will's Roadside. The name of our co-op reflected our diversity: I was black, one farmer was Hmong, and three of our members were white.

The early life of my farm stand brought days of optimism and weeks of doubt. A few weekends after we opened, I paid to have a local personality from black radio do a live broadcast at our facility. People crowded the market all day—some driving all the way across town to come—and I brought in $5,000 in gross sales on a single Saturday.

There were expenses, though, that I had not anticipated. In the early weeks, children still vandalized the facility with rocks at night, and there were repairs I had not expected. An inspection to finalize my loan from Firstar Bank also found a buried five-hundred-gallon gas tank. It had once provided fuel for floral delivery trucks. The bank would not distribute money to me until I paid to have the tank removed and an environmental assessment done of the surrounding soil. This cost me upward of $2,500.

I also wanted to keep Will's Roadside open seven days a week. There were weekdays when few customers would walk in. I hired a market manager when I first bought the property, but within a few months, she quit, citing the workload and the long hours. I could not run the place by myself, and I did not have much money to pay anybody. At first, I didn't know what to do. My home in Oak Creek was more than twenty miles away, and I couldn't be at the facility all the time. I recognized that it would be helpful to have someone always on-site, though, to discourage vandalism and offer a symbol of my commitment to the neighborhood.

I decided to talk to Karen.

∾

In 1980, Karen Parker saw a sign in a window for an assistant manager position at a Kentucky Fried Chicken. At that time, I was an executive for the Marcus Corporation and managed six Kentucky Fried Chicken restaurants in Milwaukee that they owned. When I was hired, my boss said that in those stores "more chicken was going out the back door than the front." Employees and managers were stealing raw chickens and selling them independently, sometimes to nearby convenience stores just down the street. My job was to clean up the management, end the theft, and make the stores profitable.

Karen remembers the first time she shook my hand in 1980. She says my hand swallowed her own. She was only twenty at that time, with wide eyes and hair that she had curled into an Afro—the kind "with activator and sheen, where the grease runs down and stains the couch," as she puts it. She felt intimidated by me. Along with a suit, I wore cowboy boots that pushed me upward of six foot eight. *That is one big-ass man*, she says she thought. Karen was living on her own with her then one-year-old girl, DeShell. She told me that she had previously worked several fast-food jobs before, at McDonald's and Burgers & Beans and Red Barns.

I hired her. Karen quickly proved that she was responsible—even though I quickly understood that trouble pursued her. She began work at a store at Fifty-fifth and Fond du Lac, in the city's struggling Park West neighborhood. One day, I went to the packing area where she was stuffing chicken and biscuits into takeaway boxes.

Karen was wearing sunglasses. I said to her: "There isn't any sun in here. You can't be wearing those glasses at work." She didn't listen to me, and she kept packing the chicken into boxes. So I came up and starting packing boxes alongside of her. Quickly, I snatched the glasses off of her face. I saw that both of her eyes were bloody-black and swollen.

"I'll never forget the look on your face," Karen reminded me later. "You looked at me, and you said, 'There's help for women like you. You don't have to go through this.' And I just started crying. I asked for my glasses back, and I put them back on my face, and I kept working."

She stayed with Kentucky Fried Chicken for nine years before she took a job at Hardee's. I knew she was facing demons, of which I would only gradually become aware. Yet she would almost always show up to work and do her job well. When I moved to Procter & Gamble in 1988, I hired her part-time on occasion to re-stock grocery stores in the middle of the night. As I built my farm in Oak Creek, she would help run my stand at farmers markets some evenings and weekends.

In the late summer of 1993, Karen was in her mid-thirties, and she was raising two children on her own at Nineteenth and Villard Streets, less than two miles from my roadside market. Her daughter, DeShell, was now fourteen, and she had a six-year-old son, DeShawn. I told her I had an idea. My property at 5500 West Silver Spring Drive included an old yellow duplex. I said that I would rent it to her for only $500. She could move her family there and help run my market with me. I couldn't pay her much in terms of salary. I said I could probably manage $6 an hour. Karen later told me that she was making twice that much at her current job for Procter & Gamble, where she was now a retail merchandiser, responsible for making sure that stores were stocked correctly.

Karen walked through the yellow duplex with me. There were cigarette burns in the carpet and rancid bird food on the window ledges. The house smelled of mold. While I was touring it with her, I pulled up the edge of the carpet and told her that I would tear the whole carpet out and stain the hardwood floors I saw beneath. Karen said she would talk to her children and get back to me. The next day, she called and said she would take me up on my offer.

I realize now the risks she was taking. At that time, the long-term prospects of my business were very uncertain. Karen later said that her decision was based on a feeling she had while walking through my greenhouses. She had felt peace there. *This is a safe place*, she thought. *No drugs, no fires, nothing to hurt my children.*

On the day she moved in, Karen and her kids arrived with their clothes and furniture in a small truck. Karen's teenage daughter looked skeptical about the condition of the house. As I helped them move furniture into the living room, we were watched by Karen's young son, DeShawn. He was silent.

DeShawn had piercing, handsome eyes. He was also physically disfigured. The skin on his face was ridged with deep burn scars. He had hair on the back of his head, but not on the front. He had capped silver teeth in the front. His fingers on both hands were small pink stubs. DeShawn barely spoke a word as he watched us move his family's belongings. He seemed to live in a silent world of his own.

Nearly three years earlier, on October 12, 1990, Karen had arrived at 9 A.M. at Hardee's to work an early shift. She spent that morning doing the usual work of lunch prep: roasting the roast beef, cleaning the grill to prepare it for burgers and bacon, and proofing cinnamon biscuits. Shortly after 10 A.M., one of her employees handed her the phone. Karen said hello.

"Is your mother-in-law Sadie Walker?" a man asked.

"Yes," she replied.

"Do you have a daughter named Boo Boo?" the man said.

"No, I have a son named Boo Boo."

"There has been a fire."

"A fire?"

"I am going to come over there," he said. "This is the sheriff."

Boo Boo was the family nickname for DeShawn, who was almost four. Robert Walker, Karen's on-and-off-again boyfriend, had left DeShawn that previous evening with his seventy-two-year-old mother, Sadie Walker. DeShawn's grandmother Sadie lived with her husband of fifty-six years, Jonas Walker, on the bottom floor of a small two-story house on Thirteenth Street on Milwaukee's North Side. She had always been willing to look after DeShawn when neither Karen nor Robert could.

Like many grandparents in the inner city, Sadie Walker had assumed a part-time parenting role. DeShawn slept the evening of October 11 in a sleeping bag on a couch in her living room. When he woke the next morning, he heard his grandmother making breakfast in the kitchen. It was light outside. There was a familiar clatter of pots and pans, grease popping on the stove—food getting made. DeShawn cast his eyes about the living room, looking for something to do while his grandmother was cooking. He saw a familiar cigarette lighter on the coffee table.

The lighter belonged to Sadie's husband, Jonas, who smoked. He usually took the lighter with him when he left the house in the morning. Jonas had forgotten it that day. The lighter did not have an effective safety guard. It sat on the corner of the table, along with a pack of cigarettes easily within DeShawn's reach.

DeShawn walked over to the table and picked up the lighter. He ignited it easily. The first thing he lit was the sleeping bag tag. It quickly caught on fire. He watched what he had done. Soon, the whole sleeping bag was on fire. At first the fire sounded like a whisper—not loud enough to be heard by Sadie in the kitchen. But it took on a quiet strength. DeShawn didn't understand what was happening, though he understood that it was something bigger than himself.

At first, he did not move, transfixed by what was happening. When the seat cushions of the couch caught fire, he realized that he was going to be in trouble. He needed to tell somebody. He ran toward the doorway that led to the kitchen.

"Grandma," he yelled.

Sadie came out of the kitchen and saw the growing fire. She snatched DeShawn up into her arms. By now, the flames had spread from the sofa to the carpet, and they were heading toward the curtains. Intense heat filled the room. She thought it was too late to try to stop the fire, and that the best hope was to get DeShawn out of the house and to safety.

In a moment Sadie had to make a critical decision. From where she was standing, she had two possible exits. One was a back door through the kitchen, in the opposite direction of the fire. The other option was the front door, which would have been within Sadie's line of sight as she surveyed the fire in the living room. Choosing the front door would require her to walk quickly through the burning room and avoid the sofa. That exit would also lead her and De-Shawn out to the street, where they could call for help.

Sadie chose the front door. She lowered her head and walked through the living room with DeShawn smothered in her arms. When she arrived at the door, though, she could not get it open. The bolt was stuck. Her hands were nervous and fumbling, and she decided that they would need to try the back door after all—walking back again through the burning room, which had grown even hotter in the moments she had spent at the front door.

Sadie turned around, holding DeShawn as close as she could to her, and entered the burning living room once again. Then Sadie tripped. The grandmother and grandson fell face forward. Surrounded by flames and unable to flee the rising heat, Sadie could not get up. Instead, she laid her body on top of her grandson and held him close.

DeShawn remembers Sadie smothering his tiny body with her own. After that, he remembers nothing. It was there, less than ten feet from safety, that firefighters would find them both when they broke down the front door.

The sheriff pulled into the parking lot at Hardee's. The lights on the top of his car were flashing. When he walked into the restaurant, the employee who'd taken his call and handed the phone to Karen was rubbing Karen's shoulder, trying to console her.

"Are you Karen Walker?" the sheriff asked.

Karen said yes. He had assumed she was married, and that she had taken Robert Walker's last name. The sheriff said he'd drive Karen to the hospital. She wanted to know what had happened, and yet she was afraid to know. Once Karen was in the car, the sheriff said: "I'm not going to break any laws, but I'm going to get you there as quickly as I can." He turned on his lights and siren.

There had been a fire at Sadie Walker's house, the sheriff said, and Sadie had been burned very critically, and DeShawn had also been burned. Karen took her face in her hands and said, "No no no no." She hoped that this was a case of mistaken identity.

St. Mary's Hospital was at Lake Drive and North Avenue, a twenty-minute drive away. When the sheriff arrived with Karen, there were media cameras in the parking lot. Karen saw DeShawn's father, Robert Walker, standing outside the emergency room entrance. She stepped out of the car and he bear hugged her, and he said in her ear:

"You've got to listen to these people."

It wasn't clear to Karen to whom he was referring.

"Where is my son?" Karen said. "Show me my son, and I will listen to these people."

Inside, the medical staff tried to prepare her for the sight of her son. She understood little of it. She asked to be taken to him right away.

She remembers medical staff fitting her with a gown, a face mask, and a plastic hair cap. In a small room at the end of a long hallway was a boy partially covered in white sterile sheets, with medical professionals working all around him. He was connected to IVs, which were pumping fluid into his charred body. Karen and DeShell had recently given Boo Boo black braids. All of this boy's hair had melted except for the tail end of some braids at the very back of his head.

The boy's head was pink. The skin on his neck and his upper chest had dark pink bubbles. She looked at his hands. His fingers were stubs. They looked like wax birthday candles that had melted part of the way down. The doctors estimated that he had second and third degree burns over a third of his body.

This is not my son, Karen told herself. *They have taken away my son and replaced him.*

Karen felt overwhelmed by a sense of guilt. She felt selfish and inadequate for the faults of her past life. She felt powerless to go back and correct what had happened. She wanted to believe that this was not him. Yet as she stood by the boy's side, one of her tears dropped onto his burned hand, and for a moment the boy's eyelids opened up. Karen recognized DeShawn's eyes, and she passed out on the emergency room floor.

Across town that morning, DeShawn's older sister, DeShell Parker, then eleven, was having lunch at John Muir Middle School. It was chicken patty day. DeShell really liked chicken patties, and she was looking forward to her chance to eat. Before she could sit down, however, an administrator called her out of the lunchroom and took her to an upstairs office. An older cousin of hers whom she rarely saw was there. The cousin said that DeShell would have to leave with her. As DeShell exited the office with her cousin, she felt everyone in the office look at her as if she were someone solemn and important. DeShell realized that this was strange. This was different. She got into a car that her aunt Cynthia, Karen's sister, was driving.

"Your brother has been in an accident," Cynthia said. "He's been in a fire." DeShell didn't understand. Cynthia stopped to fill the car with gas on the way, and DeShell just kept thinking: *Get me there. Let me see him.* The car finally arrived at Milwaukee's Children's Hospital—where DeShawn had now been transferred—and DeShell soon saw her mother in a waiting room. Karen had by that time revived; dark streams lay on her face where the tears had run. DeShell started crying, too. She was emotional because everyone around her was emotional. She wanted to see her brother, but her mother wouldn't let her. DeShell got angry at her mother and started yelling at her.

"If it wasn't for me," DeShell said, "he wouldn't be here."

Before DeShawn was born, she had asked her mother for a sibling. When he arrived, she felt it to be a direct result of her request.

"This is your baby," Karen told her. By this reasoning, DeShell now felt that the reason that DeShawn was suffering was because she had wanted a brother. She felt that the reason that her mother was so distraught was because she had wanted a brother. This was her fault.

"Let me see him," DeShell said. "I want to see him now."

Karen kept saying no. She didn't want DeShell to experience the shock that she had felt. Before the night was over, though, Karen relented. She walked with DeShell back to DeShawn's room in the intensive care unit. DeShell looked at DeShawn's swollen pink head, and his arms wrapped in bloody white bandages.

"That's not my brother," DeShell said. "That's not him."

DeShell turned away, and she walked with her mother back into the waiting room. There, she sat and thought about her reaction. Hours later, she told her mother that she wanted to go back to his bed again. "From then on, I was strong," DeShell said. "And I've been strong for him since."

DeShawn Parker, before and after the 1990 fire

Sadie Walker died on the afternoon of the fire at St. Mary's Hospital. Her body had protected most of DeShawn's back from burns. In her hospital bed, she woke briefly several hours after the fire and said "Where's Boo?" Her family said that Boo had been moved to Children's Hospital. Sadie took a deep breath and passed away.

DeShawn stayed in a coma for almost a month. His mother kept vigil constantly by his bedside. On the day that he awoke, Karen was sitting next to DeShawn when she heard her son's familiar voice saying: "Ice. Ice." The nurses had tied his arms to the bed so that he wouldn't accidentally fall out. Karen jumped up and ran into the hallway of the hospital, saying, "He's woke! He's woke!"

The nurses dressed Karen in a gown, and they untied DeShawn. For the first time since the accident, Karen held her son in her arms. She put ice to his lips, and he tried to suck it out of her hand. DeShawn then said: "Sell . . . Where's Sell?" DeShawn always said "Sell" when he was trying to say "DeShell," because he had trouble with the h. DeShawn had woken up on her twelfth birthday. DeShell was quickly brought to the hospital to see him.

"It had been very difficult to celebrate a birthday, needless to say," DeShell later told me. "But at the same time to have my brother wake up and ask for me, it was probably one of the greatest gifts as well."

By the time that DeShawn arrived at my place three years later, he had endured dozens of skin grafts and surgeries. The doctors had made him wear plastic masks to protect his face and splints to protect his arms. They put pins in what was left of his fingers to straighten them out, in the hopes he could regain some ability to grasp. His hair had begun to regrow on the back of his head, but not on the front. It gave the impression of an older man with hair loss, and other children had teased him about being bald. DeShell was very aware of people's reactions to her brother, and very protective of him. Once, DeShell had attacked a boy less than half her age in the park when she saw him kicking sand on her brother.

DeShawn had let his mother know that he was not happy about leaving their old house, which he liked. It was painted white, and he called it the White House. He liked living in a place called the White House. He had mixed feelings on the yellow duplex, and he didn't understand why his mother had moved. DeShell also felt that their new living situation was a definite step backward.

DeShawn went to the local elementary school, but after he came home and on the weekends he spent much of his free time in the greenhouses. The florists who previously owned the facility had left behind some of their plants, and I hadn't had time to clear those old plants out. In the second greenhouse, behind the store, there was a cactus under a table. Of all the plants in the facility, DeShawn took a keen interest in that cactus. He moved it to another table so that it could see more sun, and so that he could visit it more easily. He sometimes sat by it, and I wondered what he saw in it. Cacti are what botanists call *xerophytes*, plants that have mechanisms for storing water that allow them to survive long dry spells. I hoped that this cactus reminded him of his own resilience.

In those early months at my greenhouses, DeShawn rarely said a word to me. But he watched me as I worked. He also began to follow me into the kitchen behind the florist shop, where I liked to cook. I prepared Southern dishes like mustard greens, turnips, collards, okra, fried chicken, and fish. DeShawn sat down on a small stool and observed me silently. When I needed a spatula or a ladle, I asked him to fetch it for me, and he did so dutifully. I knew many recipes from my mother. DeShawn took in each step of the process. I let him test food as it was done. His eyes would let me know if he approved or not.

For all she faced, Karen managed to hold down steady work and raise her two kids. At the time of DeShawn's fire, she didn't understand why her son was being punished at a time when she was trying to keep her life straight.

In the neighborhood of my market, the Parkers were not the only family facing daunting challenges. Milwaukee was one of the last stops in the Great Migration. The city's black population grew from

7,500 in 1930 to more than 105,000 in 1970. During the Second World War, Milwaukee became a hub for industrial manufacturing and the headquarters for a bomb maker, the A. O. Smith Corporation. Many black people who had left Alabama or Mississippi were able to find well-paying, stable work there. They joined labor unions and even bought homes. During the 1970s, though, the city began to see an erosion of its manufacturing industries—a trend that was happening across the Midwest. Union jobs declined, and opportunities diminished. The cohesion of African American families and communities suffered in the wake of job losses.

Watching DeShawn, I began to think of how my greenhouses could be more than just a farm stand. For him and for others, my facility could be a safe place, as Karen saw it. A third of the people in the neighborhood were living below the federal poverty level. The community was 97 percent black. Almost half of the households were headed by a single parent. About half of the men did not have legitimate work. The children often had no place to go after school.

I wasn't sure what impact I could really have with a roadside vegetable stand. Yet I wanted to do what I could. There is a useful parable about a man who comes upon a sparrow along the edge of a road. The sparrow is lying on its back with its feet sticking upward.

The man asks the sparrow what it is doing.

"I heard that the sky is falling," the bird replies, "and I want to hold it up."

The man laughs at the bird. "You believe that you can hold up the whole sky?"

"No," the bird says. "But one does what one can."

During the first spring and summer, I was selling enough produce to cover my basic expenses. As the Milwaukee winter arrived, though, I began having difficulty paying my bills. An old boiler that I inherited was the market's only source of heat. It sputtered loudly throughout the day. As the weather became colder in the evenings, it began to break down almost every night at about 10 or 11 P.M. I had to go into the boiler room and try to restart it. You could hear the large volumes of gas being sucked into it. The first winter my gas bill became as high as $7,000 a month. I needed a new boiler but I was undercapitalized, and I couldn't afford one.

I did everything I could to finance my operation that winter. I drove two and a half hours northwest of Milwaukee to Coloma, Wisconsin, and picked up hundreds of white pine Christmas trees that I sold outside my greenhouses in December. I partnered with a man who had a Southern food store in Kenosha, Wisconsin. He drove down to Mississippi and Alabama with a big truck and shared with me the produce he bought there. I paid an extra charge for the delivery, which I passed on, reluctantly, to my customers.

I soon realized that I would have trouble paying Karen, DeShell, and the few other young people from the neighborhood who worked at my stand. I went back to Firstar Bank in the fall of 1994, and I said that I needed $30,000. I explained that bedding plants—trays of ornamental perennials and annuals—had become a large part of my spring income. I didn't have the money to buy the seed to create these trays, which I grew in the second greenhouse from the road, and my business would suffer if I didn't have these trays ready by early spring.

The bank approved my first loan based on my past credit rating. When I came back to them only a year and a half later, they were much more skeptical. The banker who took my application said that he needed to see a business plan and how I was going to make my business economically viable. I didn't have anyone to do that, and the bank said they could provide somebody. It would take six months to come up with the plan, they said. But by that time, I would need to have the bedding trays prepared.

Gas and electric companies began sending representatives to our greenhouses to ask for overdue payments. They often threatened to cut us off. Once, Karen remembers writing a check for $2,000 from her personal account for our electric bill, knowing that she did not have that money in the bank. When I arrived at work, she told me that I needed to cover her check. I told her I didn't have the money. Karen's check bounced, and the electric company came the next week to turn the lights off. I was able to get them turned back on a few days later. My willingness to live so close to the margin put great stress on my wife. She had grown up on the top floor of her family's restaurant, and as an adult, she had wanted to keep her personal and business lives separate. I was making that impossible.

Will's Roadside barely survived that winter. The power companies began taking only cash from me because they didn't trust my checks. I asked Karen if I could temporarily suspend paying her a regular salary. Karen agreed to make this sacrifice. I paid her when I could. I was also paying my mortgage weeks late. Because of Firstar's reluctance to provide an additional loan, I ultimately wasn't able to buy the amount of seed I needed for the spring bedding plants. I did what I could manage, but I could only prepare a fraction of the trays that I knew I could sell.

When the spring of 1995 came, I wasn't sure how I was going to survive another year.

∾

That spring, my friend Lyn Hildenbrand told me about a group of young city children at a nearby YWCA who wanted to build a garden. Lyn's boss served with me on the board of Hunger Task Force, a local charity. The children in Lyn's project were part of a Young Sisters and Brothers leadership program, and they wanted to grow enough food to sell at a market. She asked if I could be an adviser. I drove down to the YWCA facility and saw that the children only had two eight-by-eight-foot plots available to grow in. I knew right away that this would not be enough space for them to raise food to sell.

I had long been thinking about how to use the acre and a half of empty land behind my greenhouses. It was overgrown with tall weeds, which suggested to me that the land was fertile. I told Lyn that I would be glad to donate this land for the students' summer project. They decided to come. I cleared the land all the way to the back fence and tilled up the soil. With my guidance, the group of ten children and teens planted collards, 100 tomato and bean plants, and about 150 peppers, including jalapeños and cayenne. When we transplanted seedlings into the soil, the children weren't sure at first what to do with them. "Green side up," I told them. "Roots go in the ground."

Groundhogs soon wandered over from the nearby Army Reserve site and devoured all of the children's bean plants and collard greens. The young people were upset at first. But I told them that being a good gardener required adaptation and perseverance—lessons that I was still learning. We planted more tomato plants together where the beans had been. I believe that this quality of "grit," the ability to withstand setbacks and disappointments, is more important to teach children than any facts we can cram into their heads.

I enjoyed this work with kids even more than I'd anticipated. Most of the young people came from low-income neighborhoods, and none of them had any prior experience with agriculture. I carried water for them, answered questions, taught them how to seed, and planted alongside of them. A reporter from the *Milwaukee Journal Sentinel* showed up in early August and wrote an article about the children's work. One of the teens in the program was an earnest boy with the improbable name of Ronnie Turnipseed, who was thirteen. "We learned how to plant right, how to put down fertilizer, and we're looking forward to eating the crops, too," he told the reporter.

"Most kids don't get to work with the soil and learn to grow things that can mean self-sufficiency," I was quoted as saying. "This is a way for young people to learn that in hard times they can grow their own good, nutritious food."

The same summer, I also started loading up my truck with vegetables on weekdays and driving to vacant lots in neighborhoods near me. I wanted to try to bring fresh food directly to people who had no other access to it. I realized some people might be willing to come to these markets who might not be willing to come by my roadside stand. At an empty lot in the West End, I worked with a local development committee, and they set up a booth to sell my produce on Thursdays. I sold out of the back of my truck at Fortieth Street and Florist Avenue on Tuesdays, and on Wednesdays I partnered with a community center next to the Westlawn housing project. My sales were modest at these stands, but I hoped to grow these markets as I built relationships in these communities.

While I struggled financially, Karen's daughter, DeShell—who was now almost seventeen—grew more embittered about her situation. I had known her since she was a young girl, and before she was a teen, she had helped me at Sunday farmers markets. But since her mother's move, DeShell was being asked to do much more. She was expected to work on weekends and often on schooldays: running the cash register in the store, loading and unloading trucks, rotating groceries, talking to the customers. Her house was right next door, and DeShell felt like she could never escape from her mother's watchful eye.

When her mother told her that I could not pay her for a while, DeShell became quietly angry. She wanted to work at Kmart or JCPenney or any store at the mall. She wanted to visit with her friends, and not to be the girl who worked at the farm stand. She felt like the expectations on her were higher than on anybody else.

DeShell also heard complaints about me in the store. During the first year, more members of the local community began visiting the market for the first time. Many of the older residents expressed their appreciation to me. They said they were happy to have access to foods they had known as children in the South: butter beans, okra, and corn. Some of the residents, though, walked in and walked out without buying anything.

They voiced complaints to DeShell:

How can a black man be selling food at these prices?

These prices are why I don't eat this food. This is why we go to the white person.

I was also working with many white farmers, which led to resentment:

He is a black man, and he should employ only black people.

I thought these accusations weren't fair. My prices were the same as those at a typical Milwaukee supermarket. I wanted the prices to be lower. But to keep paying my mortgage on the property, I couldn't sell products for less than they cost me. I wanted to work with more black farmers, too, but the reality was that there were only two dozen of them in the whole of Wisconsin. I was building relationships with black farmers in the South, but that would take time. I tried other things to show I was sensitive to the criticism. I ran specials on greens, and I charged a dollar for three pounds hoping that these "loss leaders" would attract more local residents.

During my years selling my produce at other farmers markets, I sometimes saw black customers go to a white farmer in the stall next to me, even though I knew my produce looked better and cost the same. This was not typical, but it happened. I felt it was the result of internal racism. People had become so accustomed to thinking of the white man as superior, it was a mind-set they hadn't been able to shake. It was as if they didn't want to see me get a big head.

I didn't have a big head now. I was often weeks behind with my mortgage payment. I had allowed Karen to bounce her own checks. I was unable to pay the people who had been most loyal to me. Though I did not admit it to anyone, I wondered if I had made a big mistake.

Around this time, a black friend asked me about my farming habit. "Why do you want to do that slave's work?" he said.

It was a good question. I did not have an easy reply. To my friend, the profession was tainted with the historical legacy of slavery and economic hardship. In returning to farming, I was swimming against a current that had carried my family and millions of other black people out of South Carolina and into Northern cities. But my passion for farming had also been nourished in part by lingering impressions left from my childhood—the close observation of my parents and of a kindly older woman who owned the land where we lived, and their shared interest in plants and horticulture.

I was a reluctant inheritor of my agricultural history. It was a past that I spent most of my young life trying to escape.

Get Started

A lot of times we have an idea of something we'd really like to do, but we wait for the perfect moment to begin. I'm here to tell you that there is no perfect moment. If I had waited for a perfect time to start Will's Roadside Farm Market, I would have never begun. One of the most important pieces of advice that I give anyone wanting to start a garden is a simple one: Get started.

If you're beginning a garden for the first time, for instance, it's probably going to be several years before you get halfway good at growing anything. You're going to learn a lot in that process. Get started. You can sit around and talk for the next ten years. Talk is cheap. Start small, and then move along the long path toward your goal. You're going to have missteps, and you're going to make mistakes.

When I opened Will's Roadside, I wasn't able to have all my produce be organic. Some of it was conventionally grown from farms I partnered with in the South. But I also knew that a community that did not have access to fresh apples suddenly had them. Providing fresh fruit to that community was one early step along a path. I would work in the years to come to have as much of my food be organic as possible, though I am still not as far along as I want to be.

All big things are created by a slow and steady accumulation of small, stumbling steps. Idealism can sometimes lead to inaction. We're so afraid of doing something imperfectly that we don't do anything at all. We need to get into action. Now is not a time for us just to talk. Your work may start out a little raggedy, but if you get started, it will get better.

Roots

Rosa Bell Greene

BLACK FLIGHT

So much of my early adult life was spent in restless seeking—as a professional basketball player, as a discotheque manager, as a Kentucky Fried Chicken executive and Procter & Gamble salesman. Looking back, I now see how all of these experiences helped form my character. It has been said that every moment and every event of a man's life plants something in his soul. I understand now how I was influenced in my youth by seeds that others planted in me. Many of them took root only decades later.

My return to farming was unlikely.

My story begins before I was born, in the fields of western South

Carolina. A generation before I opened my stand, my mother, Willie Mae Kenner, came up out of South Carolina with her heart full of yearning. She was driven by contradictory longings that she later imparted to me. We both loved raising food and feeding others, but we craved independence and wanted to do it on our own terms. We felt at peace on the land, but recognized the potential of cities and colleges to provide a better future for our children.

The family that my mother, Willie Mae, left by train in South Carolina was poor, and yet for many years they were *capably* poor. They supported one another through mutual cooperation: feeding one another, coming to one another's financial aid when needed, and helping to raise one another's children. My mother's brother Benny, the oldest of my uncles, was a great believer in family. Whenever anybody did anything—good or bad—he never appeared surprised. He nodded his head and said:

"What'd you expect? Look where they came from."

My mother's family was anchored by Rosa Bell Greene, my maternal grandmother. She had married a hulking man named Henry Raiford, who was part black and part Chickasaw. The Chickasaws, a Native American tribe, enslaved African Americans for decades, even after the end of the Civil War. As the product of a biracial pairing, Henry's life was evidence that historical wrongs could sometimes be reconciled.

Rosa Bell bore Henry ten children, including my mother. All of those children grew to tower over her. She and Henry and their children lived on the edge of Ridge Spring, an agricultural community with old plantations and fields of cotton and asparagus and peaches. Henry died young of a cerebral hemorrhage, and Rosa Bell was left to support her children. She later married another man her grandchildren called "Mr. Ike," but the family often said that Rosa Bell "carried the house" by herself.

She don't know how to cook little.

That's another thing the family said about Rosa Bell. Every day, she needed to feed her large family. For many sharecroppers in

South Carolina, the main meal was at high noon. Rosa Bell called it the Big Meal; it was too big to be called lunch, and too early to be called supper. The Raiford children gathered back at Rosa Bell's house after a morning of work in the fields picking cotton. Their work clothes would be damp and heavy. She was responsible for giving them strength for more work until dusk. As they picked cotton and asparagus, the family sang spirituals together:

> *Sometimes I feel discouraged*
> *And think my work's in vain*
> *But then the Holy Spirit*
> *Revives my soul again*

Rosa Bell kept her own garden adjacent to her unpainted clapboard home, and she knew how to raise everything herself. She believed in the medicinal power of herbs, and her garden included sage, mint, and horehound—a flowering plant that could be made into a tea that helped with digestion. She grew sunflowers for their seeds and for their beauty. Rosa Bell's kitchen had two woodstoves, and she would cook with both going at the same time.

She started each day with breakfast: grits and meats like pork or fried chicken or steak. She kept chickens and pigs and cows. As her children had their own children, she dispatched the young ones to collect the eggs, milk the cows, and grab grapes and berries off the vines. Benny had a truck, and he would often bring his mother peaches from a field that he sharecropped, and she would turn them into a cobbler.

She didn't buy things, Rosa Bell. She was an expert at make-do. She made her corn flour out of corn. She got her lard from the hog. She knew how to make lye soap to wash her clothes: She saved the bones from the hogs and chickens, and she mixed them with lye. The lye digested the bones, and she stirred the mixture and stirred it until it resembled a thick dough. She let it sit overnight and then cut hard squares of soap to be used for washing.

Rosa Bell's children never lacked for food. They never went

hungry even when they were so poor in other ways. She often held picnics in the yard, especially after the slaughter of a pig, and she invited all the neighbors. It was in Rosa Bell's kitchen that my own mother learned how to cook. She also learned how the long wooden table in the dining room could bring the family together. At that table, Rosa Bell's family shared stories and gossip. As times got tougher, they also shared their thoughts of leaving.

∽

The fabric that held my family to Ridge Spring began to fray during the Great Depression. One by one my aunts and uncles left, lured by the hopes of a better life in the North.

When the Civil War ended, many former slaves remained in the South because it was unclear exactly where they should go. Upon hearing word of Abraham Lincoln's Emancipation Proclamation in 1863, some were said to have walked to the entrance of their plantations only to turn directly around and come back. It was unclear what freedom meant—or would mean. Many who remained entered into sharecropping agreements with their former slave owners. This arrangement turned out to be the primary economic relationship of blacks and whites in the South following the war. Instead of the position of master and slave, a sharecropping agreement ostensibly changed the relationship to that of employer and employee.

Sharecropping worked this way: A landowner provided land to farm, and often provided the tools—a mule, a horse, hoes, seed. The sharecropper provided all the labor. At the end of the growing season, the sharecropper "settled up" with the landlord. The landowner sold the crop that the sharecropper harvested, and then split the proceeds. The sharecropper usually got half. That's why some people called this arrangement "halfcropping."

In theory, this was a much better deal than slavery. In practice, though, sharecropping often became slavery under a different name. A sharecropper often needed to borrow money from the landowner in advance of the planting season only to find himself unable to pay that debt back after they settled up. The tenant farmer and his family could soon be caught in a cycle of debt. The worst landowners would steal from sharecroppers, withholding money they had legitimately earned at the end of the planting season. Laws in the South favored whites to such a degree that the sharecropper often had no legal right to make a claim.

During the Great Depression, sharecropping became an economic choke hold for many black people. From 1929 to 1932—the worst years of the Depression, before the election of Franklin D. Roosevelt—the cash income of South Carolina farmers dropped by two-thirds. Cotton farms in South Carolina were also being ruined by the boll weevil—a quarter-inch-long beetle that punctured the round boll (or outer shell) of the cotton plant with its long snout, laid its eggs inside, and decimated the fluffy contents before harvest.

For a sharecropper who was already in debt, this combination of circumstances meant there was little hope to break free outside of leaving. This was the dilemma that faced Major Kenner and my mother, Willie Mae. For five years, they had grown cotton and asparagus for Joseph Calhoun Watson, Sr., a descendant of a Revolutionary War veteran who was one of the early white settlers of Ridge Spring. Watson controlled three hundred acres, and he employed many of my mother's brothers.

South Carolina had been the first state to secede from the Union after Abraham Lincoln was elected president, and racial unrest lingered long after the war was over. In 1926, three members of the local Lowman family were killed by a lynch mob in nearby Aiken. Many felt that the Lowmans, who were related to my own family by marriage, became targets simply because they were successful African American farmers. They were accused of bootlegging alcohol. The local sheriff raided their home unexpectedly, and he was shot under circumstances that remain in dispute. The men who killed the Lowmans were never charged with a crime.

The Watsons, however, treated my mother and Major with respect. But there were clear boundaries. None of my family was allowed to eat in Mrs. Watson's kitchen or enter through her front door. Sometimes Mrs. Watson would make food for my mother and her two boys, which she would let them eat on her front porch but never inside. Nobody questioned these unspoken rules.

Joseph Watson's son, Joe Jr., who is now in his late eighties, says he still remembers the day in 1934 when Major settled up at the end of the cotton season. Since the price of cotton was only 5 cents per pound, his father received $25 for every 500 pounds—leaving Major only $12.50. Joe Sr. had lent Major some money at the beginning of that growing season, and Major had promised to pay it back when the harvest was done. At the end of the season, Major realized he would never be able to get ahead. His hands were cracked and raw from the picking season. Major had to pick about 50 bolls for every penny he earned—or about 64,800 bolls to earn $12.50. "When he settled," Joe Jr. said, "Major looked around, and he walked off shaking his head. He was worse off than when he started."

Joe Jr. now runs a shop in Ridge Spring called the Nut House, where he sells pecans. The population of Ridge Spring is 790, roughly the same that it was at the start of the Great Depression. The graveyards there are thicker with souls than the streets of the living.

"There were some wonderful people who lived around here," Joe said recently. "I think we had the best people that lived almost anywhere. White and black. And we lost lots and lots of outstanding black people because there was no money. They were depending on the white man for the money for the job, and there wasn't any money."

One by one they left. When the Japanese bombed Pearl Harbor in 1941, Willie Mae's brothers were eager to fight the war. Of her seven brothers, three entered the army and two joined the marines. In the armed services, my mother's brothers were suddenly earning $50 to $70 a month. They all sent Rosa Bell money while they were away.

Rosa Bell built a new two-story brick-and-clapboard house, hoping she could reunite her family in a stronger position after the war ended. One of her sons came back shell-shocked. Her sixth child, Calvin, lost his leg. Everybody else came back whole. But once they had become used to earning a good income, it was hard for them even to consider picking cotton again.

They looked north. They took trains, cars, buses to New York and New Jersey. One found a job at E. J. Korvette's, the retail giant. Another went into the demolition business. Another took a job as a hospital attendant. They had to learn new skills and come to terms with the fact that the skills they had were worth about as much to them as a heavy bag of Depression cotton.

Most of them were glad to be gone. Their children would often pretend the family had never come from South Carolina. They saw no good in being associated with sharecropping. "There was a long time when I wouldn't even talk about being from the South," one of my cousins said. "I saw my past as a stigma. People would say: Where are you from? I would say Long Island."

∽

My father, O. W. Allen, the seventh of twelve children, knew my mother in Ridge Spring before she left. He was a broad-shouldered man who usually dressed in overalls and a white cotton shirt. He began working in the fields after the third grade—typically the last grade of education offered then for black people in his county— and he was illiterate.

O.W. was good, though, at reading things besides words. When hunting squirrels to eat, he could look at the branches of a river birch tree and tell you by the bend of the branches and the torque of the leaves if a squirrel had recently been there. He loved to fish, and he knew how to read the surface of a river and tell you when the cod would bite and when they wouldn't. He knew how to build things like chicken coops and rock walls and how to make moonshine.

How well my father and mother knew each other in South Carolina is unclear. O.W. was a sharecropper who had married young and also had two children. He told me that one day when he was working in the field, he realized there was no future for him in the South. "I dropped my plow, and I left," he said. He moved his family to the same small African American community near Washington, D.C., that Major Kenner and Willie Mae called home.

Soon after the end of the Second World War, my mother and father—the aspiring schoolteacher and a man who admired her but couldn't sign his own name—left their first spouses and married each other. In 1947, they had a son named Joe. On February 8, 1949, they had a son they named Will.

The Virtue Of Making Do

George Washington Carver

One lesson I take from my grandmother Rosa Bell's life is the virtue of making do. She didn't have the money to buy irrigation systems or greenhouses or chemical fertilizer. She was a conservationist by necessity. She learned how to improve her soil by gathering leaves and animal waste and spreading it in her garden. She learned to rotate her crops so that the nutrients in the soil would not be depleted. She made mistakes and refined her practices year by year. Her knowledge was deeply rooted in generations of experience.

Many of the techniques my grandmother used were advocated by George Washington Carver, the famous black agriculturalist. Carver is a personal hero of mine. He once recalled arriving for a new teaching job at Tuskegee Institute and finding few resources at his disposal. "I went to the trash pile," Carver wrote, "and started my laboratory with bottles, old fruit jars, and any other thing I found I could use."

Carver was constantly looking for ways to solve problems from existing resources. In 1916, he published "How to Grow the Peanut and 105 Ways of Preparing It for Human Consumption." One of those new uses was peanut butter. In the early twentieth century, many Southern black farmers lacked adequate protein in their diets. By championing the peanut, Carver offered a solution that was accessible to anyone, regardless of his or her means.

Next time you encounter a problem, try to ask yourself this question: "How can I fix this with the resources that I have?" There is a deep satisfaction in learning how to make do.

Will Allen, 1949

BEGINNING

I started growing and selling food, by necessity, before I was ten years old. The work came during summer breaks in the 1950s from Rock Terrace Elementary, an all-black school in Rockville, Maryland. I remember how my brothers and I spent some weekend mornings shelling Fordhook lima beans that we had grown. Lima beans can have a tough pod to crack. First you have to string them and then squeeze the pod at the crease to open it up. Then you clear the beans with your fingers. Do this a few hundred times and your hands start to ache, and for a young person, existential questions can arise.

When I was a boy, the laws of the Jim Crow era were starting to be dismantled. In May of 1954, the Supreme Court decided *Brown v. Board of Education*, ruling that it was unconstitutional to have separate schools for blacks and whites. Joe and I returned that fall to

Rock Terrace anyway. There were fifty-seven white schools and nearly 3,000 black students in Montgomery County, Maryland, and it took the school board a while to figure out how to integrate. Although our county was once home to the former slave who inspired Harriet Beecher Stowe's *Uncle Tom's Cabin*, we were one of the few black families living in our part of Rockville.

Joe, my younger brother Tommy (born in 1953), and my parents and I lived in a small wooden house. It sat at the end of a narrow dirt driveway flanked by oak trees. We lived less than fifty feet from a larger house owned by Mrs. Ethelwyn Frank, the Canadian-born widow of a scientist for the U.S. Public Health Service. Unknown to me at the time, one of the founders of the environmental movement, Rachel Carson, had recently moved into a home only a few miles away from Mrs. Frank.

My mother, who left South Carolina with such hope, had found work as Mrs. Frank's domestic help. With our assistance, my mother and father grew food, cooked meals, and cleaned house for Mrs. Frank. In exchange for these services, we were given a place to live and have our own large garden. My father also worked odd jobs in construction to supplement his income. My parents had no inheritance. We made a little extra money by selling the surplus food we grew.

After my mother, brothers, and I had shelled lima beans, we sometimes placed them carefully in quart containers. Then we stacked the containers neatly into a red Radio Flyer wagon that my young brother, Tommy, pulled down our long driveway on sales runs. At the driveway's end, as the years passed, Tommy looked across a two-lane road toward a planned community—and a vision of how America was changing. Before I was a teenager, a new Montrose Subdivision took the place of what had been a dense wood. It was made up of small ramblers and split-level homes, built on less than a quarter acre. The streets were paved. The lawns of straw and dirt were seeded, and they changed over the years from brown to green. New cars came to rest in many of the driveways.

It was a period of rapid change. It was the era of Eisenhower's Interstate Highway System, the growth of the commuter suburb and of a new professional class. In the early twentieth century, more than 90 percent of the people living in Montgomery County made their living from agriculture. The fertile soil of the region produced corn, wheat, oats, and tobacco. That way of life began to disappear as the county's population doubled from 1946 to 1950. The area was becoming a commuter suburb for federal employees in Washington, D.C. Farmers began to sell their land to developers, who built neighborhoods as densely packed as a honeycomb. The streets of these new subdivisions were named after the things they were replacing: Green Pasture Drive, Farm Pond Lane.

Families who remained on farms were finding that their products sold for less. The way people ate was changing. Frozen food output grew fivefold in the decade from 1945 to 1955, as freezer compartments became regular features of refrigerators. Technologies that were originally designed to provide food for soldiers at war—canning, dehydration, condensing milk—now produced food for American families. A growing urban population created an increased demand for processed foods. In Southern California, the fast-food industry was being born. In 1954, a milkshake mixer salesman named Ray Kroc visited Dick and Mac McDonald's hamburger restaurant in San Bernardino, California, and soon began putting McDonald's franchises at highway intersections all across the country.

Tommy often walked door-to-door in the Montrose Subdivision with our produce. We joked that Joe and I were the growers, and Tommy was our salesman. On occasion, Joe and I made our own sales trips. I smiled nicely and handed over the produce if a customer made a purchase. I did not feel comfortable making the sales pitch. I was shy and generally didn't say a word.

Tommy was cute and good at selling. He always did well. His work was made easier by the fact that our lima beans were beautiful: plump and buttery. It was difficult for the residents to turn down a polite and well-intentioned boy selling fresh vegetables. He came home with his Radio Flyer empty and with quarters jangling in his pockets. I might have felt proud of our shared accomplishment. Instead, I felt my difference. I wanted to live on a paved road, not a dirt one. I wanted to buy food that other people grew—not grow food that other people ate.

∾

Despite my mother's dreams of teaching, she was not able to find a way. The hopes that drew her from South Carolina did not match the circumstances in which she landed. Her opportunities were so limited that the security she found at Mrs. Frank's property was its own kind of success.

When Willie Mae first arrived in Washington, Major Kenner had taken her to live in Ken Gar, an African American community consisting of six dirt roads sandwiched between Kensington and Garrett Park, Maryland. During the Great Migration, Ken Gar became a kind of way station for African Americans who left the South and were trying to establish themselves in Washington, D.C. No blacks had lived there until 1905, when two African Americans purchased land. The whites who lived nearby soon rushed to sell their property. Throughout the North, other communities experienced similar "white flight" as black people arrived in greater numbers.

Though ten miles from the White House, Ken Gar was a world away. The conditions reflected the persistence of segregation even for those black people who had left the South. The community was hemmed in by the Metropolitan branch of the Baltimore and Ohio Railroad. With a white community on the other side, Ken Gar was literally "across the tracks." Most of the homes were one-story wooden structures, and my family moved to a three-room house they shared with two other families. There would not be running water or a sewage system in Ken Gar until the early 1950s. A local women's community club—consisting entirely of white women who were ashamed of the conditions there—successfully campaigned for these basic improvements.

While my mother and Major Kenner and their two children were living in Ken Gar, residents had to hand pump their own water from a nearby well. The only bathrooms were outhouses. To help sustain themselves, many residents grew their own food in gardens outside of their homes and kept hogs and chickens. There was only one store in the community, run by a merchant who did not live there. Though Jim Crow was not codified in the North, segregation remained a persistent reality.

My mother was well liked by people in Ken Gar. They knew her as a person of warm smiles and big hugs. But she also seemed intent on moving her family away as soon as she could. The quality of her life was worse than in South Carolina. Her days were consumed with the business of caring for her family as Major Kenner worked on construction teams.

The Methodist and Baptist churches were the center of social life in Ken Gar, but Willie Mae was not a churchgoing person. She was skeptical about religious faith at a time when many black women considered faith a central focus of their lives. Willie Mae preferred playing cards and telling jokes. While at home in Ken Gar, she began to spend time with O. W. Allen. No one gave them much trouble for it.

"It was interesting back then that in this community, a lot of people were married to one person but they were living with another person, and they all got along," says Karen Jackson, who now runs the civic association in Ken Gar.

A bond grew between O.W. and Willie Mae despite her junior college degree and his third grade education. They both liked to tell stories and had boisterous laughs. They both kept gardens and loved growing food. O.W. also saw in Willie Mae a solution to some of his shortcomings.

"She had beautiful handwriting," says Ray Kenner, my mother's youngest son by Major. "That meant a lot to him."

"Willie Mae was a beautiful, smart, intelligent woman," says Marshall Stewart, who lived in Ken Gar and knew both of my parents. "O.W. was an upstanding, upright-walking man." Stewart used to set off every weekend with O.W. to go hunting in a nearby forest called Sandy Spring or fishing in the Potomac River for catfish, eel, perch, blue gill, and bass. He said my father had quiet, patient pleasures.

Sometimes they'd go night fishing with only their lantern-light to guide them. Everything they caught, they ate.

"We'd talk and talk, and tell a few lies," Stewart said. They wrapped their catch in aluminum foil and heated it with their gas lanterns. "Me and O.W. both couldn't read," said Stewart. "But we had a lot of knowledge. His bond was his word. If he said he's going to do something, you could take it to the bank."

My father, O. W. Allen

Less than two years after arriving in Ken Gar, my mother had found a way out. Her opportunity would come through Ethelwyn Frank, who was born in Canada in 1891. Ethelwyn hired Willie Mae as her domestic servant.

Ethelwyn's husband, Leslie C. Frank, had been a prominent scientist for the U.S. Public Health Service who fought for the widespread pasteurization of milk. Leslie died suddenly when he was only fifty years old, and Mrs. Frank lived after his death in the house her family called "Branches." The house in Rockville was nestled in the middle of a twenty-acre wood and accessed only by the long dirt driveway. With her children grown, Ethelwyn invited my mother and Major Kenner and their children to move to the property and to help care for the place—and her. Major built a two-story house for his family at Branches without knowing that his marriage would soon fall apart. In 1946, Willie Mae separated from Major and married O.W. At Branches, O.W. took Major's place.

The position in which O.W. found himself was as good a fate as he could have hoped for when he left Ridge Spring. He was still a tenant farmer, but he was no longer a sharecropper. He had married the woman he loved. His home was reached only by a road that looked like the entrance to an enchanted forest. Mrs. Frank, his landowner, treated him respectfully. He had ample room to plant his own garden, and he didn't have to give up half of his crop at the end of the season. He could manage to take weekends off to fish and hunt. O.W. said he felt like the king of a kingdom. He was home.

∾

If O.W. was king, my brothers Joe, Tommy, and I were his subjects. From the time we were old enough, Joe and I were working in the three-acre garden he planted. O.W. ruled the house with patriarchal authority. We had no tractor. We had no mule. Everything we grew was made with sweat equity. We created the planting rows using a shovel and plow. We grew cowpeas, okra, peanuts, potatoes, toma-toes, limas, collard greens, mustard greens, and sweet corn. From spring to summer, there was the necessary work of weeding. We hunched over the long plant beds and moved down them slowly, pulling up wayward shoots until our backs hurt. When it came time to harvest, we harvested each vegetable by hand. Throughout the year, we chopped wood to keep our mother's stove burning.

We raised our own chickens for eggs and for meat. When my mother was ready to cook a chicken, she casually snapped its neck with her wrists, and the bird's body went limp and silent. My father had a shotgun that he used on any creature unfortunate enough to rear its head out of Mrs. Frank's back woods. We ate what he shot: possums, raccoons, squirrels, and rabbits. He could spot a squirrel in an oak tree two hundred feet away and kill it with a single shot of his .22-gauge gun. If a groundhog as much as dared stick its head out of a hole, O.W. would knock it off, go fetch the animal, and throw it on a table in front of my brothers or me.

Boy, clean that groundhog, he'd tell me.

I learned to clean every animal from a muskrat to a deer to a catfish, and how to prepare it for dinner. At night or after rainstorms,

O.W. took Joe and me eeling in the nearby tributary of the Potomac River called Rock Creek. Under the glow of gas lamplight, we attached minnows or night crawlers on a hook, and we cast our lines where the trunks of sycamore trees flowed into the shallow water. When we pulled the eels up onto the bank, O.W. showed us how to step on them firmly and to put a knife directly behind the eel's head and snap quickly through the skin to kill it. When we arrived home and cleaned the eels on beds of fresh newspaper, O.W. demonstrated how to cut around the circumference of the eel's body, pull the skin back with a pair of pliers, and then divide the eels into thick chunks that looked like hockey pucks. My mother rolled them in corn meal and cooked them with flour and egg and milk.

On several occasions, my father and Joe and I traveled to the nearby C&O Canal and caught snapping turtles. We'd place a turtle in a hundred-gallon oil drum in our backyard. Over a few weeks, we'd feed the turtle with leftover vegetables, and then in its last few days we'd fatten it up with scraps of chicken and other spare bits of meat, as if we were finishing a steer. When the turtle was deemed large enough, my father called on Joe and me to assist him in killing it. I held the turtle down like I was wrestling it. Joe pulled on its tail, causing the turtle's head to pop out. My father stuck a tine of a pitchfork through the turtle's bottom lip and planted the pitchfork firmly in the ground. Joe or I pulled the turtle's back end until its head was as far out as it could go. My father then cut the head off with the swift action of his axe.

We dipped the bleeding carcass in hot scalding water, cut the shell off, and skinned what was left. My mother prepared the meat, which tasted like a combination of chicken and steak. My father always told Joe and me to bury the turtle's head right away. He said the turtle's jaw muscles could still lock down on your finger for as many as two days after it died.

There was a cruelty to this turtle business. At the time, I knew no other way of life. We wrestled whatever sustenance we could out of both animals and the earth. I performed the chores of making food in the early mornings before we left for school, and then again when we returned home. I'm sometimes tempted to romanticize the life of my parents, but I also acknowledge that it was not easy, and I often resented the work. I fulfilled my duties because I wanted to show my father that he should not be ashamed of me. O.W. rarely needed to impose any discipline on us, because we feared his strength, his occasional temper, and his gun collection. He also demonstrated a work ethic that was consistent with what he was asking from his sons.

As a family, we were almost self-sufficient. We operated largely outside of a cash economy. My mother's kitchen was a theater for skills she had learned in South Carolina. Our plates were usually mounded up with meats and fish and the vegetables that we grew. She cooked with a wood-burning stove that played a central part in the life of our home, as it offered both warmth and food. My parents slept in the living room on the bottom floor of the house, and the exhaust vent from the stove wound its way up through the second floor, providing heat to the two rooms where my brothers and I slept.

My father taught me how much work it took to raise food. My mother showed me how food could bring people together. In the summers, my mother hosted gatherings every Sunday in a park in Great Falls, where the Potomac River cascades over a series of jagged rocks and passes through a narrow gorge. My father and brothers and I arrived to fish there in the early morning light. My mother rose in the morning dark to prepare huge pots of collard greens, corn, sweet potatoes, and sweet potato pie. She laid out her feasts over several picnic tables in a grassy field by the river, with views of Virginia pine trees and flowering dogwood.

Willie Mae inherited her mother Rosa Bell's ability to cook big. Friends of my family from Ken Gar came to these Sunday gatherings at Great Falls, as well as any visiting family from New York or South Carolina. Everyone laughed and told stories together as they ate, and the children played around the picnic tables. My mother also welcomed anyone who wanted to join us. On a typical Sunday, it seemed she fed half the park.

Our frequent guests included a popular Washington, D.C., radio deejay named Al Bell. Al came by one day and said, "Oh, that food smells good," invited himself to lunch, and soon became a regular. Willie Mae was fascinated by musicians, actors, and artists, and she and Al would discuss popular music. Everyone was charmed by my mother's gracious smile, her unconstrained laugh, and the warm way that she accepted anyone as part of her extended family. When the National Park Service inherited the Great Falls park years later, the rangers reserved picnic tables for Willie Mae every weekend, though this was against the park rules.

As I ate my mother's food and worked alongside my father, I grew shamefully tall. By the fourth grade at Rock Terrace Elementary, I stood taller than my elementary school teacher. Some students in my school called me "Long Tall Sally." I felt uncomfortable in my own body. I had struggled all my youth with shyness, and my height made me unwillingly stand out.

My feelings changed only in middle school. My brother Joe came home from school one day and told me he had learned about a game called basketball. I was six feet tall and entering seventh grade. There was a flat area with a young oak tree outside our house, and Joe took a basketball rim that a friend gave him and nailed it to the tree, ten feet off the ground.

"That's how high the basket is in the professional leagues," Joe said.

Joe etched a foul line in the dirt, and he produced an old ball. Once I began to play this game, I wanted nothing else in life. I had found a physical language that was my own, and the sport spoke through me. The long and strong body that for years I had seen as a liability was suddenly an asset.

I practiced foul shots in the evening after my chores, shooting until it was so dark that I could no longer see the basket. I played against imaginary opponents and made imaginary last-second shots to win imaginary games. I slept at night with the basketball in the nook of my arm. It was an all-consuming love. I could imagine no other future for myself than one leaping toward the rim with my feet in the air.

As the years passed, the young oak tree kept growing, and I convinced myself that the rim of the basket had kept growing taller with it. I grew as the tree did. I could dunk by the time I was twelve years old. Boys who grow and can jump as I did attract the attention of men who run basketball programs. I soon had reason to hope that I had found a path out of farming and the harder aspects of my parents' life.

Going for a layup at the Maryland High School State Championships, Cole Field House, 1967

A SNORTING TERROR OF
RIPPLING MUSCLE

My father taught me that the fate of a seed can be predicted by the health of the soil where it takes root. This is true of summer crops. It can be true, in another sense, of people. We all need a healthy environment and a community that lets us fulfill our potential.

When I was a teenager, a young assistant secretary of labor in the Kennedy administration, Patrick Moynihan, wrote a controversial treatise called "The Negro Family: The Case for National Action," or what came to be known as the Moynihan Report.

"At the heart of the deterioration of Negro society is the deterioration of the Negro family," Moynihan wrote. He quoted Franklin Frazier's book *The Negro Family*. "The impact of hundreds of thousand of rural southern Negroes upon northern metropolitan communities presents a bewildering spectacle," Frazier said. "[If] families have managed to preserve their integrity until they reach the northern city, poverty, ignorance, and color force them to seek homes in deteriorated slum areas from which practically all institutional life has disappeared."

Moynihan's report does not reflect, however, the variety of the African American experience in the 1960s. The reality of Karen Parker's life reflected the "bewildering spectacle" of which Moynihan spoke. My own story is not the one presented in his report.

During my youth, I dreamed that my life would be spent on the polished hardwood of a professional basketball court. The opportunities available to me were much greater than Karen Parker's, and I was provided the space and resources to pursue this dream. I was the beneficiary of a strong family life and the well-timed help of others in a progressive community who were willing to judge me by my abilities and my character.

When I was young, I liked to think that I determined my own fate. Looking back, I recognize that I could not have found the right direction for my energies without a group of people around me who were willing to help me succeed. My personal history would later encourage me to focus on helping young people, and to try to provide a context in which they, too, could thrive.

∾

The segregated schools I attended were better than most because of the unheralded work of William B. Gibbs, a onetime principal at Rockville Colored Elementary School. In 1936 Gibbs had brought a legal case against the Montgomery County Board of Education. He had pointed out that black teachers often earned half of what their white counterparts did, and he fought for equal pay. His victory in the case, and the pay hike he gained for black educators, meant that my elementary school teachers at Rock Terrace were some of the most talented in the area.

After the future Supreme Court Justice Thurgood Marshall successfully argued the *Brown v. Board of Education* case, the U.S. government asked school boards to integrate with "all deliberate speed." In Montgomery County, it took more than five years between the ruling and its complete implementation. This delay was prompted in part by a petition of three thousand community members to the school board that asked the county to move "slowly, economically, efficiently, and reasonably" in pursuing the integration of schools. The signers accepted the Supreme Court decision, they said, but feared the consequences of integrating too quickly.

I first entered an integrated school in 1961, when my brother and I were enrolled in West Rockville Junior High. To get to our new middle school, Joe and I were picked up by a bus at the end of our driveway, and it wound its way through neighborhoods that were new to us. We were treated well—except in the lower-income neighborhoods and the trailer parks, where a few of the parents would sneer at us and call us niggers. Poor blacks and whites were competing for work in that area, and it was no doubt convenient to consider us inferior.

Children don't see color clearly unless they are taught to do so. My parents never talked negatively about people of different cultures or races, and that attitude was passed down to all of their children. The parents in the Montrose Subdivision across from our house were willing to let their children play with us. I had many white friends with whom I played baseball and tackle football. My best friend from that subdivision was Kenny Price, an athletic boy who moved there from Bethesda, Maryland, with his family. One day, Kenny pulled me aside after school and told me he wanted to tell me something.

"I'm Jewish," he said.

He had a look of shame on his face.

"What does that mean?" I asked him.

Kenny explained it was a religion and a type of person. He said that in Bethesda, his family had been ridiculed. They had moved to Rockville and changed their names so that people wouldn't know their origins. I told him it was no big deal to me, and that he shouldn't worry. Only later in life would I understand the discrimination against Jews and how he must have felt. It never seemed to occur to Kenny that I was any different from him by being black.

Mrs. Frank, who owned the property we lived on, was a small, white-haired woman who often wore white blouses and long dresses. She had intelligent eyes and a deep intellectual curiosity that had expanded in her husband's absence. Since her name was Ethelwyn, which was hard to pronounce, her grandchildren called her "Grammawyn." She kept an apartment on the ground level of her home, which she would rent out to visiting scientists, many of whom had traveled long distances to collaborate on work at the National Institutes of Health. As a young person, I was able to meet visiting researchers from Germany, India, Japan, and Sweden.

My own intellectual curiosity was sparked by these interactions and by observing Mrs. Frank. She had a genuine passion for knowledge. She took an interest in our homework and in our lives. When she had free time, she played the new word game Scrabble with us or talked us through our math or reading assignments. She developed a fascination with opera, and she taught herself Italian to understand the songs better, and later traveled to Italy. She kept a kiln in the kitchen, where she made pottery. She knew how to sew, and she planned craft activities for us and her grandchildren. Her gentle manners set an example for me.

At the back of her house, Mrs. Frank also had a greenhouse, where she grew flowers even in winter. In one faded photograph that I treasure, my mother and Mrs. Frank are standing closely together in that greenhouse. My mother is smiling toward the camera, and Mrs. Frank appears to hold the petals of a flower delicately in her right hand. Together with our parents, Mrs. Frank gave us a love of nature. My later interest in greenhouses and horticulture began in part by watching her. She often asked my older brother, Joe, or me to collect flowers for her that grew wild on her property. She laid out the specimens in her greenhouse and painted them in a white sketchbook, labeling the bottom-right-hand corner of the pages with the specimen name: Bergamot. Skullcap Grasses. St. John's Wort. Morning Glory. Bouncing Bet. Japanese Iris. Dill. Delphinium.

My brother Joe liked to sit and watch Mrs. Frank paint. To look at her art today is to be filled with respect for her and sadness for what has been lost. The land that she loved would later be cleared and covered with cement and asphalt. In its place would go several high-rise townhomes with parking lots.

My mother, Willie Mae, and Ethelwyn Frank, in Ethelwyn's greenhouse, early 1950s. Their love of horticulture planted a seed that would bear fruit in me decades later.

Between seventh and eighth grade, I wanted to find work outside of the farming chores at home. With my parents' permission, I got a job cleaning the pool at American University in Washington, D.C. The pool was adjacent to the university's basketball gym, and the college players had informal practices there most afternoons. I began to drift into the gym whenever I could, and I asked to join pickup games. I was already built like a man, and the American University coach Jim Williams let me play. He saw me as a potential recruit, and he did not want to dampen my enthusiasm. The college players dominated me. Yet the experience of playing against better players quickened my reflexes, made me learn through my errors, and strengthened me. I also learned that summer how to be a good team player; I was not yet strong enough to play a physical game under the rim.

During the fall of 1964, I entered Richard Montgomery High School as a tenth grader. My new school was the first public school in Montgomery County, and it was newly integrated. Of the roughly two thousand students, about one hundred were black. Richard Montgomery High had recently added a $3 million section with sparkling classrooms, a new band room, and modern shop classes. I saw an opportunity at this big, gleaming public high school to have a larger stage for my ambitions.

The year before I started high school, Martin Luther King, Jr., delivered his "I Have a Dream" speech on the steps of the Lincoln Memorial, less than fifteen miles from our house. Rachel Carson, the author of *Silent Spring*, also testified on Capitol Hill before President John F. Kennedy's Science Advisory Committee about the dangers of chemical pesticides. She said, "We shall have to begin to count the many hidden costs of what we are doing," and she tied the fate of human beings to the contamination of the environment. "The world of air and water and soil supports not only the hundreds of thousands of species of animals and plants," Carson said, "it supports man itself."

I would like to say that as a young man I cared about the civil rights movement and the dangers of which Ms. Carson spoke. But I had been shielded from the worst kind of racial injustices and had not yet developed an environmental conscience.

All I could think about the first months at my new school was the upcoming basketball season. Tenth graders were typically not allowed to play for the varsity basketball team at Richard Montgomery. I showed up at the junior varsity tryouts, and I quickly demonstrated in the first few minutes that I could dunk the ball. Many of the other young players auditioning were almost a foot shorter than me and completely hapless when trying to guard me. The junior varsity coach sent me right away to see the varsity coach, Earl Walthall.

∾

I was named the varsity starting center. I scored 349 points in twenty games that season and was named by *The Washington Post* as a

First-Team "All-Metropolitan"—one of the top ten players in the D.C. area. By my junior year, at six-six and 230 pounds, I helped lead our team to the Class AA state championship.

Almost every week, my picture was in the local papers. The captions: "Jumping Willie." "Big Willie." "Allen Scores." "Richard Montgomery center Willie Allen demonstrates why he is clearly the best in Montgomery County." "Allen demonstrates brute strength to return this rebound to the cylinder." I was often recognized when I went to Howard Johnson's or the Congressional Shopping Plaza. One local sportswriter said that in civilian clothes I was a "quiet, always smiling and unassuming clean-cut" young man but that in a basketball uniform I was "a snorting terror of rippling muscle."

My athletic success helped me become popular outside of the court. When Jackie Robinson broke the color barrier in baseball in 1946, he set a standard both on and off the field that made it easier for those who followed him. I also recognized there was a power in being both huge and polite; I invoked fear in people and allayed it at the same time.

My mother carefully cut out each newspaper article about me and pasted it in a scrapbook. My father supported my basketball, but I recognize now how the sport also created an unspoken distance between us. I remember him attending only one game during my entire high school career.

It wasn't his nature to sit in a crowded auditorium. Though he had moved to the edge of a city, I realize now that O.W. never felt entirely comfortable with the sprawl that was beginning to surround Mrs. Frank's property—or with the values of urban life. The land was his place of skill and competence. He had different, older rhythms. He liked to see people busy doing practical things. When O.W. saw a bunch of black boys hanging out on a corner, he'd sometimes point them out to my brother and me and say: "I don't want to see you boys hanging out with those jitterbugs."

By my junior year, O.W. was suffering from a heart condition that slowed his work and made the effort of planting more difficult. He spent more time at home, tending when he could to Mrs. Frank's property. His way of relaxing was to sit by the stillness of a river, fishing for bass, with a flask of gin beside him. He had always been ashamed that he could not sign his own name, and Mrs. Frank sat with him one day and taught him how to write his initials.

My mother, meanwhile, compensated for my father's decline, and she poured her life's effort into me and my brothers. Whenever we had chicken, my mother would make an entire bird just for me. I was the only member of my family who was accorded that privilege.

I had grown so muscular from my mother's food, farm work, and from basketball that I unintentionally broke things. More than once I snapped off the chain of a hanging lightbulb when I went to pull it. Riding in the passenger seat of a car one day, I reached out of the window to extend the radio antenna and yanked it clear out of the hood.

One of my yearbook photos as an underclassman shows me standing at the back of a group of tidy young women as part of the "Interior Display Club," a "service club that helps to improve the internal appearance of Richard Montgomery." The club decorated the school's hallway showcases and bulletin boards for PTA nights and school events. I am one of only a handful of men in the picture, and the only black face.

I had joined the club for one reason: I had grown fond of one of its officers, and she had grown to like me. She was white, and my first girlfriend. We are standing nowhere near each other in the photograph, so as not to let on. My parents welcomed her in our home, but I was never welcomed in her home. When she told her parents about our relationship, they immediately demanded that it end. The ultimatum was "something that was very hard to take given our youth and idealism," she remembered recently. "They were very concerned that I would be the target of some kind of retaliation from other whites and their hatred."

The relationship later ended for good when we went to different colleges. It was still illegal at that time in Maryland for blacks and whites to marry. The state's miscegenation law would not be repealed until 1967, a few months before similar laws were struck down nationally by the Supreme Court's decision in *Loving v. Virginia*. Only a decade before, fourteen-year-old Emmet Till had been murdered after allegedly flirting with a twenty-one-year-old woman in Mississippi. His body was dumped in a river with a cotton gin fan tied around his neck by barbed wire. Decades later, my girlfriend's father apologized for his angry response to me. But at that time— even in a progressive community where old perceptions of race were changing—there were still lines you were not supposed to cross.

I benefitted, though, from other sorts of kindness that extended across racial lines. Bob Guy, then a twenty-four-year old stringer for *The Washington Post*, provided me with a crucial opportunity to improve myself. As a journalist, Bob covered high school basketball games in Virginia and Maryland. He thought the young players in Maryland were not receiving the coaching or resources they needed. After my sophomore year at Richard Montgomery, he asked me to join other local players for a summer-league team he was putting together called "The Maryland All-Stars." Bob persuaded the owner of a linen company to sponsor it.

The Maryland All-Stars included other young players of promise, such as an explosive guard from Hyattsville named Harold Fox. Our team was racially mixed, with three black players and two white ones. Bob picked up team members who didn't have a car, and he ferried us to games held at a boys club in Washington, D.C. He also cared about us as people. He visited my family's home on many occasions. At that time, it was not common for blacks and whites to fraternize in each other's houses. He noticed that I had flat feet—"the flattest feet that God ever put on a kid," he told me—and that I kept getting corns. He took me to a podiatrist, who made inserts for my shoes.

Bob's role as a mentor in my life meant that on the court I faced the best competition in the entire D.C. area. "I used the team as a tool to keep kids active and productive and responsible," Bob told me recently. He said that he also learned lessons from his visits to my parents' house. "It was therapeutic," he said of my mother and father, "to see people with so little be so happy. Yours was a happy family, and you had nothing."

∾

Willie, now that your basketball season is over, I would like to take this opportunity to congratulate you on a fine season and to let you know that I have been following your progress with a great deal of personal interest. . . . Willie, I am very interested in your future educational endeavors. . . . Dear Willie Allen, I imagine you are beginning to think about your future education. . . .

By my senior year, I had received more than one hundred similar letters from colleges. My mother read them with pride, anxious that I get the four-year education she never had access to. Her journey from the South resembled, in some ways, that of many first-generation immigrants to the United States. She had sacrificed her own ambitions to support those of her sons.

I signed a letter of intent in May of 1967 to attend the University of Miami as their first African American basketball player. I would be provided with a full, four-year scholarship. *Jet* magazine reported the event: MIAMI UNIVERSITY SIGNS WILLIE ALLEN, NEGRO CAGER. My parents both attended the signing ceremony.

Bob Guy picked me up late that summer to drive me to the airport for my trip to Miami. My mother put her hand upon my face and told me she was proud. My father shook my hand. Though he was not a man to express feelings, his eyes conveyed the bittersweet emotion of seeing a child go. When the car pulled out of the driveway, I glanced back out the rear window for a last look at the life I was leaving behind.

I felt confidence as I set off for a new city. I was defining myself on my own terms. My future would not be living in a wooden house on someone else's property, growing food. I had made myself into something. I thought I would never have to farm again.

Patience

Agriculture provided lessons to me as a young man that made me better at basketball. One important lesson was patience. Farming does not provide instant gratification. It can take more than fifty days to bring an eggplant from seed to harvest. A seed is not like an iPhone or a computer, instantly responsive to your touch. It requires time. On the day you harvest a fresh vegetable that you planted weeks before, you understand that patience matters—and that anything worthwhile cannot be done all at once.

This lesson helped sustain me in my basketball career. I did not expect success right away. I wasn't naturally good at shooting foul shots, for instance. My hands were large and clumsy. But I practiced from the free throw line over and over again, and after many years I became proficient. People also complimented me in high school on my vertical leap and my rebounding ability. They didn't know that I wore ankle weights on my legs during many high school practices. They didn't know how I did drills every day to strengthen and quicken my hamstrings, calves, and quadriceps. Through steady practice, I slowly developed the skills that would make me a competitive player. I improved not over a matter of days, or even months, but over the course of years.

The benefits of the hard work that you do now may not be felt for a very long time. But if you plant seeds and continue to tend to them—and keep faith in the harvest—good things can come.

With my daughter Erika in Miami, July 1970

GUESS WHO'S COMING
TO DINNER

When I arrived at the University of Miami, I was one of two students that year integrating the school's athletic programs. The other was Ray Bellamy, a six-foot-five-inch football wide receiver who was the son of a migrant picker. One of the frequent criticisms of black athletes during this period of integration was that we were benefitting from "black favoritism." There was a commonly held belief that black players were being provided places on teams because of affirmative action and not because of our actual abilities.

Ray Bellamy and I both began to receive threatening letters soon after we moved into Coral Gables, the small college town southwest of Miami. My first letter came to the dorm room I shared with Mike Hutslar, an easygoing Californian who was a sophomore guard. The letter was tucked inside of a small envelope without a return address. It was signed "KKK," and offered some blunt advice: *Nigger Go Home.*

Around the same time, a letter addressed to the football team's head coach promised "four years in hell" if Ray Bellamy played. It was signed "Patriotism, Inc." Not long after Bellamy arrived at school, he'd been dragged out of the passenger seat of a car by a Miami policeman after a routine traffic stop. The only reason: He was alone with a young white woman who was driving the car. Ray called the university's president, Dr. Henry King Stanford, after he was detained, and Stanford drove to the scene and made sure that one of the school's prized football recruits was released.

In many ways, Ray Bellamy faced challenges that were tougher than mine. He had arrived the year after an all-star class of receivers had graduated, and all of them had been drafted into the NFL. He would be competing for playing time with three white upperclassmen who already had strong careers at the school.

The University of Miami's basketball program was in a period of uncertain transition. Its longtime head coach, Bruce Hale, had retired the year before I arrived, and a twenty-nine-year-old former Miami player named Ron Godfrey had taken over the head coaching position. The team had no home arena, so it played its home games in an assortment of local venues: a former airplane hangar, the Miami Beach Convention Hall, Miami-Dade Junior College North, and even Coral Gables High School. It was often too difficult for students to travel to these games, and as a result we did not have the committed following that the football program did.

Despite the threatening letters I received, I had no trouble making new friends. I began to practice with a red-shirt basketball team comprised of other freshmen recruits. The National College Athletic Association had rules in place at that time that said that freshmen could not play at the varsity level, and so I would spend a year playing with other freshmen against local junior colleges. I spent much of my free time enjoying the weather and the beaches with Mike Hutslar and other friends. I also fell in love.

∾

It was the late fall of 1967. Although the Supreme Court had made it legal for blacks and whites to marry, many still viewed the mixing of the races as a fearful sign of moral degeneration. United States senators still spoke in the halls of Congress about the need for "racial purity."

Many others were beginning to rethink these old prejudices, however. In December of 1967, Columbia Pictures released a film called *Guess Who's Coming to Dinner?* starring Sidney Poitier, Katharine Hepburn, and Spencer Tracy. In the movie, a young white woman falls in love with Poitier's character, an African American physician, and intends to marry him. She brings him home to meet her parents, as portrayed by Tracy and Hepburn. The film captures the discomfort of the young woman's father, even though he is more liberal than most. At the end of the movie, Tracy's character comes to terms with the relationship and tells the couple that they are "two wonderful people who happened to fall in love and happen to have a pigmentation problem."

The same month that this movie premiered, I met a beautiful young woman named Cyndy Bussler. She was a senior and three years older than me. A mutual friend introduced us at the Varsity Inn, a small hangout off campus. Cyndy was from Oak Creek, Wisconsin, and she had long blond hair. I'd had every intention of focusing all my energies on basketball and on school until I met her.

I called her several times on the telephone. She brushed me off. Finally, she agreed to a date. I pursued Cyndy with the same focus that I had used on the basketball court. I invited her to campus dances, as well as to parties off campus. We crashed a party one night at the home of Sam & Dave, the famous R&B duo. We saw the gold record of their hit single "Soul Man" on the wall and were surprised by how small the house was given their fame.

I felt at ease with Cyndy. She was interesting. She liked R&B music, as well as folk singers like Bob Dylan and Joan Baez. She was intrigued by art history. I found out that our families shared an agricultural past. Her parents were of Polish and German descent, and her father's father owned a large farm in Watertown, Wisconsin, which he lost during the Great Depression. Cyndy's father, Ray Bussler, had tried to escape his own farming background through athletics. He was a popular right tackle for a fabled 1932 Watertown High School football team, which did not allow a single point—defeating their eight opponents by a combined score of 223 to 0. Ray went on to enjoy a prominent football career at Marquette University. While he was there, the film star and figure skater Sonja Henie named Ray to her "All-America Adonises" football team for being one of the best-looking college gridiron players in the country.

Ray became an ensign in the U.S. Navy during World War II and then had a short professional football career playing for the Chicago Cardinals. Cyndy's mother, Ann, had been recruited to be a fashion model before she married Ray. When I met Cyndy, her parents were operating a popular steak house together in Oak Creek, called Bussler's Restaurant, that benefitted from her father's local celebrity.

No black people lived in Oak Creek, according to Cyndy. Her only exposure was listening with her sister Abby to soul music on WAWA, the Milwaukee radio station, at AM 1590, that catered to African Americans. She treated me no differently, however, for my race. She admitted that she had noticed me in the Student Union before she met me. "You were hard to miss," she said. She also spoke to me of her love for Wisconsin. She talked about how she grew up on her parents' property surrounded by animals.

After Cyndy told me of her fondness for dogs, I visited a pet store. I had little money at that time, but I wanted to make a statement of my affection. In a cage, I saw an affectionate puppy, a mutt, looking lonely. I bought it for her on impulse, hoping it would make her happy. Knowing her interest in art, I also bought her a small replica of Rodin's famous sculpture *The Kiss*.

Cyndy Bussler in 1967

She named the dog Pucci, after the famous Italian fashion designer. I did not know at the time that the apartment where she lived off campus in Coconut Grove did not allow pets. She adored the dog, though, and appreciated the sentiment. She kept it secretly at her place for a few weeks. During a school break, she flew home with Pucci to Wisconsin in the hopes that her family would keep it.

When Cyndy told her parents the source of the dog—and that she was dating a black man—they refused to take it in. The mutt was passed off to a football player who was friends with Cyndy's father, and Cyndy never saw Pucci again.

A little more than a year later, on February 5, 1969, the *Miami News* reported on why the University of Miami's basketball team had lost its game the previous evening, 87–83, against the Stetson University Hatters.

"The Hurricanes' problem last night could rest on sophomore forward Willie Allen," reporter Jim Huber wrote, "who scored only eight points and got nine rebounds. He appeared to have other things on his mind and was not playing with his usual muscular authority.

"There could be a reason," Huber continued. "Willie is to be married Saturday. The bridegroom seemed a nervous fellow. But Miami was left sitting on the church steps last night."

Many things of national importance had happened in the previous year. Martin Luther King, Jr., had been shot on the balcony of a motel in Memphis. Bobby Kennedy was shot a few months later in the Ambassador Hotel in Los Angeles after winning the California Democratic primary. With the war in Vietnam escalating, the campus of the University of Miami roiled with protest. Students held frequent rallies to protest the draft and the role of the U.S. government in Southeast Asia.

Yet these events played to me like distant music. In the summer of 1968, during the school's break, I had taken Cyndy to Rockville to meet my parents. My mother prepared a giant meal our first night, and she accepted Cyndy gracefully. On the second day of our visit, I stopped the car halfway down the six-hundred-foot-long driveway from Montrose Road to my family's house. I proposed from the driver's seat, surrounded by the shade of the tall oak trees. Cyndy accepted. We chose not to tell my parents while I was home, for fear of their disapproval. I was still only nineteen years old.

It would be several months later, once we had returned to Miami, that we finally informed our parents of our plans. We set the wedding date for February 8, 1969, my twentieth birthday. When I called my mother to tell her the news, she voiced no disapproval. My father, when he got on the phone, said simply: "Boy, you're a fool." When Cyndy told her parents, her mother, Ann Bussler, called her back to say that she would be coming to Miami to see us—not for the wedding, but for a meeting before it happened.

Ann was forty-seven, with wide eyes and a prominent jawline, the same qualities that had attracted several modeling offers when she was younger. She had been born in Krakow, Poland, and had come with her brother to the United States in the 1920s, passing through Ellis Island. She sat down with Cyndy and me to talk in a Hallandale, Florida, apartment that she owned with her husband. She was very charming and not unkind. Yet for more than an hour, she tried to persuade us that getting married wasn't a good idea. She said repeatedly that we were too young.

As she spoke, I felt the real problem was that I was too *black*, though this could not be said. Ann had married Ray when she was twenty-two. In 1969, the typical American got married for the first time between ages twenty and twenty-one. I was going to be twenty on my wedding day, and Cyndy was twenty-three. We decided to go ahead with our plans, and I hoped in time I could earn her family's trust.

❧

We exchanged vows at a Catholic church on the edge of campus, with one hundred of our friends in attendance. None of our parents attended the wedding—mine for financial reasons, Cyndy's because they disapproved. Years later, Cyndy reflected that in some ways she felt cheated of the experience of having her father give her away and of having her mother there to help dress her and fix her hair. It was not my intention to deny her those things. I couldn't change the color of my skin or the simple fact that I loved her.

The night of the wedding, I played a basketball game against Florida A&M, the first time that this historically black college had played the University of Miami. When my team played away games in the Deep South, I began to witness the deeper racial prejudices I had never experienced in Rockville. At the University of Florida in Gainesville for the first time, I walked into the gym and heard the sound of monkeys. Young men stared at me and scratched themselves as if they were trying to rid themselves of nits. Their eyes were wide and taunting—secure in their anger and in the company of others who were like-minded in their bigotry. When we played at the small gym of Centenary College in Shreveport, Louisiana, spit rained down on the court in front of me as I entered. Signs in the stands read: GO BACK HOME, NIGGER and KKK, and I heard shouts of "Gorilla."

Whenever I heard taunts, I tried not to attach any emotion to it. I simply renewed my focus on my game. At the time, we did not have scouting reports on teams we were playing. I knew little about the skills and weaknesses of a team until I was on the court. I had to make quick assessments in the first five minutes of a game. Every time I heard insults from the crowd, I tried to focus on the task at hand.

I had trouble initially finding a groove. "Willie Allen is UM's 6'6" center who has been plagued by inconsistency," one article said the week after my wedding. "When he is on, however, Miami is tough to beat."

∾

My life outside of basketball suddenly felt more important to me than my life in it. Before year's end, my first child, a daughter named Erika, was born in a Miami hospital. Her skin was the color of coffee with cream. When I held her for the first time, I felt that it was true—as I have once heard said—that to have a child is to allow your own heart to live outside of your body.

The Hurricanes lacked that indescribable thing that transforms a group of talented individuals into a team that consistently wins. We entered the last game of my junior year against the nationally ranked Jacksonville Dolphins with nine wins and sixteen losses. I was matched up against Artis Gilmore, a seven-foot-two-inch center who was considered one of the top players in the country. Full of frustration after a disappointing season, I summoned all of my heart and muscle for that final game. I won the opening tip-off against Gilmore despite his seven-inch height advantage. I battled him with my elbows under the rim all night. I wanted him to respect me. I finished that game with nineteen points and ten rebounds; Gilmore's statistics were exactly the same.

"He's a big man," Gilmore told a reporter about me after the game. "And a good man. He plays to win and so do I for that matter." We lost the game 108–97, but I felt pleased with my performance. As the losses mounted, I realized that I was playing in part for my own self-respect.

∾

My first leadership experience came to me by accident. In October of 1970, during the fall of my senior year, the University of Miami leaked a report by a special committee that had been convened to study the school's athletic programs. The committee talked about the financial losses of the basketball team—and it recommended that the entire basketball program be discontinued. When this news reached my teammates and me, we were worried for our futures. I quickly convened a meeting with a dozen varsity members of the team and two freshmen. We needed to organize ourselves if the school administration was to take us seriously.

As players, we did not have much power. The season was not scheduled to begin until December, but we had already begun early practices. I suggested to my teammates that we should boycott official practice—though we'd still work out on our own to stay in shape in case the university changed course. The other members agreed, and they appointed me as their official spokesman.

After we committed to the strike, we demanded a meeting with the university's president, Dr. Henry King Stanford, about his intentions for the team. In late October of 1970, our team crammed into his office. Stanford, who wore glasses and a fresh carnation in his lapel, was one of the first presidents at a Southern university to ban the marching band from playing "Dixie" at halftime. I appreciated his respect for civil rights, but the team felt that he had much less commitment to the sport of basketball.

I told Stanford, as did other team members, that this meeting was about dignity. Everyone in his office had received scholarship offers from other schools, and we had invested our faith in the

University of Miami. We felt we had not been treated with the same respect. We had learned about the possible elimination of our basketball program through press reports and not from the university. Our potential futures in professional basketball were dependent on having a team to demonstrate our abilities. We told Stanford that we needed to plan our own careers, and we just wanted some sense of his thinking, off the record, about the future of the program.

Stanford looked uncomfortable. He said he could not promise us that the basketball program would continue, but he wouldn't say it would be canceled either. After he spoke, several members of the team raised their hands and asked questions. After only a few players had a chance to speak, Stanford cut us off and said he had to go. We came away feeling that he had no interest in either basketball or in us. I issued a statement to the press saying that the "general consensus of the team is that the situation looks bleak . . . and individual action by the players may start taking place." We held a press conference to announce our displeasure. We wanted the university's leaders to understand that its best players could soon begin transferring to other schools.

In December, the university announced that it would continue the basketball program for at least one more season. That would allow me to complete my senior year, but the news was little consolation to the players who were underclassmen. There was a clear sense that the university had every intention of disbanding the team after my final season. Several of our best prospects decided to leave and play at schools more committed to their basketball programs.

I spent my senior year trying to attract the attention of the NBA. We entered my last college game, against top-ranked Jacksonville, with a dismal record: seven wins and eighteen losses. One of our home games had been attended by only seventy-five people. But I had assembled strong personal numbers. I had scored nearly five hundred points that year. My rebound total over three years had grown to more than nine hundred, second only to future NBA Hall of Famer Rick Barry in the basketball program's history.

The game against Jacksonville was played at Miami's Dinner

Key Auditorium on March 2, 1971. The day before, our coach, Ron Godfrey, had announced that he would resign following the game, citing the stresses of the job on his family. Jacksonville was soon headed to the NCAA Tournament. With two minutes left in the game, we were down by nearly twenty points. I knew that pro scouts were in the audience, and that this could be my last opportunity to impress them. Near the foul line, I caught a pass from my teammate Rob Spagnolo, dribbled once and launched myself into the air. Artis Gilmore, who would later play in six NBA All-Star games, was directly in my lane. He tried a late jump. I sailed straight into him and slammed the ball through the rim. All seven-plus feet of Artis Gilmore went crumpling onto his back.

When I landed, Gilmore looked up at me from the floor with a startled expression on his face. For a moment, I felt like I was Muhammad Ali standing over Sonny Liston. "To put it mildly, the crowd went berserk," a columnist for our university's student newspaper wrote.

The referees called a technical foul against me. It was against NCAA rules at that time to dunk the ball. Yet in one play, I had given voice to years of frustration—both my own and for fans of the Hurricanes. A month later, the university's board of trustees agreed to drop the basketball program "temporarily until such time as a permanent field house can be constructed on the main campus." The school would not have a basketball team for another thirteen years.

I thought a career in professional basketball would allow me to be master of my own fate. In reality, I saw now how much I was subject to the whims of other men. In April of 1971, I was chosen sixtieth in the NBA draft by the Baltimore Bullets. I would have been chosen higher but for the liabilities in my game. I did not start playing basketball competitively until I was thirteen, and I hadn't developed a classic jump shot. I could score against anybody within fifteen feet of the basket. Yet I was not the kind of player who could stand twenty-five feet from the rim and sink shots reliably. I was big by any standard, but in the world of the NBA, six-foot-seven—the height at which I finally settled—was not so tall as to overcome my weakness at shooting from the perimeter.

The deal with the Bullets was for three years and paid around six figures, but it was contingent on me making the team. I played exhibition games that summer with the Bullets against other NBA teams, and I thought I did well. Yet a day before the regular season began, I was let go. Veterans of the team told me that I deserved to make it, but that the Bullets were forced to commit to three rookies with no-cut contracts.

My wife remembers me coming home after the Bullets cut me. "You knocked on the door instead of coming inside," Cyndy said, "and I opened it. You looked like you had five hundred pounds on your back. You said, 'I didn't make it,' and you cried. It was hard to watch you. I saw how hard you had worked. It meant so much to you."

I wanted to keep playing in the hopes that another NBA team would recognize my worth. So I joined a team from Hartford, Connecticut, in the semiprofessional Eastern League. When I had expectations of making the Bullets, Cyndy and I had moved to a small apartment in Gaithersburg, Maryland, near my mother's property. Cyndy was now expecting our second child. For home games, I commuted nine hours by car from Gaithersburg to Hartford. For away games, I drove to Hartford, caught a bus with the team, and rode to small markets like Scranton, Pennsylvania. After one Scranton game, the bus brought us overnight to Hartford through a heavy snowstorm. I arrived at 6 A.M. and then made the nine-hour drive back to Gaithersburg.

In December, the struggling Miami Floridians, a team in the American Basketball Association—the NBA's rival at the time—called me and made an offer. They did not have reliable rebounders. The team's coach, Bob Bass, had seen me play both in college and during my brief stint with the Bullets. Yet when I arrived again in Miami, I sat on the bench. I played in only six games, averaging two minutes of playing time per game, and I felt I didn't have an opportunity to show my strengths. The team consistently lost, and the players were suffering from low morale. In January of 1972, the same month that my son, Jason, was born, the Floridians released me. The team disbanded later that same year for financial reasons.

I was not sure what to do after the Floridians cut me. Don Shula, the head coach of the Miami Dolphins, asked if I wanted to try out for his professional football team. I had not played much football in my life, and I never felt entirely comfortable tackling or being tackled—a liability in football. I joined the Dolphins practice squad nonetheless. By early August, I was released.

During this period of difficulty, I turned to some of the lessons I had learned growing food with my father. Sometimes you can do all the right things to prepare for a good harvest, but fate does not smile on you—it rains too much or too little, the sun shines too hot, or you have some other problem that you didn't foresee. He taught me that all you could do was control your preparation, learn from your mistakes, and accept the losses.

Not long after I failed to make the Dolphins, I received a call from my mother telling me that my father was in the hospital after a heart attack. O.W. did not let my mother call an ambulance, so my brother Joe drove over and helped him into the backseat of a car. Joe said that my father did not say a word on the way to the hospital. He simply held his chest, his pain visible on his face.

I boarded a plane from Miami to Washington, and I was able to see him while he was still alive. He had his eyes open even though he was only partly conscious, and I wanted to think he recognized me, though he couldn't talk. Seeing him, I remembered what he had told me so often while working on the land: *Everybody wants to go to heaven, but no one wants to die.*

It was unsettling for me to see my father in an intensive care room, surrounded by the trappings of modern civilization that he had always avoided. I knew it had been a long journey from the South Carolina cotton fields to a big city emergency room. He died soon after I arrived. He was not yet sixty. Though he ate healthfully, my father always smoked, and there was a history of heart disease on his side of my family. I felt time had caught up with him too soon.

∾

Soon after my father's death, my agent called to tell me that I had an offer from a team called BC Sun Charm in the Belgian city of Aalst. The team was named after a fruit juice company, and the idea of playing in Europe did not match my vision for myself. Yet the agent also said the team would agree to pay my travel there and back to the United States, and it would provide free housing for my family. The salary was generous enough that it would allow me to care for my two children.

I discussed the offer with Cyndy. I knew that her relationship with me had brought instability to her life in ways that she could not have anticipated. She nonetheless agreed to go to Europe with me, and she embraced the move as an adventure. As I boarded a plane for Belgium, I worried that my dreams of playing in the NBA were falling out of my grasp. Half a world away from home, I found my love of the land again.

The manager of the Nine-Mile Disco, Oak Creek, Wisconsin, 1978

BACK TO EARTH

I arrived in Aalst on Sabena Airlines, Belgium's national carrier, and I played my first game the evening I stepped off the plane. I did not speak any Flemish except for a few words I had gleaned from a guidebook, such as *Ik begrijp het niet* ("I don't understand") and *Hallo* ("Hello"). My teammates spoke serviceable English, and we communicated as well through the common language of basketball. I understood most of what I needed to know through the coach's diagrams, hand gestures, and eye contact. My coach and fellow players told me through their smiles that they were pleased to have me.

Our games were played in gymnasiums that were not much larger than the one at my public high school. The few American players in the Belgian basketball league were paid more than the local players. Most of my teammates had to supplement their income with day jobs, and they arrived in the evenings after work for practices and games. We traveled by bus together to play other teams; the country was roughly the same size as my home state of Maryland.

Because I could support my family on my basketball salary alone, my schedule was light. In a typical week, we practiced three times and had two games. I rose early each morning to go jogging on the streets of Aalst, or on a nature path that wound its way through the city. I also had a key to a practice gymnasium where I practiced shots and did calisthenics.

I had never had so much free time before. My family and I spent it in exploration. Cyndy dragged me to art museums when she could. In the market square in downtown Aalst, there was also a beautiful open-air bazaar every Saturday, with fresh vegetables, cheeses, and baked goods. I still remember the faces of the farmers, chefs and craftspeople there. I sensed pride and joy inside of them. They seemed always to be laughing and smiling.

On other free days, I drove through the Belgian countryside, where I saw sharp differences from the agricultural landscape of the United States. There were large farms, but many families also kept farms of an acre or less. In small fenced spaces, these families often grew dozens of different fruits and vegetables. I was impressed by the land's fertility and the diversity of the crops. I also took notice of the rich brown color of the soil. At almost every Belgian garden, I saw wooden compost bins.

My father had taught me as a boy how to compost: to transform decaying organic material into a natural fertilizer. He took chicken poop and vegetable scraps (materials high in nitrogen) and mixed it with dry hay and dead leaves (materials high in carbon). He let these piles sit for many months. The piles gave off steam as they were decomposing. I remember reaching my hand in and feeling their warmth. In the planting season, O.W. tilled the cooled and finished compost by hand into his garden rows. The small farms in Belgium used compost instead of chemical fertilizers.

When I returned to Aalst or traveled to other cities to play basketball, my thoughts often drifted back toward the countryside. I began to feel that my heart was there. In June of 1974, I left BC Sun Charm for a new team called Bus Fruit, in the Belgian city of Lier. My contract, written in broken English, ensured me 40,000 francs a month, a car, and asked that I do "everything nessecary to be in good moral and fysical condition." I felt that my ability to meet those requirements would be helped if I could live in the country. My wife was pregnant at the time with our third child, and we also needed more room.

The father of our babysitter found us a two-story brick house in Kessel, a tiny town nestled between two rivers. Kessel was also home to a popular flower garden called Vredehof. The house had a small plot of land to its east behind a brick wall.

Soon after we moved in, I tilled my first garden. I started very simply. I planted a few rows of beans, peppers, and squash. While planting, I often thought of my father. I remembered the shape of his strong back. I also felt a new respect for his abilities. He possessed skills with his hands that were of little economic reward to him but left a lasting impression on me. Every spring, O.W. made twenty planting rows that were one hundred feet long and forty inches wide. Most people I knew who made planting beds tied a piece of rope between two poles and followed the line in order to make them straight. My father could till perfectly straight rows simply by sight. If he needed to finish cutting three dozen bushels of firewood in three hours, he also worked with the precise amount of efficiency and effort required to get the job done.

In Kessel, Cyndy and I invited the American basketball players in Belgium to a Thanksgiving dinner at our home. We prepared a large feast. At that time, a friend had given me twenty-five chickens to raise. I put the birds in an old shed in the back of our property, and I made an enclosed area with some chicken wire around the shed door so the birds could get some fresh air. For Thanksgiving and family meals, I killed a few of these chickens and harvested vegetables.

With my friends and family around my table that Thanksgiving, I felt the sort of pleasure that my mother must have felt when she fed others. There was a satisfaction that I had not found in other parts of my life. Once my parents left South Carolina, they no longer saw farming as slave's work. When I tilled my first garden and hosted meals, I realized that growing food no longer felt like slave's work to me.

With my teammates from Bus Fruit, where I played from 1974 to 1976

After several seasons in Belgium, I felt gravity's pull. The landings after my rebounds felt harder. My jumps felt creakier. The Belgian courts were often made of concrete, which had caused damage to the cartilage in my knees. I also felt the weight of my circumstances. I had kept my wife separated from her own family for too long. My older daughter, Erika, now seven, spoke Flemish as well as she did English. I began to think of returning home.

During my last season, in 1976, I noticed that I had some trouble swallowing water during my basketball games. I felt pressure on the nerves on one side of my neck. I decided at the time not to go to a doctor, and I pushed the issue to the back of my mind. When the Bus Fruit season ended, I retired from basketball. Cyndy and I decided to take our family to Oak Creek, Wisconsin, where she had been raised. Her mother, Ann, still operated a restaurant there. Cyndy's father had passed away suddenly in October of 1969, the same year that Cyndy married me.

When I came back to the United States, my wife and I had little money to our name, and few prospects. Ann, who had tried to persuade us not to marry, had come to accept that I was not going away. "Her initial feeling toward you was not so much maliciousness," Cyndy says now. "It was lack of exposure. It was lack of understanding."

My relationship with my mother-in-law would always be complex. Publicly, she was often charming. In her best moments, she reminded her family of Rosalind Russell, the fast-talking, no-nonsense star of *His Girl Friday*. Privately, though, Ann could be controlling and verbally abusive to the help in her restaurant. Yet she also played an important role as Cyndy and I tried to reestablish ourselves in the United States. When we left Belgium, we had no place to go. We were starting over with three children. Ann took us in. She offered us the top floor of a two-story restaurant along Highway 41, a four-lane road that had once been one of the major north-south thruways in Milwaukee, before Interstate 94 was built a few miles away. We lived in the same rooms where Cyndy had grown up.

Behind the restaurant, there was a quarter acre of rocky soil. Soon after we moved in, I planted some tomatoes, collard greens, and lettuces there. With my basketball career ended, I was forced to imagine a new life. My first job in Wisconsin was as a teacher's aide at a local high school. As I looked for steady employment, I began thinking about an empty restaurant that Ann owned on Nine Mile Road in Oak Creek. It was 1977, and John Travolta's *Saturday Night Fever* was a hit in theaters.

I asked Ann if I could transform the restaurant into a discotheque. She agreed. Cyndy and I bought mirrors and disco balls. The building had two floors; I set up the basement as a small jazz club, and we put the disco floor upstairs, where I built a small DJ booth with two vinyl turntables. We called it the Nine-Mile Disco. I hired bartenders, and I often DJed myself.

Former members of the Milwaukee Bucks basketball team soon

came to dance, and we were busy nearly every weekend. The business was successful, but I became disillusioned with the disco lifestyle. I didn't like having to break up fights, or arriving home on Sunday mornings at 3 A.M., with my clothes saturated in cigarette smoke. I often got up only a few hours later to care for my kids.

Not long after I started the Nine-Mile Disco, my mother-in-law provided us with a family house on fifty acres in Oak Creek. Ann and her husband had bought the property years earlier as an investment when Bussler's Restaurant was thriving. She allowed Cyndy and me to live there rent-free. The plot included a small farmhouse on the rise of a hill. In my first summer there, I planted crops on two acres. I wanted to grow more but was limited by not having any large farm equipment. We had an old station wagon at the time, and I soon decided to drive it to a local junkyard. I traded it in for parts and purchased my first tractor. Soon after, Ann helped my wife and me acquire a new car. "You wouldn't think she would be so helpful," Cyndy says of Ann. "I think it was difficult for her to express her better nature verbally. It was easier for her to *do* things."

I began having more trouble swallowing while managing the Nine-Mile Disco—the problem I had first noticed in Belgium. I saw a doctor, who told me that my muscles were simply sore. I went for a second opinion, and that doctor told me that I should have a CT scan. The scan found a growth. A biopsy determined that I had thyroid cancer.

I was twenty-nine years old. The doctor was puzzled how I could have developed cancer so young. He asked my medical history. I casually mentioned that when I was seven, I got ringworm, a fungal infection of the scalp that is common in children who live in farming communities. I was given a novel treatment at that time: radiation therapy of the scalp. My community in Rockville, Maryland, was close to some of the country's leading research institutions. Scientists were flocking to the area because the National Institutes of Health was headquartered there, and they brought the latest advances with them. Many hoped to become the next Jonas Salk, who developed the polio vaccine.

I had been taken to an office and placed in a leather chair. My head was placed in an orb resembling a hair dryer at a women's salon. I remember sitting there patiently for twenty minutes. I felt nothing. Within days of my first session, my hair began to fall out. The doctor laid strips of tape over my head and then ripped it off, pulling out the rest of my hair. At school, I wore a stocking cap over my head. Only two months after the radiation treatment, the ringworm was gone, and my hair began to grow back again.

After I was diagnosed with cancer, I discovered that a generation of young people in the 1940s and the 1950s who had low-dose X-ray treatments for ringworm developed thyroid and skin cancer at rates dramatically higher than their peers. One study showed that a young person was four times more likely to develop cancer after the radiation treatment than a child who did not have it. The doctor in Oak Creek operated on my thyroid, removing a tumor the size of a turkey egg. A follow-up surgery a few months later removed the rest of my thyroid after my doctor detected additional cancer that he had not caught the first time. The doctor said I would need to take a daily medicine to replace the missing hormones. With these surgeries behind me, though, I hoped that I would remain cancer free.

I kept searching for a career. When I decided to close the disco after two years, I saw an ad in the newspaper from a local hotel and restaurant group called the Marcus Corporation. They needed a regional manager for half a dozen of their Kentucky Fried Chicken stores. I interviewed with a gentleman named Peter Helf, whose brother had been a manager of the Green Bay Packers. We quickly fell into a discussion of sports, and I was hired before I left his office.

The Kentucky Fried Chicken stores that I inherited were all in African American neighborhoods. Many of those communities were beset by crime. At one of the KFC stores—at Nineteenth Street and West Atkinson Avenue in Milwaukee—the employees and the customers did not even breathe the same air. The staff stood behind a large sheet of bulletproof glass, and they passed the food to the customers through revolving windows.

I poured my competitive energies into my new job. I wanted to make my six stores the most profitable ones that the Marcus Corporation owned. Within six months, I fired all of the existing managers and brought in new ones, including Karen Parker. I promoted several women to top positions. I came from a family of strong women—and I felt that in many cases, women could enforce greater accountability than men could. I imposed a zero-tolerance policy for theft, and I spent time learning KFC's business model. The company called it the science of "chickenology." I insisted on attention to cleanliness. I visited each of my stores every day, and I reviewed the daily sales and inventory reports to make sure that no chicken was being shuttled out the back door.

Within a year, the six stores that I managed accounted for nearly half of the total sales from Kentucky Fried Chicken's thirty-five restaurants in Wisconsin. The store at Nineteenth and Atkinson became one of Kentucky Fried Chicken's top 100 grossing stores in the nation. I won several sales awards. Yet I felt little attachment to this success. To me, the most fortunate aspect of my job was that KFC did not serve breakfast. This allowed me to devote my morning to farming. I'd often get up at 4 A.M., farm for several hours, change clothes, and visit my six stores beginning at 10 A.M. I'd also farm in the evening before catching a few hours' sleep. With the tractor that I bought, I was able to till most of the fifty acres that my mother-in-law owned.

As I grew more food, I looked for places to sell it. My oldest children, Erika and Jason, helped set up a small farm stand outside our house on West Drexel Avenue, which we opened on Sundays. I also became a "truck farmer"—a person who filled the back of his pickup truck and drove it to busy intersections or farmers markets.

I didn't have any retail customers until I got the courage to visit a small grocery store called Lena's Food Market on West North Avenue in Milwaukee. Bezelee and Lena Martin, a local couple, had started the store in 1965. One July morning, I pulled up with the back

of my truck filled with the best collard greens I had harvested. I
went inside and asked Lena to come out and see what I had brought.

I've always believed that you need to let a product sell itself. You
can talk all you want, but if you don't have the goods to show, your
talk isn't worth anything. When Lena came to my truck, I grabbed
a batch of collard greens I had, and I said I was interested in forming a business relationship.

"Those look like the collards that I knew growing up in Okla-
homa," Lena said. She quickly agreed to buy my produce. In the
years to come, Lena's sold my collards, kale, and sweet corn.

In the spring of 1980, a week of heavy rains arrived just after I had
finished most of my planting. Part of my land was low-lying and
flooded, and I realized that almost all of the income that I had expected from my early harvest would be lost. I didn't know at first
what to do.

I reached out to the local branch of the U.S. Department of Agriculture's Agricultural Stabilization and Conservation Service.
Along with the Farmers Home Administration, which had an office
in every county, the agency was entrusted with helping farmers keep
their businesses alive in hard times. It provided reimbursements in
the case of catastrophic crop losses like my own. I filed a detailed application that showed the amount of income I would have expected
to receive had my crops been harvested. I included pictures of my
fields that showed the damage. A gentleman from the local USDA
office soon visited my farm and surveyed the damage. My fields
were ankle-deep in water. Yet my application was quickly denied.

I have always been hesitant to look at events in my life through
the prism of race. Yet I felt that the color of my skin had played a
part in my application's denial. At the time, I was one of the only minority farmers in Oak Creek. The farmers who made up the county
committee were elected by the community, and their families had a

long-standing history there. I had just arrived in town, and I felt my presence was not entirely welcome.

I experienced similar feelings of unease a few years later when I first sought to bring my produce to Fondy Farmers Market in Milwaukee. Located in a North Milwaukee neighborhood that was almost exclusively African American, the market was administered by the city government. It operated under a large steel awning that kept the stalls dry even on days of rain. I remember walking through the market for the first time and feeling that I could do well there. Though the community was black, all of the farmers who had stalls in the market were white.

I saw older customers walking through the aisles and perusing the tables, and I knew that they were members of the Great Migration. They were searching for the flavors of their youth, and they could not find them there. The farmers weren't selling the produce that black people liked and that I was growing now in large quantities: collards, curly-leaf and slick-leaf mustards, and turnip greens.

The Fondy market stalls were full at that time, and I was put on a waiting list for a space. In the meantime, I decided to start my own stand a few blocks away at Twenty-seventh and North Avenues. I only had a narrow space on the sidewalk—twelve feet by eight feet—and I set out some long tables and bought market umbrellas to keep my vegetables shaded and dry. I did well my first weekend. Besides the greens, I did a brisk business with okra, peas, and lima beans.

After I had spent a few weeks on the sidewalk, a representative from the city's common council told me that I was first on the list for a stall at the market. When one of the farmers passed away, I heard that his daughters were not interested in continuing the stall. I expected to be invited to join the market. I soon heard, instead, that the daughters had sublet the stall to another white farmer, from Racine. I issued a complaint to the city, because I knew that the market's rules did not allow a farmer to sublease. I felt that the decision could have been a collective effort by the other farmers to shut me out.

The city did not give me the stall but agreed to provide me a space for my stand next to a band shell outside of the market. I was able to set up large tables, and I began to pull in $3,000 to $4,000 on a single weekend. Feeling shunned by the farmers in the market, I became determined to outsell them. Some of the customers began to visit my stand and bypass the market altogether.

I felt the resentment of farmers who had a long history there. I saw it in their glances. I soon received a call from an administrator at the city who said that one of the farmers had complained about me. He had questioned whether I had grown all of the food I sold—a requirement for being a vendor at Fondy. He said that someone from the city would need to come out and inspect my fields. I told them that I would welcome a visit. A city official pulled up one morning at my house in Oak Creek, and I walked him through my planting rows so he could see the quality of my collards, kale, and other vegetables. As he left, I told him: "If you are doing this to me, you need to be inspecting everyone's farms."

Within a year, I was given a stall in Fondy. I began to form friendships with the other farmers there. The tensions that had grown in those early days lessened. I see now how the mutual suspicions between me and the other farmers were due, in no small part, to that narrow road that separated my stand from the rest of the market. Once we began speaking to each other face-to-face, we no longer felt distrust.

∾

My experiences reflect the uncomfortable truth that black farmers have faced discrimination for generations, even to the present day. They have also often been hurt—rather than helped—by the U.S. Department of Agriculture and its policies.

A crucial turning point in the relationship of black farmers and the federal government came when the Union general William Tecumseh Sherman marched through the South toward the end of the Civil War. Slaves abandoned their plantations and joined his army. To handle the challenge of so many refugees, Sherman issued a special directive to resettle the black families on the coast of Georgia, saying that "each family shall have a plot of not more than forty acres of tillable ground" and that "the military authorities will afford them protection until such time as they can protect themselves." Sherman's army also provided mules to some of the first settlers protected under this directive.

Freed slaves soon embraced the hope that the federal government would help them establish their independence with the guarantee of "forty acres and a mule." Yet when President Abraham Lincoln was assassinated a few months later, his successor, Andrew Johnson, abandoned any commitments of the U.S. Army to protect black people who were resettled under Sherman's directive. He returned all land that had formerly belonged to slave owners, and the Freedmen's Bureau Act of 1866—passed over Johnson's veto—did not provide forty acres and a mule. The act focused instead on trying to make sure that labor contracts between black people and their former slave owners were fair. The law provided few resources to enforce even this much more limited goal.

A racist cartoon from the post–Civil War era attacking the work of the Freedmen's Bureau as an "agency to keep the Negro in idleness."

Without protection or assistance, former slaves faced severe obstacles if they hoped to obtain land. Few had any inherited assets or much if any cash. The reason that so many African Americans still speak nostalgically of "forty acres and a mule" is that the policy, if properly carried out, might have provided a chance for thousands of former slaves to establish themselves independently of white landowners. It could have given former slaves and their descendants a path to self-sufficiency. Most black people in agriculture had to turn instead to sharecropping—a business relationship that seemed like wage slavery. Many Southern whites, however, perceived the policy of "forty acres and a mule" and even the modest work of the Freedmen's Bureau as a handout to lazy blacks who didn't have the discipline to work hard enough to buy their own property. These sentiments were often expressed by people whose economy had been built by slaves.

For black farmers in the twentieth century who outlasted the upheaval of the Great Migration, there were more subtle forces that drove them off their land. In 1982, the bipartisan U.S. Commission on Civil Rights issued a report called "The Decline of Black Farming in America" that attempted to understand why black farmers were leaving the profession at a rate two and a half times greater than that of whites. The committee found that one important reason was that black farmers were small farmers. The average commercial farm owned by a black man in the South was 128 acres. The average farm of a white landowner was 428 acres. Almost all of the technological innovations that the United States government had subsidized over the previous decades, the authors acknowledged, were geared toward increasing the productivity of large farms—and not to making small farms sustainable.

"The cost of basic equipment minimally necessary to run a commercial farm is much greater in proportion to the number of acres of land held by the average black farmer than it is for white farmers," the authors wrote. "Black small farm operators who cannot afford . . . new large-scale technology to increase their output fall behind."

The authors also found that the government's income-support

programs had the indirect effect of pushing small farmers off their land. These subsidies were first established by President Franklin D. Roosevelt during the Great Depression to help farmers who were suffering. Prices for things like wheat, corn, tobacco, rice, and milk had declined sharply in the 1930s. Roosevelt's New Deal program encouraged farmers to allow some fields to lie fallow or to kill excess livestock; the decreased supply increased prices for these commodities. The government, in turn, compensated farmers for the money they would have made had they continued to farm at full capacity.

This idea was well intentioned. The unforeseen trouble with the income-support program as decades went by was that it benefitted those who needed it the least: the largest farms. The policy later shifted emphasis so that farmers were less often encouraged to let fields lie fallow, but were simply compensated directly with payments if corn or wheat prices fell below a certain minimum. This meant that the more food you could produce, the larger your income-support payment when prices fell too low. By the late 1970s, payments for participating small farmers were as low as $365. Farms with more than 2,500 acres, on the other hand, received as much as $36,000 a year.

These policies, the authors of the 1982 report wrote, allowed larger farms "to borrow and invest capital in more land and improved technology, resulting in increased production on their part" and provided for an "increasing disadvantage for small farmers." The U.S. Department of Agriculture, in a separate report on the structure of agriculture, acknowledged that these income-support programs could be contributing to the loss of small farms.

As black farmers have tried to compete with larger farms, they have also needed progressively larger lines of credit. Farmers are paid only after a crop is harvested, which can be many months after they need money for seeds, equipment, and fertilizer. When farms were smaller and communities were more closely knit, black farmers could sometimes turn to local farm supply stores for credit, borrowing from people who knew them personally. As the agricultural economy became more concentrated in the hands of fewer and fewer companies in the twentieth century, most of these local stores were absorbed by national chains reluctant to extend loans.

The lender of last resort for black farmers became the federal government. Decisions on such loan applications were often administered by local offices of the U.S. Department of Agriculture's Farmers Home Administration, or FmHA. Local farmers were elected to sit on the county committees of the FmHA, and they made decisions in the communities where they lived. I later served on one of these committees, where I learned that the system was largely a good ol' boy network where farmers supported their friends and punished their enemies. It was a system that encouraged corruption because the committee had great power and little accountability.

These county committees rarely included African Americans, and black farmers' interests were rarely protected. During the same year that I applied for disaster insurance, a fourth-generation farmer named George Norman and three other black farmers filed a discrimination complaint to the USDA's Civil Rights Office against the supervisor of the FmHA in Gates County, North Carolina. The complaint said that black farmers in the county often received loan payments from the department in June, well into the planting season—long after white farmers in the county received their payments. The black farmers said that they were routinely given less than they needed to stay afloat, while white farmers in the county were awarded the complete amount of their financial need. The black farmers said they had been forced to sell their livestock at a loss in order to make loan payments after threats from the FmHA of foreclosure.

Before the 1980 harvest, George Norman died of a heart attack. His wife says that when she contacted the Gates County FmHA supervisor, she was told that no help would be forthcoming because of the complaint he had filed. The bank foreclosed on their farm. The FmHA bought the Norman property and resold it.

A subsequent investigation by the USDA found a "pattern and

practice" in Gates County "of black farmers being foreclosed, liqui-
dated, or being forced to sell their property" by the county supervisor. Black farmers were not informed of debt restructuring loans
offered by the FmHA. Their land was appraised at less than its real
value. Waiting periods for loans were much longer for blacks than
for whites. Black farmers were told that if they sold their farms, they
would be given money to build homes outside of Gates County.
When black farmers did sell their land, their property was usually
purchased by a "select group" of white landowners or timber entrepreneurs. One black farmer told investigators that when he approached the FmHA office to ask if there were any loans for
economic hardship because of high production costs, he was told
there were none. Yet in 1979 and 1980, a twenty-one-year-old white
male received $237,000 in "economic emergency loans" from the
Gates County FmHA office to purchase and maintain a thirty-acre
farm.

Across the South, stories similar to the Gates County lawsuit
flooded the U.S. Department of Agriculture's Civil Rights Office in
the 1970s and 1980s. But in 1983, President Ronald Reagan closed
that office, and the USDA stopped responding to claims of discrimination. In 1984 and 1985, the agency lent $1.3 billion dollars to
farmers in order to buy land. Sixteen thousand farmers received
these loans. Only 209 of them were black.

In the little more than two decades between the beginning of my
college basketball career in the late 1960s and the start of Will's
Roadside in 1993, about 115,000 black farmers left the profession.
By the last decade of the twentieth century, the typical African
American farmer who remained on the land was sixty years old. He
often had a precarious livelihood. If he was finally forced off his land
by necessity, it was all but impossible for his descendants to become
farmers again. The costs were simply too high to compete against
farms of four hundred acres or more. By the end of the 1980s, there
were fewer than five hundred African American farmers under the
age of twenty-five in the entire United States.

❧

One morning in 1983, as I was shaving I felt the right side of my face and touched a hard nodule below the skin near my ear. It felt like a marble. I rolled my hand around it, and I pushed down on it. It hurt a little bit to touch but not too much. I decided to go in for a scan just to be safe. My doctor found that this mass was cancer in one of my parotid glands—the largest of the salivary glands—near my right ear.

My doctor warned that the surgery to remove the cancer in the parotid gland was even more dangerous than the surgery on my thyroid. Several crucial structures run through the gland, not least of which is the facial nerve, which controls the muscles that provide for facial expression. If the doctor was not careful, I could be left with facial paralysis. He said that the surgery was essential. The parotid gland was very close to the brain, and the cancer could spread there quickly if left untreated.

As I was wheeled into surgery, Cyndy squeezed my hand, and I realized that once I was asleep, I would have no control. I like to be in control. People might assume because of my size that I am immune to fear, but I was afraid. I faced the prospect of losing the ability to control my face. The surgeon made a long cut behind my ear so that the scar would be less prominent. In a matter of two hours, he folded over the skin, removed the tumor, and sewed me up. After I awoke from surgery, I realized that I had some difficulty moving my lips on the right side of my face. The doctor explained that the facial nerve had been touched but not severed. Within a few months, I had regained about three-quarters of my former ability. I still have some trouble moving my mouth on my right side. Some of my relatives say that I was more expressive before, but I hardly feel a difference now.

I returned to work at Kentucky Fried Chicken within a week of the surgery. Peter Helf, my boss at the Marcus Corporation, had suggested that I take more time. I wanted to get back to work. My ongoing treatment required doses of radiation to the right side of my face in order to eliminate any cancer that had not been caught by the surgeon's knife. The doctors laid me down on a flat table and covered my left side with a heavy shield. They left one side of me exposed and pointed a machine at my jawline near my ear. The machine did its silent work. Within a day of this treatment, my whole mouth was so raw that I had trouble eating and chewing.

Along with my athletic disappointments, cancer rid me of my youthful arrogance and belief that I was invincible. My illness made me realize that life was not guaranteed, and it raised the possibility that I could die as a young man. I felt a sense of urgency to make good use of time.

My cancer also contributed to a lifelong skepticism of unnecessary technology. When I was ill, I was entirely dependent for my care on technological therapies, even though an elaborate technological solution to my ringworm had got me into this trouble in the first place. Radiation caused my cancer, and now radiation was its cure. In my agricultural work, I have always looked for common-sense solutions. I try never to use a more expensive, energy-intensive technology when a simpler one can serve the same purpose.

After a decade of managing Kentucky Fried Chicken stores, I was tired of the chicken business. It was 1989. A new opportunity came to me by chance. My son, Jason, was sixteen at that time. I had forced Jason to farm with me since he was young enough to help. Like his father, he had developed a passion for basketball instead. He was also quite good, and his Amateur Athletic Union basketball team won the 1988 Wisconsin state tournament.

Jason's team needed to raise $22,000 for all of the players to attend the national championships in Las Vegas. Many of the high school kids on his team were from low-income neighborhoods in Milwaukee, and I knew this opportunity would be a rare chance for them to be seen by college recruiters who could potentially provide them athletic scholarships and a chance at higher education. On my own I was able to raise $19,000 of the money the team needed.

The father of one of my son's teammates was a district manager for Procter & Gamble, and he was impressed by my fund-raising ability. He asked me if I was interested in applying for a sales job with his company. I spent a day shadowing another salesman while he made five sales calls, and I immediately saw the benefits of this job. I would no longer be coming home to Cyndy smelling like chicken grease. As long as I met a sales quota, the company said I could do the work on my own time, allowing me to farm. Procter & Gamble also offered substantially more money than KFC, and the retirement benefits were very generous. I said yes.

By the time I had joined Procter & Gamble, my farming operation had expanded. The city of Oak Creek had fifty acres of empty land near my own property that looked fertile, and I began to lease it. Though Oak Creek had long been almost exclusively white, it was slowly changing. Several Hmong refugees had moved into the area. The Hmong have a long history in subsistence farming, and I hired a gentleman named Mr. Chu and his family to help me farm the additional acreage. I paid him in cash but also provided him land to grow on for his own purposes. I also hired a young man who had once worked for me at KFC. He had recently gotten out of jail after pulling a gun at a bar on a guy who had pulled a gun on him. He was having trouble finding work after his conviction, and I paid him and a few of his friends to help me cut greens and prepare them for market.

One Friday afternoon in mid-October of 1990, I drove by the Hardee's where Karen Parker worked to ask if she could help at some of my farmers markets that weekend. Her employees said that her son, DeShawn, had been in a fire, and that a sheriff had come and taken her to the hospital. In the aftermath of DeShawn's accident, I was able to help Karen find part-time work at Procter & Gamble.

When a grocery store bought one of our planograms, we needed to reset the items on every shelf of the store. The work could only be done when the grocery store was closed, and it often involved a frenzied rush of activity between midnight and 6 A.M. Karen frequently came to these resets after long shifts at Hardee's, where she was now a manager. She worked very hard, and she never complained. She was raising her two children on her own, and she never turned down work. She was later able to find full-time work at Procter & Gamble, where several people were sympathetic to her situation.

My primary venue to sell my produce continued to be Fondy Farmers Market, where I now had a presence seven days a week. In the early 1990s, an increasing number of Hmong farmers were applying for spots at Fondy. I felt the same cultural resistance among some of the farmers toward the Hmong that I had once felt toward me, though this attitude was not universal. I fought to include Hmong farmers at Fondy. I knew that agriculture was one of the few ways that people in this community could provide for their families when their English language skills were limited.

∾

In 1992, Milwaukee's Common Council acted on a recommendation from the city's mayor to stop sponsoring the Fondy Farmers Market. It was costing the city $73,000 a year, and the council decided to sell the market to a private owner. Many of the farmers at Fondy were worried by this news. It cost a farmer $300 a year to rent a small stall, and a private owner of the market was likely to double that fee in order to make a profit.

Although so many of the Fondy farmers had initially rejected me, several of them now turned to me for a solution. They felt I had clout in the African American community, and they suggested I help organize the neighbors there to oppose the city's plan for privatization. I had a different idea. I proposed that all of the farmers at the market join together to form a cooperative and that we run the market ourselves.

I was able to secure a small grant and hire Joan Jacobs, a friend who had served with me on the board of the Wisconsin Farmers Foundation, to be executive director of our cooperative. The three dozen farmers in the market held an election, and I was chosen president of the newly created Fondy Farmers Market Co-op. The city of Milwaukee agreed to lease the market structure to us for $1 a year. We brought in fifteen additional farmers to help us defray our operating costs, and we shared the expenses of cleaning and maintaining the facility together. We were able to keep our stall fees lower than $300, and the market survived.

By the following year, I felt the familiar restlessness that had dogged me my whole life. I have always liked to do hard things, and my job at Procter & Gamble was not hard. I would walk into a grocery story or a wholesaler, and as soon as I walked in, some guy would say, "Wow, you must have played basketball," and I would say yes, and we would talk about sports, and before you knew it, I had sold my quota of diapers or napkins or toilet paper for the week. Procter & Gamble also had incentives for buyers that often worked in my favor. My record sale of 25,000 cases of Pampers came with a wholesaler in Racine, Wisconsin, when Procter & Gamble was offering a "buyback" of $4 per case. This meant that when a wholesaler bought a case of diapers and then resold it to another store, they were offered $4 for each case that was resold. Given these rewards, my sales pitch was not a hard one to make.

Procter & Gamble restructured in 1992, and my local office moved farther away from my home, to Oak Brook, Illinois. I did not like the nearly two-hour commute each way that I had to make a couple of times a week. Planograms had become a large part of my business and sales pitches, and I knew I did not want to spend my life selling planograms. When I drove the Procter & Gamble company car, I sometimes looked down and saw that my belly had begun to progressively obscure my view of my hips. I wanted to spend my life entirely in the active and physical work of agriculture. Though I was committed to the Fondy market and the success of the new co-op, I also longed for some degree of independence.

With these unsettled thoughts, I found myself on a cold January morning in 1993 driving down Milwaukee's West Silver Spring Drive. When I spotted the greenhouses at Fifty-fifth Street, I did not know that this small lot would absorb the attention and energies of the second half of my life. My desire to do hard things was the source both of my joy and of my trouble.

PART 2

Sweat Equity

At my farm market, worms soon became the largest part of my workforce. To create food on damaged city land, I needed first to heal the soil.

BLACK GOLD

Two years after I started Will's Roadside, my stand was still open. I could say that much. In late August of 1995, Ronnie Turnipseed and the other children from the YWCA youth program harvested their tomatoes and peppers on my back lot. I helped them set up tables at the Fondy Farmers Market. The young people made several hundred dollars, and we distributed their earnings between them. I said that this experience should teach them that hard work brings rewards, though the payoff can often be a long time coming.

I hoped my own story would ultimately offer proof of this lesson. I loved the program with the YWCA children, and I wanted to have the opportunity to work with them again. That summer, I was able to pay my mortgage and expenses, though not always on time. I began to see a way through the fall and winter. I sold produce from my one hundred acres at a dozen other farmers markets around the city—including at the Fondy market—and I committed whatever I had left over to cover the expenses on my Silver Spring Drive mortgage and utilities. Belatedly, I also received a $30,000 loan that I had requested from Firstar Bank. It had not arrived in time to help me with my bedding plants that spring, but I used part of it to buy a new boiler.

After the article on the YWCA youth appeared in the *Milwaukee Journal Sentinel*, I started getting calls from teachers and program administrators who wanted me to create gardens with their children. My work with young people had so far been as a volunteer. I thought that if I formalized a youth program, however, I could charge schools or social service agencies for my services. I had a better understanding now that I needed to develop several different income streams to support my operation. My greenhouses could be not just a selling space but also a teaching space—where young people could come, even in the bitter Milwaukee winter, to learn the lessons of horticulture. To help support these ambitions, and with the encouragement of friends, I started a nonprofit organization called Farm-City Link.

At Kentucky Fried Chicken and Procter & Gamble, I had worked in the for-profit world, and I had believed in it as a model. It was not my nature to accept grant money. I knew that the decision to form a nonprofit could invite criticism from those who value profitability as the only important social value.

I faced a simple economic reality. Most small farmers I met had one or two jobs outside of their work on the land. Few of these farmers were making enough money, and many were deeply in debt. The percentage of farmers who work somewhere outside of their farms has tripled since 1959. In 2008, 90 percent of total income for all farm households in the United States came from work outside of the farm. For farmers whose annual sales are $100,000 or less—and who often operate at a loss—off-farm income often accounts for 100 percent of their yearly income. At larger farms, with $250,000 or more in annual sales, off-farm income is less than a quarter of annual pay on average.

The money that small farmers earn from second or third jobs is often spent servicing the large debt they have incurred from farming equipment, land, and livestock barns. These farmers often stay in the profession out of a sense of duty. They do not want to be the person who breaks their family's history on the land.

I did not want to work a day job again. But I understood the challenges that I faced as a small farmer whenever I drove my truck out of Milwaukee toward Madison. Traveling west on Interstate 94 in the mid-1990s, I saw fields of corn and soybeans that stretched all the way to the horizon, covering thousands of acres. The fields often looked lush and beautiful. Yet these images were paired in my mind with more disquieting scenes: small barns and farmhouses that were abandoned or in disrepair. Many of these small former farms had "For Sale" signs.

So many rural areas across the United States had come to resemble the scene along Interstate 94. This was not inevitable. One crucial turning point came in 1971, when President Nixon appointed Earl Butz as secretary of agriculture. Mr. Butz had ties to several agricultural business firms, and he opposed the policies of Franklin D. Roosevelt's New Deal that fought to contain overproduction. Butz fought for foreign markets for America's excess corn and soybeans. He encouraged farmers to plant "fencerow to fencerow" and to "get big or get out." He spoke of America's "agripower": its ability to develop huge stockpiles of commodity crops, which it could unleash upon the world markets when it wanted.

These new policies put considerable financial pressure on small to mid-sized farmers. After paying for fertilizer, seed, insecticides, fungicides, fuel, crop insurance, and labor, small farmers faced significant pressures in a farm economy where margins could be only a few cents per bushel. They no longer were competing against just local farmers but were increasingly part of a global economy. From 1970 to 1980, the total farm population in the United States declined by almost thirty percent. The average size of a single farm grew, however, to nearly 430 acres. When Butz resigned his position in 1976 after making a racist joke, he wrote to President Ford to say that "American farmers will always be grateful to you for your solid support of our efforts to raise their incomes and to permit them to manage their farms without excessive government regulation."

The trouble with Butz's argument against the meddling of big government is that his policies required the largest government interventions in agriculture in U.S. history. His fencerow to fencerow policy led to an eventual collapse in corn prices from overproduction in the 1980s, requiring large taxpayer-funded support for farmers—a dependence that has continued to this day. In 2000, nearly half of the net income for corn farmers in the United States was paid for by subsidies. In 1972, by contrast, the average annual federal subsidy to a corn producer was less than $100. And while the income of some farmers has increased by these supports, these gains have not transferred to those who are unable or unwilling to "get big." By 2011, three-quarters of government commodity payments were given to the same top 10 percent of recipients. The beneficiaries of this new system of cheap corn and grain were companies like Archer Daniels Midland, who stood between farmers and food companies. They took raw commodities like corn and wheat and turned them into products that could be used for processed foods and beverages: high-fructose corn syrup, frying oils, flours, and gums.

I was trying to create a model that was the opposite of the Butz system. I had not yet figured out how to make it work financially. The choice to leave a for-profit model felt to me like a kind of capitulation. I wanted to prove to everybody, not least myself, that a small farm stand working with small farmers and selling a diverse array of produce to the inner city could be commercially viable for everyone involved. I took comfort that my nonprofit would depend mostly on the private sector rather than grants or loans from the federal government. I wanted to rely on outside support as little as I could. In the meantime, I saw the potential to do work on Silver Spring Drive whose value could not be measured in money.

When I founded Farm-City Link, I began to think in a more focused way about how to make my fresh fruits and vegetables available to those who had the least ability to afford them. I was sensitive to complaints about my prices.

In the mid-1990s, the model of community-supported agriculture, or CSA, had become increasingly popular. A typical CSA at that time involved a group of people committing their labor and capital to a single farm. In exchange for providing some workdays on the farm— and a monetary investment of several hundred dollars at the beginning of the planting season—the owner of the farm would provide weekly seasonal produce to its members during the harvest season.

I believed this was a promising model, but not for poor people. They did not have the money to pay $500 or $600 at the beginning of the planting season for food they would only receive later in the summer. People in low-income communities also had larger families, and they were not going to be able to survive on the few items that became available early in the planting season. They need twenty pounds of fruits and vegetables a week. They were also not going to have the leisure time or transportation to travel to a rural farm and work in the fields there.

I began to imagine how the CSA model might be modified to make it work for people with little income. I approached the members of my Rainbow Farmers Co-op, which I had founded on my own after the Fondy Co-op. It had now grown to more than a dozen members. I asked the members if they would be willing to give me, at a sharp discount, the excess produce they grew. My plan was to combine these vegetables with apples and oranges and peaches that

I purchased from small regional wholesalers, and place them in what I called a "Market Basket." All the food in this basket would be food-stamp eligible.

I made arrangements first to sell these boxes of food outside of Neighborhood House, a Milwaukee-based early-childhood education and child care service. Late in 1995, I had begun working with children from Neighborhood House in my greenhouses, teaching them the basics of planting and germination. In the summer of 1996, we planned for the children to help me sell the baskets out of the back of a van at Neighborhood House on Friday afternoons, when parents picked up their children from day care or after-school programs. I priced a basket with twenty pounds of fruits and vegetables at $10. The baskets could be purchased on a week-to-week basis, so families could make decisions based on their income at the time. I told farmers who worked with me that they couldn't depend on the market basket structure for steady income. It could simply be an alternative source of revenue for produce that would otherwise go to waste. I was able to pay the farmers who participated in the market basket on delivery; when farmers sold to a wholesaler, they often had to wait up to ninety days until they got a check.

From the first day, the program was well received. Kids engaged their parents, who told me that they appreciated how much food they were getting for so little money. I started to reach out to other community centers in the hopes that I could bring my baskets to other neighborhoods without grocery stores.

During this time, I met a kind young woman who had an unusual problem. Alison Meares Cohen took a job in 1995 with Heifer International, a nonprofit organization that funded projects in forty countries. Her office was based in Chicago. Alison had at one time intended to pursue a Ph.D. in English literature. On a trip through southern France, she saw how her North African boyfriend faced discrimination everywhere they went. The experience awoke in her a social conscience. She came back to the United States seeking work that could make a difference in the lives of others.

The goal of Heifer International was to help end hunger and to increase the self-sufficiency of people with little economic means. Typically, Heifer's work in Africa was carried out through livestock—donating a goat, for example, that could in turn provide a family consistent milk and a modest income. In 1996, Heifer had received some money from the W. K. Kellogg Foundation to fund urban agriculture projects in the United States. The sticking point was that Heifer wanted Alison to use livestock in her project, just as the organization had done in Africa. Alison had good intentions, but she was running up against roadblocks while trying to figure out how to introduce animals into American cities. Keeping goats was often illegal in urban areas. Cows were both illegal and impractical. She was describing her challenges to a friend when he told her that the USDA classifies worms as livestock. Alison thought he was kidding at first.

Alison knew nothing about worms. She didn't understand that they could be cultivated or that they had any intensive agricultural uses. Neither did I. Yet she reached out to an expert on red wigglers in a suburb of Chicago, who soon gave her a demonstration in his backyard of "vermicomposting." He showed how the red wigglers could convert food scraps and newspaper into fertilizer. He explained how the worms ate through organic material, digested it, and pooped it out into "worm castings" that were rich in beneficial bacteria and nutrients. When sprinkled on top of the soil, he claimed, these castings were the best fertilizer a person could buy.

I had already begun to do some composting without worms in my back lot on West Silver Spring Drive. I used food scraps I had on hand, as well as moldy hay that some of my rural farmer friends offered me. When I met Alison at an agricultural conference, she soon started discussing the idea of a worm project with me.

"I'm not a worm farmer," I told Alison on the phone. "This is kind of ridiculous."

"I know it sounds ridiculous," Alison said.

She argued that the reality of city politics, however, meant that it was going to be a lot easier to get a project funded with Heifer money and approved by local government if I did it with worms. It was going to be much harder to get municipal approval for goats or other animals.

"Do you think Heifer would really fund a project with us if we just do some worm composting?" I asked.

"I don't know," she said. "But I want us to try."

Alison made her case. She said this worm project could involve local kids and the community. She argued that it could strengthen the work with youth that we were already doing at our facility. It could also give Heifer (and herself) a model for how the organization could work in American cities.

I was skeptical. I knew that in the 1970s and 1980s some ill-intentioned companies had tried to sell people on the dubious idea that you could make millions of dollars from worms because of their rapid rate of reproduction. I didn't see how the project fit into the larger work I was pursuing. Yet despite my doubts, I decided I was willing to give the worms a chance for Alison's sake. She wrote a project proposal and soon secured nearly $50,000, which was to be spent over three years to teach children from a local YMCA about vermiculture.

"If you love it enough," the agriculturalist George Washington Carver once said, "anything will talk to you."

To my surprise, worms began to talk to me.

Our first order of red wigglers was sixty pounds' worth from a company in Florida. When I opened the boxes, I found them writhing inside a soil mixture in transparent plastic bags. I looked at them with some fear and pity; I wasn't sure their future was in good hands.

I followed what I had learned from books and from one demonstration at my greenhouses. I showed the young people from the YMCA how to drill holes in about a dozen Rubbermaid bins to allow for aeration. They ripped newspapers into inch-thick strips to create a bedding material for the worms and then moistened those strips and squeezed them partially dry. We added some dirt and a handful of food waste and then poured several pounds of worms into each bin. I tried not to let the students know that my experience in this area was about as deep as theirs.

Despite our good intentions, the worms soon began to die. Only two weeks into the project, I opened up the Rubbermaid boxes and found many of the newspaper strips soaking wet—and many of our worms lying on the top of the pile, lifeless. In other bins, the worms seemed sluggish. I saw few signs that they were reproducing. I knew the worms had Goldilocks-style needs: Their bedding needed to be moist enough but not too moist. The temperature of the material they lived in needed to be between fifty and seventy degrees.

The children were having trouble getting the balance of these demands quite right. Worms breathe through their skin, and they need some moisture to be able to take in oxygen. Too much moisture, however, and they drown. The reason they end up on a sidewalk after a heavy rain is that they are making a desperate attempt to gasp for air. When the children were asked to remoisten the worm bins, they often overwatered them and killed the worms. Some of the bins had too much decaying fruit for them to eat, while others had too little.

Within a few weeks, rather than growing our population of worms, as intended, we had killed off most of them. The students had another type of reproductive success, though, in growing a fruit fly population. The flies were feasting on the decaying fresh fruit we were placing in the worm bins. We soon had so many fruit flies that I had to swat them away as I walked through the greenhouses. I understood that I had to make some changes fast if I wanted to keep this project alive. I decided to temporarily suspend the children's participation until I could fix the problems.

I spoke with Jan Carroll, a friend who I knew raised worms in her basement. "I can't have people come in here and see flies," I told Jan. "We've got fresh fruit in our retail store." She said she struggled with flies as well, though not to the degree that I did. Jan suggested burying the fresh produce that we fed the worms underneath the bedding material. This would make it less accessible for flies.

I reached out to another friend, who suggested that instead of adding fruit that was recently fresh to the worm bins, I should let the fruit decay for a few days in a sealed environment so that it was broken down. This would make the fruit less attractive to flies, and easier for the worms' small mouths to eat.

Jan brought over some of her own red wigglers to help me start over. I constructed a couple two- by four-foot worm boxes using wood. Instead of using newspaper scraps in my bins, I decided to experiment with my own method. I laid down several inches of my own compost in each wooden box. I added a layer of worms from Jan's supply and the lucky batch the children had managed to keep alive. Then I added about three inches thick of food waste that I had sealed for two weeks in a five-gallon bucket. The fruits had already become slimy, though they had not broken down entirely.

To my delight, I saw that the worms were rapidly eating through the composted and pre-composted material. And I began to find small brown cocoons in the bins—signs that the worms were reproducing. I became interested in which pre-composted foods the worms liked the best. I began testing different types of food in different corners of the boxes. In one box, I put pre-composted bananas in a corner, sweet potatoes in another, brewery waste in another, coffee grounds in the fourth. I watched closely which foods the worms gravitated to—and on which sides of the boxes I was getting the best reproduction. I covered the boxes with burlap bags in order to protect the worms from light, which they don't like. The bags also detracted flies.

The worms particularly liked the partially decayed bananas. Sometimes I'd pick up the remnants of the banana and find dozens of worms in that area. The worms also thrived with other types of pre-composted vegetables and fruits, such as old cucumbers, tomatoes, and nectarines. They appreciated small amounts of material that had some grit, like brewery waste and spent coffee grounds. In a proper environment, the worms ate through their entire weight in a single day and deposited the waste in little black globules. In the gut of the worm, I soon understood, the beneficial bacteria in the soil multiplies by as much as fourteen times. This bacteria "fixes" nitrogen for the plant's roots: It takes nitrogen from the air and dissolves it so plants can use it as energy.

These worm castings were a rich brown color and beautiful. We called them "black gold." When I began to sprinkle the castings on plants in my greenhouses, I saw that the plants thrived. I thought that if I could grow my worm population, the castings could be my only fertilizer. They could replace the need for synthetic products that are by-products of fossil fuel. Synthetic fertilizers can destroy the soil's worm population and its natural fertility. Worm castings, in contrast, were a renewable resource.

The worms taught me. I couldn't expect to put them in a box with inadequate resources and have them do well. They required husbandry, and they demanded the kind of attention and care you would pay to sheep or pigs. The worms also made me reflect again on what it took to improve the lives of people. You couldn't place folks in the middle of a blighted neighborhood—without a strong family unit and without easy access to healthy food—and expect them to thrive. If you could create an environment in which people felt secure and healthy, though, you could provide the possibility of a better life.

In the years since DeShawn's fire, Karen Parker had poured her life into the care of her son. She wanted to compensate for what had happened to him. She attended to his wounds, drove him to surgeries that grafted skin from his stomach to his face, bought him whatever clothes or video games she could afford, and filed a lawsuit on his behalf against the Bic corporation for product liability. She felt that the company should not create a lighter that could be so easily ignited by a three-year-old boy. If the case was successful, she thought it could cover DeShawn's medical expenses, give him some economic security, and also make sure that a similar accident did not happen to another young boy or girl in the future.

DeShawn was deposed in the case, even though he was little more than five years old at the time. Lawyers asked him to recall the details of the fire. In his deposition, DeShawn said he remembered taking a green lighter off the table near the couch, and that he remembered throwing the lighter into the fire as it grew. The lawyers from Bic argued that no green lighter was found at the scene— though investigators did find a *red* Bic lighter and a pack of cigarettes on the floor. Bic accepted that DeShawn could have indeed thrown a green lighter into the fire; they said this green lighter could have been completely incinerated by the flames, since no traces of it were found. No evidence suggested that their company's red lighter was responsible, the lawyers said.

In October of 1996, a Wisconsin appeals court upheld an earlier court decision that dismissed DeShawn's case. In telling the story of the fire to his family, DeShawn sometimes said the lighter was red, and sometimes green. DeShawn's grandfather said the lighter he had left behind that morning was red. In his deposition, DeShawn chose the wrong time to go with green.

By 1997, when DeShawn was ten, the florist who first occupied the retail store at my facility had left her business, and I began to use that space to expand my store. In the kitchen behind the store, De-Shawn and I sometimes cooked meals together. When DeShawn came into the greenhouses while I was working, I also taught him when I could the names of vegetables or how to plant seeds in plastic trays. He was very quiet, but he would listen attentively to me. He would rarely share his feelings.

Strangers sometimes stared at DeShawn when they first saw him. He was not unaware of this attention, and it clearly made him uncomfortable. If he felt someone gazing too long, he sometimes stared back and said "peekaboo" until the person looked away. He was struggling in school. He was often teased there, and he felt little connection to the material taught him. He valued his time alone.

"When I came in after school and walked through the greenhouses, I got my mind at peace," DeShawn explained later. On his schoolwork, he said, "I'm not a person where you sit down and put a book in front of me, and I'll learn. The teachers always wanted me to write something. I don't learn that way."

Like my father, DeShawn was a good visual learner. When he cooked with me, he began to anticipate when I would need a spatula or a spoon, and he handed it to me before I asked. He had little opportunity to demonstrate this type of intelligence at his public school. In his free time, unknown to me, DeShawn began to cook things on his own. He thinks the first meal he prepared independently was a steak in his mother's kitchen. He was only eleven. By the holiday season, he was trying more elaborate recipes: cornbread, purple-hull pea dishes, candied yams.

In May of 1997, while I was still experimenting with worms, Alison Cohen attended the International Conference on Sustainable Urban Food Systems in Toronto. Alison was looking for ways to expand Heifer's work with me, and she hoped the conference would provide some ideas. At the time, "sustainable urban food systems" still seemed more like an academic exercise than a legitimate ambition.

On the first day of the conference, Alison gave a speech on the potential of introducing livestock into American cities. She also discussed the obstacles. She told an anecdote about her efforts to start a dairy goat project at a school at Cabrini Green, the Chicago public housing project. A few days after the program began, police squad cars descended on two teenagers walking the animals down the street. The cops took the goats into custody. Alison explained the misunderstanding to Chicago's Animal Control, who returned the goats to her. The principal of the Cabrini Green school made a special announcement over the intercom that the goats had been "released from jail," and a cheer went up among the students.

After Alison's speech, a man she didn't know approached. He asked if she knew about a hunger organization in Toronto that was growing fish in barrels. Alison was intrigued, asked for the address, and immediately took a cab across town to the small warehouse operated by a nonprofit called FoodShare Metro Toronto.

FoodShare's facility sat in the Port Lands district, a former industrial area that was now largely abandoned. Inside, Alison met Jonathan Woods, an entrepreneur in his late twenties. Jonathan had struggled for years with opposing ambitions: He wanted to live in the city, but he also wanted to grow his own food and to live in a self-sufficient way. So he began to read everything he could find about growing food in urban environments. He obtained a degree in zoology with a specialty in fish, and founded a company in 1995 called Annex Organics. The company's goal, according to its mission statement, was to be "a model urban farm designed to challenge the North American myth that food must come from the countryside."

Jonathan gave Alison a tour of the FoodShare warehouse, where he was using vacant space to grow food. On the roof, he was growing Turkish orange eggplants, a dozen varieties of tomatoes, and other specialty greens. The plants were rooted in a thin layer of soil in small pots. These pots sat in a trough filled with a complex microbial soup created by water, composted vegetable waste, discarded fish heads, wood ash, and other recycled organic materials. When the root systems outgrew the pots, they extended into this murk. Somehow, improbably, the vegetables grew healthy and strong.

Inside, Jonathan and his partners grew trays of sprouts under lamps: alfalfa, pea shoots, radish greens, and spicy lentil crunch. Jonathan sold his specialty fruits and vegetables in Toronto, to health food stores and to chefs at high-end restaurants. He delivered the produce by subway, bicycle, or bus instead of using trucks. One of the advantages of growing inside cities, he told Alison, was that it eliminated the dependence on fossil fuels.

Jonathan also showed Alison his fish system. Inspired by the work of Dr. John Todd, a Canadian biologist, it was called a "living machine." It cost less than $250 to construct and maintain. The hardware for the system was made up primarily of three interconnected fifty-five-gallon plastic barrels, PVC pipe, and an aquarium pump. One tank was used for growing submerged and floating plants, algae, and zooplankton—small aquatic organisms. It emptied into a second tank that contained about two hundred tilapia,

an African freshwater fish that is popular for food. A third tank took
the fish waste and broke down the ammonia in it with snails, bacteria, and fungi, before returning the water back to the first barrel
again. Jonathan knew that his work was viewed as countercultural.
In his mind, though, he wondered how trucking in food from thousands of miles away had become the new normal.

Alison called me to tell me about this fish system. I was immediately interested. We decided to invite Jonathan to Milwaukee to give
a workshop; Alison was able to secure some money from Heifer to
fund the visit. Children from Neighborhood House and the YMCA
were asked to participate. We obtained fifty-five-gallon barrels for
$40 each from a local car wash called Scrub-A-Dub. We cleaned
them out thoroughly so as not to kill the fish with any soap residue.

At the workshop, Jonathan explained the living machines, and
the children helped build them. I made a special point of teaching
the young people to use power tools, hoping this experience could
provide a practical skill outside of agriculture. By the end of a weekend, we had three fish systems set up in my greenhouses.

These fish barrels struck distant chords of memory in me. One of
the great pleasures of my father's life was fishing. I had spent many
happy hours as a boy with him at Sycamore Landing, a shallow
stretch of the Potomac River near our home. I knew it was a far different thing to grow fish in barrels in the city of Milwaukee, and
O.W. no doubt would have laughed to see me. *That ain't real fishing,
boy*, I could imagine him saying. Yet for all the ways our lives were
different, I felt this fish barrel project connected us.

Out of economic necessity, I was accepting whatever work came to
me. The first year of my nonprofit, in 1996, I brought in only $10,000
in grants and fees for services. With the help of a grant from the
Milwaukee-based Helen Bader Foundation, I hoped in 1997 to secure four times that much. But I knew that even this money could
hardly sustain a single full-time salary. My board and I were all

serving as volunteers. Joan Jacobs, who was executive director of my co-op at Fondy, also became Farm-City Link's board chairman. In the early 1990s, Joan and I had worked together to develop a micro-loan fund for small farmers who were in financial situations like my own.

Joan helped me with my payroll for my nonprofit and for my roadside stand. My expenses included salaries for Karen, DeShawn, DeShell, and a handful of other young people from my neighborhood. "You were always hiring people when there was no money for them," Joan recalled. "I'd say, 'Will, we don't have money for five new people.'" When she walked into my office for the first time, Joan saw receipts all over the place. She often didn't know how we were going to pay the bills.

I pumped whatever money I earned from my own farm sales back into covering my roadside stand's expenses. Joan said that thinking over my predicament sometimes deprived her of sleep. Yet she believed as strongly as I did in the benefit of what I hoped to do. "A lot of kids from the neighborhood would arrive at your site in the summer," she reminded me. "It was a place where they were coming to be safe, frankly." Joan encouraged me to make my youth program more structured, and to provide job training and transferrable skills. I didn't yet have the resources or the right people to make that happen.

During this time, I developed a closer relationship with Neighborhood House, the Milwaukee family service agency. The organization owned ninety acres of land outside the city that they primarily used for recreation and hiking. I started a small gardening program on this site. Youth from Neighborhood House's after-school programs continued to come to my greenhouses to learn about worms and plant germination. I undertook some neighborhood beautification projects with their kids, such as laying compost and seeding flowers in abandoned or derelict city lots. We hoped by planting flowers in lots that attracted drug dealers, we could draw the eyes of the community to the plants and that the criminal elements there would feel less welcome.

An educator with the State of Wisconsin's Division of Juvenile Corrections heard about this work, and he contacted me in the summer of 1997. With his help, I began an agricultural program for youth offenders who were transitioning out of the detention system. Farm-City Link was compensated $100/hour for this work. At the time, this was a not-insignificant amount of money for my organization.

One day a week for four hours, I visited a transitional school for young people with some of my compost. I worked alongside young men, making planting beds and teaching the basics of cultivation. We created raised beds of vegetables on the edge of a basketball court at their transitional school. We drove to neighborhoods where some of them had been arrested and planted flowers. I hoped that this experience could give the young men an opportunity to feel that they were a positive part of communities where they had been seen as trouble.

As I helped the young men till the soil, they told me their stories. One thin boy, who did not yet look twenty, told me how he stole an automobile, led a police chase, and then ditched the car while the officers chased him on foot. When the fastest officer caught up with him, the teen turned around and hit him. He was charged with car theft and assaulting an officer. His family could not afford a private attorney and had to depend on a court-appointed lawyer. He spent three years in prison.

He wore an ankle bracelet that monitored him, as did many other teenagers in the transitional program. Sometimes they lifted their pant legs to show me, half with shame, as if it were a tattoo that they had since reconsidered. I could not help but feel that if some of them had been white—and if they could have afforded their own attorneys—they would have been sentenced to community service at most. When they got out of prison, these boys had a record and a difficult future ahead of them. Employers were wary of them, and they had little training or skills. They had better incentives to find illegal work than to live straight.

I wanted to expand the program with the juvenile offenders. I was disappointed when the administrator who hired me was transferred and my program ended after a single year. I knew it was naive to think that gardening could turn around the lives of young men whose circumstances were so difficult. By discussing my own basketball career, though, I hoped I could present one model of a life that did not seem unbearable to them. Many of these young men had no future vision of themselves that was stable and hopeful. I also thought that planting flowers could provide the experience of being a positive part of a community rather than a destructive one.

In the summer of 1998, after this program was canceled, I sat around a campfire one evening at Neighborhood House's ninety-acre natural site in Dodge County, outside of Milwaukee. It was twilight. After nightfall, I planned to drive home to Cyndy in Oak Creek. Middle-schoolers were roasting marshmallows before camping overnight. Sitting next to me were Bradley Blaeser, an earnest young man who was a program director for Neighborhood House, and Heifer's Alison Cohen, who was visiting my garden project at the site. I talked a lot that night about the future of my work.

"Where can we go with this?" I said. "What can we do with this?"

Looking back, I realize that I had some pieces of my puzzle already in place. I was refining a system with worms to create organic fertilizer. I was working with young people in an effort to transform their view of agriculture and to introduce them to fresh and healthy foods. I was growing fish in barrels indoors. I had begun a market basket system to bring inexpensive food to low-income communities.

I had added all of these parts of my operation one by one, mostly by chance. I didn't have a clear idea of my future. As I was struggling with these questions, my path intersected with a young community organizer whose name was appropriate to my needs. Hope.

Be a Do Tank

I visit groups who receive grants to build urban gardens but after a year, their money is all gone, and they have not made any compost or grown a single fruit or vegetable. They have spent all their time in meetings. I tell people that they need to be a *do tank* and not a think tank. It's pleasant to talk about a garden you might build, because your idealism has not yet been tempered by the difficult process of actually doing anything. It's another thing altogether to start a project, to get your hands dirty, and to have some inevitable setbacks and disappointments.

I know from experience that it helps to make a good plan before you launch into any project. Don't spend so much time on your plan, however, that you never get around to doing something. As Teddy Roosevelt once pointed out, it is better to be the man or woman in the arena—the one whose "face is marred by dust and sweat and blood"—than it is to be a person who just talks about doing things. Be a person of action.

With Hope Finkelstein in 1999

A LITTLE HOPE, A LOT OF WILL

The first time I shook Hope Finkelstein's hand, I looked at her with no understanding that she would become a part of my future. Hope heard of me through a mutual friend, and she had arrived at my greenhouses interested in a tour. I walked her quickly through my facility and showed her my fish and worm systems. I was still using only two of my five greenhouses. Hope was five-foot-one, thirty-four years old, and the top of her head fell well short of my shoulders. She wore oversized glasses, and she absorbed everything quietly.

"I thought you were doing great work and had a big heart," Hope told me later. "The greenhouses were an amazing resource. I also thought: 'This guy needs a lot of help.'"

When Hope was twelve, in 1976, her father was driving her home along the Long Island Sound when he asked her what kind of work she hoped to do. "I am going to organize programs for the community," she said. She was a petite Jewish girl with wide eyes and straight brown hair. At a time when many young girls wanted to be a ballerina or an actress, she dreamed of becoming a community activist.

As an undergraduate at Cornell, Hope became fascinated with the Federal Art Project, a program created by President Franklin D. Roosevelt's New Deal to employ out-of-work artists during the Great Depression. The project led to the creation of one hundred community arts centers across the United States. In a period of only eight years, these centers yielded a tremendous creative harvest of more than 2,500 murals, 100,000 paintings, and 17,000 sculptures. After Cornell, Hope moved to New York City and wrote her master's thesis at the City University of New York on Augusta Savage, a talented African American sculptor who founded a community art center in Harlem and who later became director of the Harlem Community Arts Center. Savage had not been content to create her own art, but fought for equal access for black people to arts education.

In her study of community art centers, Hope understood that if people had support and a context to express their creativity, it could enrich their lives and build a sense of place and community. She started to work in museums and community art centers in New York, but she quickly became disillusioned by what she perceived as the snobbery and pretension of the New York City art world.

She moved to Madison, Wisconsin, where she soon became involved by chance in a growing community gardening scene. Hope was particularly intrigued by a community gardening project along Madison's Troy Drive, where a large field had been converted into small plots leased for a small fee to residents of Madison. The project had attracted Hmong immigrants from Laos and Vietnam, middle-class whites, and a handful of African Americans. At a harvest festival there, Hope saw that the project provided an opportunity for interaction between cultures—communication that would have been unlikely to occur in any other context.

There were several community gardens in Madison, but Hope felt that they were doing little to work together. She thought that they could be strengthened through collaboration: applying for grants together and sharing resources and lessons learned. She dreamed of a different food system that brought people together, and where power was not concentrated in corporate interests.

Early in 1998, Hope rose one morning from a dream. In it, she saw a long line of people holding hands. They were all ages, shapes, colors, and sizes—tall, short, fat, thin, black, and white. She felt the people were drawing strength from one another. Their feet were rooted in the earth. She remembers that a simple name was on her lips as she woke: Growing Power.

Soon after her dream, she reached out to her artist friend Ricardo Jomarron. They discussed her vision for an organization she hoped to create, one partly inspired by her dream. Hope's idea was to start her nonprofit in Madison, but to build her group nationally and internationally. The organization would be multigenerational and multiethnic, Hope told Ricardo. People would work cooperatively together. No single person would be more important than another.

Ricardo designed a logo with Hope's help. It pictured a globe that was contained within the petals of a sunflower. Figures of different sizes and shapes held hands across the equator of the earth. All of the figures were on the same level. The logo was accompanied with a tagline: "Together . . . We Are Growing Power."

The image of the sunflower was particularly important to Hope: "The sunflower is a flower of beauty," she later told me. "It is also a flower of food." Hope could not have known, but sunflowers had been important to my mother, Willie Mae, and her mother, Rosa Bell. The women in my family always kept them in their gardens, as I did in mine.

∾

During her visit to my greenhouses, Hope told me about Growing Power, and I soon offered to be a board member. She invited me to her inaugural event in Madison. I brought a garbage bag full of my greens for people to eat at the reception. At a multi-faith chapel, Hope introduced a Cuban government official, Eugenio Fuster Chepe, who delivered a speech indicating how the U.S. embargo on his country had spurred people to grow food in city centers. He said there were now more than seventeen hundred urban gardens in Havana, providing a large percentage of the city's food.

In the spring of 1999, Hope and her board members gathered with me for a day-long meeting at my greenhouses. Hope was pregnant with her second child at the time, and she was trying to find a way forward for Growing Power. At the same time, I was trying to find a way forward for Farm-City Link.

Hope was soliciting advice from those close to her. She had recently organized an interracial youth garden with thirty children at a Madison early childhood learning center. She hoped to do similar projects in the future, but she was dependent on other organizations to provide her land. She wanted to ground Growing Power at a place, to give it a home. She did all of her grant writing, planning, visioning, and office work out of her house. By the afternoon of our meeting, Hope said she looked at me and something clicked inside her.

"You had a physical space that needed an organization," she told me later. "I had an organization that needed a physical space."

I loved the name "Growing Power." It was better than Farm-City Link. It felt true to my own mission: to make people stronger physically and spiritually through agriculture. I also knew that I needed someone to help me plan, strategize, write year-end reports, apply for grants, and organize. I felt competent as a farmer but not at managing my organization. Hope possessed skills that I lacked. She had a vision and was passionate about her cause.

We agreed that afternoon to merge and become partners. Hope felt strongly about the idea of shared leadership, so we chose to call ourselves "co-directors" of Growing Power. After our larger meeting with half a dozen others was over, Hope came back to my small office. We talked briefly about our next steps. I ended the conversation by saying: "Let's do this!"

I saw the joy on Hope's face. She extended her small arms for a hug around my midsection.

"There is a part of the Jewish wedding ceremony called the *yichud*," Hope explained to me later, "when the bride and groom are left alone in a small room for the first time. Ours was a strictly professional relationship, but that moment kind of felt like that to me."

In Milwaukee, I had often encouraged young people and their parents to plant their own gardens. When I tried myself to plant in city land, I realized that this advice was not practical. The soil was almost always dry and infertile. An urban environment messes with the ways that nature replenishes the earth. When you displace animals and trees, you also deprive the soil of manure and falling leaves that offer new sources of carbon and nitrogen—essential components for any plant's growth. Chemical fertilizers give plants and lawns the nitrogen they need, but they can lead to dependence by damaging the soil's earthworm population and its natural fertility.

Soon after Hope and I became co-directors of Growing Power, I was approached by the executive director of a Milwaukee organization called WasteCap Wisconsin. Jenna Kunde was trying to reduce the amount of food that was going to landfills. Food waste is the major reason why trash needs to be collected so often in cities. If allowed to sit and rot, the waste attracts insects and rodents, and it can pose a public health hazard. A full one-quarter of all food that is created in the United States ends up in the waste stream—more than sixty billion pounds a year. In the landfill, when it is not combined with substances heavy with carbon, food waste emits methane as it rots. Methane changes in the atmosphere into carbon dioxide, a gas that contributes to global warming.

Jenna and WasteCap had worked in Milwaukee to encourage the recycling of housing construction and demolition materials. Now they were turning their attention into how food waste could be converted into soil and into energy. WasteCap did not have its own truck, though, or the capacity to compost waste even if they retrieved it. So Jenna approached me with an offer to help me find waste streams that could amp up my compost production. Following my father's example, I was already doing some composting on my back lot at Silver Spring Drive. I used food scraps I had on hand as well as moldy hay that some of my rural farmer friends offered me. I started on a small scale.

With Jenna's help, I visited a grocery called Sendik's in the upscale Milwaukee neighborhood of Whitefish Bay. The store was immaculate and had carpeted floors. In the produce aisles, the vegetables and fruits on display were always perfect. Unseen to the customer, several employees worked in a back room of the store, trimming any imperfections from produce that was shipped to them. They also threw out any fruits or vegetables that they felt would not meet the customers' high standards: celery stalks with small blemishes, or lettuce that was even slightly brown on the edges. All of this organic waste was ending up in the city landfill.

I made the produce manager at Sendik's an offer. I said that I could save them hauling fees to the dump if they would allow me to come three times a week and pick up all of their fruit and vegetable waste. I explained how I planned to use this trash as a nitrogen source for my compost—converting it back into soil to create raised planting beds where people could grow fresh food.

The manager said he appreciated the spirit of what I hoped to do. Yet he also had some practical concerns. He wondered whether I was going to be there on time and whether I would never miss a pickup. Waste Management came when it was searing hot, and when the windchill was forty below zero. Could he expect the same from me? If I didn't show up, it would create problems for the store.

I said I would be there. With the help of WasteCap, I soon provided the store with several purple twenty-plus-gallon Rubbermaid totes. The store's employees were instructed to dump their fruit and vegetable waste and trimmings there. The Sendik's staff stacked these filled containers in a loading bay where I arrived with a truck three days a week. With the Sendik's produce and old straw, a small, steaming volcano of compost began to grow near the back fence of the lot behind my greenhouses. I soon built a relationship with Alterra Coffee, a local brewery, to collect their used grounds at their main location on North Prospect Avenue. These were added to the compost pile as well.

Kids from the nearby Westlawn public housing complex began to hang out at my facility after school, and I told them if they were going to stay, they needed to help me turn my compost to keep it aerated. I felt there was a lesson for young people in compost. The process showed how you could take something that others considered to be trash and transform it into the basis of life. I also thought that composting could be a new income stream for me. I began to imagine a new kind of urban ecology where I could intercept organic waste before it reached the landfill and grow it into healthy soil.

When we first joined forces, Hope was in the last stages of her pregnancy. Her second daughter, Barae, was born in June of 1999. Hope continued to live in Madison, a two-hour drive away, and worked mostly from home. She wrote grant applications, and we began to talk about our plans for the new year. She sometimes worked out of our office: a small room with a concrete floor that sat behind the kitchen and front store. Though I hired some local youth from the community to help run my store, I could only afford to maintain a skeleton staff. Karen Parker continued to be my main employee.

Karen's daughter, DeShell, who was now almost twenty, had enrolled at the University of Wisconsin in Madison two years before. DeShell says part of her motivation to work hard in high school was to escape her life at Will's Roadside. She didn't like the demands I put on her or the constant watchful eye of her mother. As a teen, she was very opinionated about politics or people, and I usually tried to take the opposite position of most of what she said just to sharpen her debating skills.

To my surprise, DeShell returned home during her second year in Madison. She decided to enroll at the Milwaukee Area Technical College, and to move back into her mother's house. "I had wanted to leave as soon as I could," DeShell explained to me later, "but I realized as soon as I left that I missed my mother and brother deeply."

While DeShell attended college, she also worked occasionally in the store to relieve her mother. While she seemed on a good track, I began to worry more about DeShawn. He was entering his teen years, and he had become very withdrawn. He spent long periods locked in his room. Some of his second cousins would tease him about his burns and about being bald. Once, when he went with a cousin to a salon to get his hair braided, the hairdresser didn't charge DeShawn any money when she finished.

"Why aren't you charging him, because he's only got a half head of hair?" one of his second cousins asked the hairdresser.

DeShawn held these things in his heart. I would sometimes see him walking through the greenhouses, looking at his cactus and the other plants, trying to collect himself. I saw that he was not just sad, but he was angry. He would occasionally yell at people in violent outbursts. He was not doing well in school. He was also grappling with questions that were at the core of his identity.

DeShawn allowed himself few close friends. In his eighth grade year, though, a thin boy his age from the neighborhood started visiting his house after school, and they began to spend a lot of time together in my greenhouses and in the store. DeShawn was intensely shy and did not always like working in the store. When the boy was there, he seemed quite willing to work.

One day Karen passed by the kitchen door in her house, which was partially open. She saw DeShawn kissing the thin boy on the mouth. Rather than confront them both, she walked quietly out of the house, collecting her thoughts.

Later that day, she approached DeShawn.

"Boo Boo, you don't want a girlfriend?" Karen asked.

"I don't like girls like that," he said.

Karen told him what she had seen through the kitchen door. DeShawn was silent for a moment.

"I want to kiss boys," DeShawn said. "Boys make me feel good."

"Have you always felt that way?" Karen said.

DeShawn nodded his head yes. Karen looked at her son's face and felt the heaviness in his heart. She reached her arms toward him and pulled him close to her.

"It don't matter to me what you decide," Karen said quietly in his ear. "I don't care if you love a man or woman, your momma's always going to love you."

∾

As Karen came to trust me, she told me that she had divided her past and present life into stages: the older men stage, the beating stage, the drugs stage, the fire stage, the Will's Roadside stage.

The older men stage began at age thirteen, when a member of her extended stepfamily, who was thirty-one, came up behind her in his sailor's uniform at her great-aunt's house and told her she shouldn't have her comb like that, sticking out of the back of her hair, and pressed his whole body up against her back.

She loved him. She felt their age difference was okay because when you flipped the numbers 1 and 3 around, they were the same. He got what he could get out of her and then left.

She moved from Milwaukee while still thirteen to live with grandparents in Detroit. Her grandmother was a maid for Warren and Nancy Zide, a wealthy couple who owned movie theaters in Detroit. Karen began to babysit for their son Warren Jr., who later in his life would go on to produce the *American Pie* movies. The Zides had a screening room in their house with a real film projector, and sometimes when Warren Jr. was sleeping, Karen turned it on and dreamed that she was a director watching the film she had made.

The reality of her life was different than a Hollywood movie. Her mother had died when she was five, her father was not a consistent support, and she always needed to make her own money. She had started on a paper route at eleven, and then a job at McDonald's on

8 Mile Road in Detroit when she was fifteen, handling the fries and shakes and eventually moving up to the cash register and becoming a crew leader.

At sixteen, she decided to move out of her grandparents' home and to share a place with a single mom from her job at McDonald's. She added a job as a waitress at a joint called Burgers & Beans. Holding down two jobs, exhausted, still in high school, she'd often come home crying at nights. It was then that her roommate introduced her to a reverend at a missionary Baptist church that operated out of a one-story, windowless building in downtown Detroit. The reverend and his wife agreed to take Karen into their home, rent free.

That summer, before Karen's senior year, the reverend called Karen on the phone while she was at her job at McDonald's. He told her he could drive by and pick her up from her job so that she would not have to take the bus. By this point, Karen was calling the reverend "Daddy." She felt like he was more her father than her real one.

When the reverend picked her up at the restaurant that day, several other boys from church were in the car, and Karen sat on the middle partition between a boy in the passenger seat and the reverend. She had changed out of her McDonald's uniform, and she was wearing shorts. Karen began to feel the reverend's right hand quietly running up and down her exposed left leg and thigh. He guided the steering wheel with the other hand. When he dropped the last boy in the car off, he drove her to a motel on Woodward Avenue and had sex with her for the first time.

Karen went to church with his family on Sundays, and she watched him preach the gospel. When his wife and children were not at home, he called for Karen and asked her to come downstairs and do "laundry" with him, or to come into his bedroom. She accepted what was happening to her.

"I was always looking for attention," she says, "even if it was the wrong attention."

She decided to leave the house not too long after she heard a noise in the reverend's bedroom, and she quietly got down on her knees and peered under the door. She saw one of the reverend's daughter's pants and underwear on the floor, circling her tiny legs. Karen realized that the attention she was receiving wasn't special to her.

When Karen returned to Milwaukee, she entered the "beating stage." That's when I met her. She briefly sold herself on Fond du Lac Avenue, and she had more than one boyfriend who hit her. "I thought that beating meant they loved you," she says. "Because they showed their love afterward. They did better after they had beaten me than before." She was pistol-whipped across both sides of her face by one man. Because he feared he would go to jail, at his request she did not go to the hospital.

Only once did she fight back against one of her abusive boyfriends. It was in a bar, and when he lunged at her, she grabbed him by the hair and threw him against an ice cooler. He was briefly knocked out. The next time she came into that bar, the staff started calling her "Muhammad Ali," and when the boyfriend got word of it, he beat her worse than he had ever done.

"You think you're Muhammad Ali now, bitch?" he said as he hit her. "You think you're Muhammad Ali?" He blackened both of her eyes until she couldn't see. "I wasn't Muhammad Ali no more," Karen told me.

Then came the drugs stage. "Drugs were my new man," she said. "I ventured off into that world." Even as she struggled with drugs, she did a good job for me at Kentucky Fried Chicken, and her stores were often rated the highest by secret shoppers who visited on behalf of the company.

DeShell said that when she went away to college at Madison, she gained a new respect for her mother. "You know, my mom has always been a hardworking, strong, phenomenal woman," DeShell told me. "But her life shifted when she made the decision to move her family here. My mother was always trying to please everyone. She had never made her own needs paramount. Her move here was different. It was as if she was saying, *This is what* I *need. My family is most important.* She knew we would be safe here."

Karen's history would only become known to me over a period of many years, as I earned her trust. She wants me to tell her story now.

"Don't pretty it up," she said.

Sometimes on the sidewalks of Milwaukee, there will be a flower or a tall weed sticking defiantly out of the tiniest crack in the concrete. I realize that human lives can be like that. People find a way to persist even when they are provided the narrowest possibility.

∽

During the winter of late 1999 and early 2000, Hope and I often sat in my first greenhouse and plotted our future. Hope came up with a slogan that played on our names: "It takes a little bit of Hope, and a whole lot of Will." She drafted fund-raising letters that we both signed. *Dear Friend*, one of them read. *In an age and time when so much seems out of control, there is an organization called Growing Power. Power that comes from synergy. Power that comes from the earth. Power that comes from fresh, healthy food.*

One frequent discussion that Hope and I had was how best to fill my underused greenhouses. Each of the five greenhouses was thirty feet wide and a hundred feet long. We no longer needed the first greenhouse as a selling space; the store had long since moved inside the small building adjacent to it. I was keeping my worm boxes, fish barrels, and bedding plants in the two greenhouses closest to the road. I grew very little food inside except for some seed starts that gardeners could buy and transplant to their own yards. The back two greenhouses mostly stored my farm tools and bedding-plant trays. The glass in the back greenhouses still had holes that I had not yet gotten around to repairing.

Hope brought out a diagram of the five greenhouses, and together we sketched our future use of the space. We decided that the first greenhouse would be our primary classroom, where youth groups and adults could gather. We knew that education would be an important part of our revenue stream. We decided to offer hands-on weekend workshops that spring to teach composting, worm breeding, indoor fish farming, and cooking basics. We would place the fish systems and worm systems in the second greenhouse. We would create a year-round organic vegetable garden in the third greenhouse, where youth and adults could come to learn simple planting and harvesting.

Hope and I started calling our facility a "community food center." The idea built on Hope's knowledge of community arts centers from the New Deal era. Ours was a place where you could buy fresh food or compost food that was no longer fresh. It was a place where you could learn to plant a garden or learn the basics of cooking.

I also began to think about the greenhouses as a place where I could grow food intensively. During the cold Milwaukee winters, I was reliant on Southern farmers in my co-op for vegetables. I knew I could reduce some of the shipping costs I had if I could grow them myself. Root vegetables like carrots or yams need a deep bed of soil, however, and they did not seem practical to grow inside. I wondered how I could raise enough food inside to break even on my costs, let alone make money.

∾

That people in cities should mostly eat food grown within a few miles of their homes was not always a strange idea. Kings and Queens Counties, which neighbor Manhattan, ranked as the number one and number two largest producers of vegetables in the United States as late as 1880. Someone standing in the heart of Brooklyn during the American Civil War would have seen, according to one account, "a vista of the finest farmlands in America, almost treeless for six miles and beyond, in full view of the Atlantic Ocean." These farms fed the city that was rising on the Hudson River. By 1949, however, the *Brooklyn Eagle* ran a story on the area's "last farmer," who grew squash and broccoli on three acres soon to be overtaken by an apartment complex.

Across the United States, the local agricultural system was

dismembered piece by piece in the twentieth century. As urban areas expanded, property prices rose in areas on the edge of cities. Farmers sold their land and often relocated to places where land prices were cheaper. City planners never made an attempt to incorporate agriculture into the fabric of urban life. Technological innovations that arrived over the course of several decades—the canal system, the railroads, refrigeration equipment, tractor-trailers, airplanes, canning and freezing processes—meant that farmers and consumers were no longer yoked together geographically by necessity.

The average item of food consumed in the United States today travels fifteen hundred miles from producer to consumer, and it is buoyed on a sea of oil and gasoline. To feed just one American, the industrial agricultural system requires, on average, the equivalent of 530 gallons of oil a year. The long journey from farm to consumer also has nutritional effects on the foods we consume. Fresh green beans, for example, have been shown to lose nearly 80 percent of their Vitamin C within a week of being picked.

A family living in an inner-city community today faces a radically different food environment than their ancestors did. Less than half of one percent of the food they eat comes directly from farmers. This family often lives two miles or more from a supermarket, which abandoned inner cities in the 1960s and 1970s as part of a tide of urban disinvestment. If the family is poor—and the father and mother are working one or more jobs—they contend with the daily struggle of nourishing themselves using as little money and time as possible.

In many inner-city communities, the only companies that meet these specific demands of low-income families are corner stores and fast-food restaurants, with their dollar menus, 99 cent bags of chips, two-for-one offers, and twenty-piece boxes of chicken nuggets. One recent study has shown that a two-thousand-calorie diet can cost as little as $3.50 a day if it consists entirely of junk food, while healthy foods that are not as energy dense can cost more than ten times as much.

"If you have $3 to feed yourself," a researcher at the University of Washington recently told *The New York Times*, "your choices gravitate toward the foods that give you the most calories per dollar. Not only are empty calories cheaper, but the healthier foods are becoming more and more expensive. Vegetables and fruits are rapidly become luxury goods."

The problem with the current price structure for unhealthy food is that the food is *deceptively* cheap. The prices for unhealthy foods rarely reflect the costs they impose on the rest of society. The health costs associated with obesity have been estimated at nearly $170 billion annually, for instance, and these costs disproportionately affect communities of color and are often paid by federal programs like Medicare and Medicaid. Though the Center for Consumer Freedom, a lobbying group for the fast-food industry, has characterized some of its opponents as "anti–free market do-goodnicks," the industrialized food system has long been propped up with federal subsidies for industrial farming and taxpayer money for health care once people get sick.

I believe in personal responsibility. In many low-income neighborhoods, though, it is hard to make good choices even if the desire is there. As wealthier Americans have become more health conscious, fast-food companies have also reoriented their advertising campaigns to grow their business in low-income communities and communities of color. A 2006 analysis compared eleven hundred ads on Black Entertainment Television, the WB, and the Disney Channel during afternoon and evening hours. Two-thirds of all the fast-food ads on those channels were on Black Entertainment Television. A 2011 study by researchers at Yale found that black children and teens were exposed to 50 percent more fast-food advertising than their white peers—partly because black youths watched more TV.

Corner stores are often the only alternative to fast food in inner-city communities. The owners of convenience stores rarely offer fresh fruits and vegetables because they are highly perishable, require a large amount of refrigerator space, and sell poorly in relation to processed food. Many people also do not know how to prepare fresh foods, and they often feel they have no time. They have also come to prefer the taste of processed food to nonprocessed food: strawberry bubble gum over strawberries. The "natural flavors" in potato chips, ice cream, and most of our fast foods have been carefully engineered by scientists at flavor companies, many of them headquartered along the New Jersey Turnpike.

I wanted to help provide affordable alternatives to junk food in inner-city communities. I knew that providing access to healthy food was not a solution in itself. It was one step of many in offering people a chance to heal themselves. But I no longer thought of my operation as just a roadside stand. I wanted Growing Power to control the production, marketing, and distribution of food on a community level—and to strengthen the neighborhood in the process. I saw my work as trying to create a new model for the food system: one that was better for small farmers, customers, and the earth.

I met someone in the late 1990s who would be crucial to me as I tried to advance this vision. Hope introduced me to a faculty member at the University of Wisconsin in Madison named Jerome Kaufman. Jerry was then in his mid-sixties, with gentle eyes, a full beard, and thinning gray hair. He was a professor in the department of urban and regional planning. He came by my greenhouses one day in May of 1999 with one of his graduate students.

As I spoke to Jerry, it became clear to me that he had spent his professional life grappling with some of the same questions that I was now considering. He had long been interested in how to create environments that provided people with the chance for better lives.

The first urban planners were landscape architects like Frederick Law Olmsted, who designed Central Park. They believed that if you made cities more beautiful, it could have an effect on people's behavior. Jerry had become interested in planning as a young man when he read Lewis Mumford's *The City in History*. The book offered a dire view of how large cities and their suburbs—"megalopolises," Mumford called them—were expanding recklessly without respect for the human relationship with the natural environment.

"Instead of regarding man's relation to air, water, soil, and all his organic partners as the oldest and most fundamental of all his relations," Mumford wrote, "the popular technology of our time devotes itself to contriving means to displace autonomous organic forms with ingenious mechanical (controllable! profitable!) substitutes. Instead of bringing life into the city, so that its poorest inhabitant will have not merely sun and air but some chance to touch and feel and cultivate the earth, these naive apostles of progress had rather bring sterility to the countryside and ultimately death to the city."

Jerry had a social conscience inspired in part by the memory of his older brother, Arnold. The two boys were raised together by immigrant Jewish parents in New York City. Arnold had been active in civil rights causes as a young man, and he went on to a brilliant academic career on the faculty at the University of Michigan. In the 1940s, Arnold worked with the Congress of Racial Equality, a nonviolent, interracial group that organized sit-ins and later coordinated the "freedom rides" that carried blacks and whites side by side on interstate buses into the Deep South, where they were attacked by angry white mobs. In 1968, Arnold published a book called *The Radical Liberal*, in which he argued that a good society should provide everyone "equal opportunity to develop his potentialities as fully as possible." He encouraged people to put their principles into concrete action, and he argued that there was an "enormous gap between the rhetoric and practice of most American liberals."

Three years later, Arnold was flying from Los Angeles to Salt Lake City to give a speech at the University of Utah, when his DC-9 passenger plane was struck in midair by a Marine Phantom II jet with faulty radar. Both planes plunged to earth in the San Gabriel Mountains, near Duarte, California, and Arnold was among the forty-four passengers in the DC-9 who died.

Jerry had long operated in the shadow of his brother. In Arnold's absence, he wanted to invest his planning work with his brother's

passion and concern for civil rights. He sought to have a positive impact on the world outside of the ivory tower.

In 1997, Jerry agreed to head the Madison Food System Project,
an assessment of the food environment in Madison and surrounding
Dane County. While doing this work, he began to understand how
the food system was connected to almost every part of civic life. He
saw how runoff from dairy farms affected algae growth in Madison's lakes and created problems for the fish population. He recognized that a large part of the burden on the city's transportation
network was owing to food: transporting it, disposing of it, purchasing it. He saw that a full third of the waste that ended up in the
county dump was from food waste and packaging.

He also saw great differences in access to healthy food. Madison's best neighborhoods offered multiple options: a popular cooperative, health food stores, restaurants, large grocers. In one of the
city's poorer neighborhoods in South Madison, residents had only
one chain grocery store, along with convenience stores and fast-food
restaurants. Jerry understood that this uneven distribution of healthy
and affordable options was not unique. It was part of a broader national problem of food access and food security. A study from the
United States Department of Agriculture from that time found that
roughly thirty million American households were "food insecure"—
meaning that at some time during the previous year they weren't
sure of having, or were unable to acquire, enough food to meet their
basic needs.

"I was always interested in areas of planning where not much
work had been done," Jerry told me later. "When I began this work,
I didn't know much about food." He was surprised as he searched
through the major trade journals of his profession that he was not
alone. He could not find a single article that addressed how communities might build healthy and durable food systems.

In 2000, Jerry wrote a paper with a visiting professor in Madison
for the *Journal of the American Planning Association* called "The Food
System: A Stranger to the Planning Field." He laid out a passionate
argument, citing Lewis Mumford's vision of a city as a place "for

Jerry Kaufman and me

active citizenship, for education, and for a vivid and autonomous personal life." Jerry wrote that "it is difficult to imagine any of the above goals being realized without secure, ongoing, and socially acceptable access for all citizens to high quality, nutritious food."

Jerry soon received a grant to conduct a survey of the fledgling practice of urban agriculture in the United States. He saw vegetable and fruit production in Rust Belt cities with vacant land as potentially one piece of a more sustainable, locally controlled food system. He started visiting Growing Power more regularly, and I enjoyed speaking with him. I recognized his value to me as a strategic thinker.

Jerry had a vision. He wanted a food system that was centered on a regional and local level rather than on a national and international level. He wanted a food system that strengthened small farmers, community gardens, urban farms, farmers markets, community-supported agriculture projects, and food cooperatives. He wanted to build relationships between regional farms and low-income communities and schools. He believed in what I was doing, but I knew that he also maintained a healthy skepticism about whether my operation—or even the idea of urban agriculture and community-based food systems—could succeed. "My hopes for a better food system were based on optimism," Jerry said. "But reality said: 'Show me.'"

∾

I lost my father when I was young, and Jerry became a father figure for me. In July of 2000, my older brother Joe called me to tell me that my mother, Willie Mae, had passed away. She was ninety. My work in Milwaukee had so consumed my life that I was rarely able to visit my mother in Maryland. I regretted it now that it was too late. I had kept in touch frequently by phone, and she came once in the 1980s to see me in Milwaukee.

My mother had encouraged me with my roadside stand, though she was surprised at my interest. She knew that I liked farming the least of my three brothers as a child. When I went back for Willie Mae's funeral, I felt how the world had changed around her. The Washington metropolitan area had become the "megalopolis" of which Mumford spoke. Where farmland had once been were large big box stores and even larger parking lots. New roads had names such as Executive Boulevard. An 800,000-square-foot mall and Cheesecake Factory had arisen close to where Tolson's Nursery, a family-owned business, once had been. A small shopping center about a mile from my former home had once been made up of local businesses, like Lockerson Lumber. This center was now more than three times its original size and consisted mostly of national chains: Bed Bath & Beyond, Hooters, Ruby Tuesday. In a sense, this was economic progress. Yet I could not help but feel that something had been lost.

My mother had remained at our small house at Branches for more than a decade after O.W. died in 1972. In that time, she had grown closer to Mrs. Frank. The two widows occasionally went to the ballet or to plays together. Willie Mae also allowed herself certain freedoms that she would not have been allowed in the presence of my father. O.W. shot any raccoon that dared walk onto his property. Willie Mae began to feed the raccoons her table scraps instead. She gave them names. They sometimes scratched at her kitchen door, waiting for her, and she greeted them with a soft and sympathetic voice as if she were welcoming a neighbor's children.

Mrs. Frank had a stroke in the early 1980s. She told her children that she didn't want to be placed on life support, and she spent her last few days on the couch of the home she loved, with Willie Mae beside her. Around the time of Mrs. Frank's death, my mother fell and broke her femur while attending a wedding. This accident was the first step of a gradual decline. She soon felt lonely at Branches, though Mrs. Frank's children had allowed her to stay there. At Willie Mae's request, Joe moved her to an assisted living facility. She had a survivor's benefit through the Social Security Administration that would pay for her care.

Willie Mae was popular at this facility, though she was not always happy there. She always enjoyed the company of young people. When she had her own stroke, my brother Joe's wife, Joyce, remembers rushing to her side to find her flirting with the emergency workers. "She just saw herself as young," Joyce said. "Even in the midst of a stroke, her personality was intact."

My mother had always been an independent thinker, but her life was bound by the historical realities of her time. She had escaped sharecropping, but she had not been able to escape her role in the servant class. My father loved her but had a patriarchal view of men's and women's roles. I think her personality was never allowed the full fruit of expression. Willie Mae told Joe how she had once traveled to New York before she moved to Branches, on a visit to her cousins, and how she had met the actor and singer Paul Robeson, and what a handsome man he was. She might have been happy in New York City, surrounded by poets and actors and singers.

Recently, my brother Ray found a photograph of Willie Mae from before I was born. She sits against a backdrop of a waterfall and mountains in a photographer's studio. She wears an immaculate floral dress with an open neckline and white heels. She smiles with warmth. The photograph was taken after my mother arrived in Maryland. She would have paid for a photographer at a time when my family had little extra for luxuries.

I think my mother must have wanted an image that captured her escape from the South, and her arrival in the New World. The reality of her life did not always match her dream, but she accepted whatever circumstances she was given with grace. Her generosity to others continued even in death. Before she passed away, she requested her body be donated to the Georgetown University Medical

Center for the use of science. After her body had served that purpose, she asked that her ashes be sprinkled on a garden.

One of Willie Mae's greatest legacies to me is that she taught me that food was a celebration. It brought people together who might differ otherwise because of race, religion, or politics. To this day, whenever I eat something she would cook—pumpkin pie, baked chicken, braised collard greens—I think of her. I remember how her meals attracted people of different races and backgrounds

together in Rock Creek Park and how everyone was welcome at her table. I remember her strong hands and how they gripped the handles of her iron cooking pans. I remember how if I came home even in the early hours of the morning, after she had fallen asleep, she would rouse herself and cook something for me.

My extended family from South Carolina and New York came to her funeral, and we held a large feast in her honor. We celebrated her life with toasts to her memory, good food, and laughter.

Erika Allen, with young people in Chicago

HOMECOMINGS

Soon before my mother passed away, Hope was riding with me in my truck to pick up compost materials. She grew quiet and told me she needed to tell me something: Her husband had been offered a research professor position at the University of Alaska in Anchorage. He had long wanted to move to the state, she said, and she knew that this was a rare opportunity for him. She wanted to join him there. They had two young daughters together, and the job would allow him to provide better for his family.

Hope said that she still wanted to be the co-director of Growing Power. She had recently obtained a renewal of a $20,000 grant from the State of Wisconsin. She wanted to build on that momentum in the coming year. She felt that the work of our organization could be international in scope and that perhaps in the future we could even have programs in Alaska. She said she would fly back to Milwaukee periodically to help me run our spring workshops.

I thought it would be difficult for us to manage the organization together while she lived so far away. We had been working as co-directors for only a year. I was focused on farming and on trying to improve our operation on Silver Spring Drive. I felt it was too soon to think about expanding. Yet I was willing to see.

"We can make this work," I told her.

The day before Hope left for Alaska, on a cloudless day in late July of 2000, she arrived at my greenhouses with her husband, two daughters, and a small North Star cherry tree. I dug a hole in a patch of grass near our greenhouses, a few feet away from the drive-way to Karen Parker's house. We set the tree in the hole, and Hope went to her car and brought out her daughters' two placentas, which she had kept in a freezer.

Hope felt they were symbols: the vascular tissue of the placenta

Hope; her husband, Brian; and her daughters, Aviva and Barae, after planting a North Star cherry tree outside Growing Power, July 2000

provides a child oxygen and nutrients in the womb. Hope saw Growing Power as her child, too, and she wanted to nourish it. She placed the two frozen organs next to the tree's roots, and we took turns shoveling the dirt back on top. Her daughters used their tiny feet to press the soil down. Hope hugged me as she left.

"I knew that I was definitely letting go of a lot," she said recently. "I was going to see what happened. And what has happened to you since is a big story. Yet I have my own story in that big story."

As the cherry tree grew over the years, Karen began referring to it as the "placenta tree." Every year, beginning in mid-July, it yields nearly a bushel of beautiful ripe fruit.

∾

I had no ambitions while my children were growing up that they would pursue a life in agriculture. I knew how hard it was to make a living as a small farmer. I did think, however, that the work of cultivating food offered useful lessons for each of them, no matter what career they ultimately pursued.

You're going to thank me for this someday.

That's what I told my eldest child, Erika, whenever she complained about farming when she was young. "It was like we were training for the Olympics," Erika said recently of her youth. "It was ridiculous the amount of physical work you had us do."

On Saturday mornings after I started selling vegetables at Fondy Market in 1980, I often woke my kids as early as 3:30 A.M. Erika was about eleven and Jason was eight. I mostly spared Adrianna, my youngest, since she was only six at that time. I have always been as competitive in farming as I was in basketball. I needed a team, even if they were unwillingly drafted. My wife often helped me, but she also worked full-time as a psychiatric nurse.

I knew that most of the farmers at Fondy harvested their crops on Thursday for the Saturday market. I felt that if I could push back the harvest one more day—picking and washing my produce on Friday evening—my vegetables would be the freshest among my competition.

The trouble was that the work of washing the produce often lasted until 11 P.M. I had two household bathtubs set out in my fields for those purposes. On Friday evenings, Erika and Jason and I scrubbed cabbage and collard greens, stumbled into the house a little before midnight, got a few hours of sleep, and then loaded up the truck together in the early morning black. We drove to Fondy, bleary eyed, and stacked our piles of produce so that we were ready to sell by 6 A.M.

Erika's least favorite thing was picking beans.

"I didn't like row crops," Erika says. "I didn't like the endless, tedious hard work."

She admits to me now, decades later, that sometimes she would put bean leaves (the inedible part of the plant) inside the bushels she collected in order to fluff them up.

Erika's passion resided in art. She loved painting and drawing, and she was quite good. When she left for college at the Art Institute of Chicago in 1987, she felt like she was finally able to define her life on her own terms. She returned the first couple of summers to help me on the farm because she needed the money. Yet I could tell she was also unhappy and that her heart was in Chicago. "After that second summer, I essentially said to myself: I don't need to come back here anymore," Erika says.

Erika's feelings reflect an uneasy reality that confronts many black farmers who have stubbornly remained on their land. Their children often have no desire to stay in agriculture. According to the National Agricultural Statistics Service, the average age of all farm operators in the United States has increased from fifty years old in 1978 to fifty-seven years old in 2007. Among African Americans, the typical age of a farm operator in 2010 was sixty. The survival of small and medium-sized farms is often dependent on the transfer of farmland from one generation to the next—and on the younger generation wanting to farm. Young people can rarely begin a farm or ranch on their own because of high start-up costs: The average price of an acre of American farmland is now more than $2,300. To buy a typical commercial farm of four-hundred-plus acres today can cost $1 million or more.

I do not blame young people who choose not to remain on their parents' farms. In the new farming economy, sons and daughters have often witnessed their mothers and fathers lose money year after year and be forced to work one or two additional jobs to make ends meet. They have seen their friends flee rural communities and seek work in cities. For young African Americans, the work of agriculture carries the added stigmas of sharecropping and slavery.

After Erika decided not to come back to Milwaukee in the summers, she graduated from the Art Institute and then pursued an M.A. in art therapy from the University of Illinois in Chicago. She started working with children and elderly people at social service agencies, encouraging her clients to work out some of their feelings through painting and drawing. Erika was surprised to see that several children in her art program spoke of not having enough food to eat at home.

"When you taught me how to grow things, you said, 'You'll know how to do this someday, and no one else will,'" Erika told me. "I realized that was true. I saw in Chicago how very few of my peers knew how to do what I naturally know how to do."

When Hope left for Alaska, Erika began to help me write grant applications for Growing Power. She also began to speak to me for the first time about her hopes to start her own urban agriculture project in Chicago. She built a relationship in 2001 with members of the Fourth Presbyterian Church on Chicago Avenue, who had purchased an old, unused basketball court across the street from Cabrini Green—the Chicago public housing project famous for its gang violence and poverty. The church wanted to turn the lot into a community garden.

The high-rise Cabrini Green apartments were constructed in a period of "urban renewal" from the 1940s to the 1960s, when blighted areas of cities were demolished and replaced with low-income housing. These efforts were well intentioned, but in reality the housing projects often became "warehouses for the poor," in the words of Vincent Lane, who was the head of the Chicago Housing Authority from 1988 to 1995. In the mid-1990s, the City of Chicago began a process of demolishing the old Cabrini Green buildings to make way for new mixed-income housing.

The Fourth Presbyterian Church hoped that the garden across the street from Cabrini Green could be part of a healing process in the community. Erika saw an opportunity. She soon had secured a role to help design the garden, to serve on its planning committee, and to supply the compost and seed. By the time the Chicago Avenue Community Garden near Cabrini Green opened in 2002, my daughter had assumed the role of Growing Power's Chicago projects manager. I drove down with a truck full of finished compost to help her get started, and I was filled with pride for her. This was our organization's first venture in the Windy City.

At the community garden near Cabrini Green, Erika soon started an after-school program with young people from the projects. In the years to come, she would refine a curriculum with the educator Laurell Sims that used the lessons of agriculture to teach life skills. Laurell was a young mother who had worked in Boston for several years at a shelter called reVision House, where homeless women with children grew food on abandoned city lots.

Each week at the Chicago Avenue garden had a different theme. In the week devoted to pollination, the young people observed bees at work and learned lessons about the interdependence of species. In the week they learned about the reproductive cycle, they did a scavenger hunt for caterpillars. During the week devoted to compost, Laurell taught about the necessity of teamwork—that it takes many partners in a community to gather the raw materials for a healthy compost pile. At the end of each day, Erika and Laurell gathered the young people and asked them to describe their "rose" and their "thorn": the best thing that happened to them that day and the thing that was the most difficult.

Many social service workers had come to Cabrini Green with good intentions only to leave after a few months or less. When Erika first arrived, she sensed skepticism from the community about her staying power. It was also difficult to keep many of the young people in the program in line. One summer day, a young boy named Quentin was jumping from picnic table to picnic table and disobeying requests to settle down. After Quentin ignored two warnings, Laurell decided she needed to take him home. Laurell felt like she understood many of the harsh realities of urban life, but she was not prepared for what she saw when she entered the Cabrini high-rise where Quentin lived.

"It was a gorgeous sunny day outside, and when I walked inside it was the scariest place I have ever been," Laurell says. "None of the lights in the hallway were on. We walked up to the fifth floor, and there was graffiti everywhere. Except for the entryway, the stairwell was almost pitch-black. On one wall, I saw the words 'Kill or be killed.' How can you raise a child in a building where they see that every time they walk up the stairs?"

As Laurell came out of the building, someone approached and told her that the police often wouldn't go in that building for fear of being shot. The experience changed Laurell's sense of her priorities. Whatever lessons she hoped to impart about agriculture and healthy eating, she realized that simply providing a space for the young people to be safe for a few hours was its own accomplishment.

"I realized it was a challenge for these kids just to stay alive," she said.

∾

In Milwaukee, I met young people whose families were struggling with other basic needs, including putting enough food on the table. My early work with youth had come through other social service organizations, like the YWCA and Neighborhood House. Soon after my arrival on West Silver Spring Drive, though, I began to formulate the idea of my own "youth corps."

My idea was to pick a few young people in challenging circumstances who were eight or nine years old. The children were not hard to find. Parents often came into my store asking if their kids could spend time at my facility. Other young people visited through church or community programs. Some young people wandered onto my back lot from the Westlawn public housing facility or the surrounding neighborhood.

I wanted to provide a few of these boys and girls with a consistent apprenticeship all the way to college. I thought that if they could learn to do the hard work of farming—composting, planting, harvesting, marketing, customer relations—that they could meet many of the other challenges that life brought. The grant money I was able to obtain to support the program allowed me to provide a stipend. As the children grew older, I planned to pay the young people for their work at the store and in the greenhouses. Karen Parker agreed to oversee the program, and she took responsibility for the children, who came to call her "Mama Karen."

By the time that Erika started working at Cabrini Green, our Milwaukee youth corps program had grown to more than half a dozen young people. Our youth corps members were initially all African American except for Lulu Rodriguez, who found her way to Growing Power through a paid summer program at her church. One of ten children from a Puerto Rican family, Lulu was fourteen when she first visited Growing Power in 2003. The church compensated her and other youth for an entire summer of work to plant gardens and assist part-time at Growing Power.

Lulu's siblings and parents lived together in a small apartment on the city's west side. Her father suffered from advanced type II diabetes and had to rely on Social Security. Both her father's father and one of her father's brothers had already passed away from diabetes, and Lulu was told that she was at risk. One of Lulu's older sisters suffered from severe mental retardation and had occasional violent outbursts. Neither of Lulu's parents spoke English, and few of the people in Lulu's family were able to work. At fourteen Lulu was already trying to help support herself. Karen Parker recognized all that Lulu was going through. We started paying her to work soon after she joined us.

"The first few weeks I was here, it was kind of awkward," Lulu says. "I was totally new, trying to find my place here. Most of the kids in the youth corps were younger than me."

Over her first year at Growing Power, though, Lulu began to establish a close friendship with DeShawn, who was two years older. Lulu started calling DeShawn her brother, and he started calling her his sister. They understood each other in part because their lives had not been easy.

I noticed that the members of our youth corps constantly chomped on chips, soda, and candy. They had grown up in families where this was the only food they knew. I had no illusions that I could change their diets right away. I didn't pretend to be a perfect eater either. Yet I also believed that the experience of growing food could ultimately do more good than any nutrition lectures I delivered.

My own love of farming and fresh vegetables grew in part because of the vivid memory of tastes from my childhood, and my hands-on education of planting and harvesting food. When I grew older and began to eat more processed food, I was aware it tasted nothing like the fruits and vegetables that had nourished me as a young man.

Children often come into my facility for the first time with their pockets filled with candy, acting wild. Something changes in them when they walk up to my worm systems and put their hands in the soil for the first time. They mellow. It can be a spiritual thing simply to touch the earth if you have been disconnected from it for so long. I have also seen the faces of children come alive when they eat their first tomato or sunflower sprout freshly picked from the soil. If the child planted the vegetable and watered it, the experience is particularly vivid. Most young people from the inner city have never had a face-to-face encounter with a vegetable that has just been plucked from the earth. They have never planted a seed.

The experience of eating a fresh tomato is not likely to change a young person's eating habits dramatically in a matter of months, particularly if those habits have been established since the person was born. Yet I think early experiences with fresh food can shape a person's diet when that person is older.

One recent study of one hundred sixth-graders compared students who had participated in a hands-on, garden-based nutrition education program with two other groups: students who were taught nutrition lessons in a classroom and those who were given no nutrition education at all. The researchers found no significant difference a year later in the vegetable and fruit consumption of children without nutrition education and those who received nutrition classes. The students who received hands-on training in a garden, however, increased their fruit and vegetable intake by more than two servings a day. My own experience tells me that if we can expose young people more often to fresh, delicious food—and create positive emotions around those experiences—that we increase the chances that they will adopt more fresh food into their diet as they begin to make independent food choices later in life.

∾

The journey of Robert Pierce, a farmer in Madison, Wisconsin, offers proof of how early experiences with fresh vegetables can have distant effects. He was introduced to me in 2002 after a speech that I gave about my work. As I came off the stage, a mutual friend came up to me and said, "Will, here's another black farmer."

"I thought I was the only black farmer in Wisconsin," I told Robert. He said the same thing to me. He said that he was surprised to hear I was composting and creating fertilizer with worms, because he had been doing that himself for years.

Robert was then fifty years old. I soon came to know his history. In the early 1980s, he was a single father raising three young children. The youngest was only three and a half months old. He was trying to attend business school while he was working at a call center and caring for his kids.

Robert's skin was constantly breaking out in allergic reactions. He began to think that his health problems were related to the food he was eating, and he decided to start eating a diet of mostly organic fruits and vegetables—the foods he had known as a boy. Within a few weeks, he says, his allergies had improved dramatically. In 1984, he told the administration at his business school that he was quitting, and that he was going to become an organic farmer.

"What is that?" he was asked.

"I'm going to start growing foods without poisons," Robert said. He was able to lease twenty acres outside of Madison. He could not afford day care, so he put his kids in a tent on the property while he went about his work. Robert traced his interest in farming to his childhood. When he was growing up in South Madison, his grandmother often sent him out in the fields to fetch wild mustard greens. His grandmother's friends were too scared to gather the greens because they feared snakes, and word soon spread that Robert was happy to do the work. He often returned from fields of tall grasses with a bushel of mustard greens in a satchel, and his grandmother slipped him money for his efforts.

"She was paying me to pick up weeds," he remembers.

When he was nine and ten, Robert also helped an uncle who found work planting gardens in people's yards. The uncle promised Robert and his brother that if they assisted him, he would take them fishing. Robert loved gardening and tasting the food that his uncle picked fresh for him. Whenever Robert's uncle had leftover flower bulbs from the landscaping side of his business, he gave them to Robert, and Robert planted them in empty lots along Madison's South Side. Some of those flowers are still growing today, he says.

Robert's return to growing food was a homecoming, as it was in my own life. Robert suffered from post-traumatic stress disorder from a trauma he experienced as a young man. He felt that the physical work was therapeutic and that it was unnatural to sit in front of a computer screen all day. He began to work out some of his emotions in the fields.

"If I got angry," he told me, "I'd go out in the field and I'd plant up a whole acre by hand. If it wasn't right, I'd take it out and go do it again."

Robert began selling his food for the first time at the Duane County Farmers Market in 1984. Hosted every Saturday on Madison's Capitol Square, the market has long held the distinction of being the largest in the United States. Robert's greens and root vegetables were as good-looking as any in the entire market. He noticed that many customers glanced at him, though, and walked to other vendors. When the farmers market closed at 2 P.M., half of

Robert's produce often remained unsold. He could not help but feel that the reason was the color of his skin.

"I was the first person to grow blue potatoes and sell them on the square," Robert said. "No one bought them from me. The next year, another white farmer in a stall near me started selling them, and they sold out. From that point on, I knew exactly what was going on. I said, 'I don't need this.' I left."

Robert decided as an alternative to create his own small stands throughout South Madison, the poorest part of the city. Often he simply parked his truck in underserved neighborhoods and sent his young children down the street to beckon people out of their houses.

We got sweet corn! We got watermelons!

His youngest daughter, Shelly, particularly loved yellow watermelons, and she knew that if she dropped a watermelon in the street while delivering it to a customer, she was able to eat it.

"I would always hear her saying, 'Uh-oh, I dropped it!'" Robert said.

When I met Robert, he was establishing small farmers markets in Madison for the communities that needed his food the most. He had reached out to other local farmers to join him, many of them Hmong immigrants. He was barely getting by financially, but he was happy. He was doing work that he loved.

I asked Robert to come aboard the Rainbow Farmers Cooperative so I could sell some of his produce in Milwaukee. I was grateful to have another farmer who shared my vision. His life story also reinforced for me the lesson that a love of healthy food is something that can be planted in people when they are very young, only to bloom late, after many seasons.

Robert Pierce

ҩ

Robert and I both recognized that our economic survival as small farmers depended on developing multiple income streams. One important bit of good fortune in my own efforts came when I obtained some warehouse and refrigeration space for the Rainbow Farmers Cooperative that I split with SHARE, a Milwaukee hunger-relief organization. The space allowed me a staging area for my market basket program, which was now providing fresh food to several hundred low-income residents. Karen and DeShawn and the youth corps and I assembled the baskets for pickups at community centers throughout Milwaukee. The warehouse and packing area allowed us to expand the program to meet the demand. Soon we were delivering baskets to more than two dozen locations in the city where there was little access to fresh food.

I was also creating more compost than ever before, and I began selling it to gardeners by the truckload out of my back lot. After refining my techniques of worm composting for five years, I felt ready by 2003 to bring a worm-castings product to market. When worms finished digesting the compost in a bin, I laid a sixteenth-inch mesh screen on top of the pile and placed pre-composted bananas or other recently fresh food on the top of the screen. More than three-quarters of the worms in the bin would routinely crawl up through the screen to eat the new food source. I then transplanted the harvested worms to other compost bins, where they could begin the months-long process of reproducing and eating their way through another pile. When people asked me how many staff members I had, I started saying that I had millions. I explained that my red wigglers were my hardest working employees, and that they never talked back to me.

A finished worm compost bin held eight hundred pounds of worm castings. I sold bags of these castings as organic fertilizer for $2 a pound. Erika designed the label. I also created another product from the castings called Milwaukee Black Gold Tea. We dried the castings and placed them in large tea bags with green sand and a little honey. A customer added a gallon of water to this product, allowed it to leach overnight, and then had a very effective liquid fertilizer. These Milwaukee Black Gold Tea bags used only a half pound of worm castings and sold for $10. I used the tea and castings on my own plants, and I had never experienced such intensive fertility. A single worm bin could yield several thousand dollars in products before expenses.

By 2003, we had also begun selling our own urban honey. One of our volunteer beekeepers-in-training was Sarah Christman, who had arrived at my facility two years prior and spent most of her free time there. Sarah was rail-thin, in her late twenties, and had an infectious enthusiasm. She grew up in Milwaukee with a family that kept a large garden to help reduce the cost of their grocery bills. Sarah had become interested in urban agriculture during a bike trip in the Netherlands, when she saw city residents keeping intensive gardens in their backyards. She was allergic to bees but was fascinated by them. From books and from other beekeepers, she taught herself the complex science of honeybee hive maintenance.

Our hives sat in my back lot on Silver Spring Drive. The bees could take advantage of wildflowers in the 230-acre Army Reserve base adjacent to our property, a facility that had once housed Nike missiles during the Cold War. As I better understood the life of the hives, I realized how dependent human beings are on bees and how bees offered several lessons about the importance of community.

Honeybees do not exist for themselves but work together for a common good. The queen bee devotes her entire life to laying as many as two million eggs. Scout bees are the first that are sent out from the hive to search for food—nectar and pollen. If the bees find the food more than a hundred feet away, they will return to the hive and perform a "waggle dance" for the other forager bees. The dance is one of the wonders of the natural world: a complicated bit of vector calculus that communicates where food is located.

The orientation of the waggle dance in relation to the top of the hive indicates the food's direction. If the food source is directly in line with the sun, for example, the scout bee will dance in a straight line toward the top of the hive. The bee is somehow smart enough to adjust for the sun's constant movement in the sky, altering its dance direction one degree for every four minutes that have passed since it was at the source's location. The frequency with which the bee "waggles"—gyrates its little body—indicates the distance of the food from the hive.

The recent collapse of bee colonies teaches us the necessity of humility toward the natural world, and how we cannot tamper with one part of nature without affecting another. According to the National Agricultural Statistics Service, there are forty percent fewer honey-producing hives in the United States as there were in 1980. Scientists are concerned that the widespread use of certain pesticides throughout the U.S. and Europe is impacting the central nervous system of bees, impairing their ability to perform the waggle dance effectively or carry out the other delicate tasks that are necessary for their ability to survive as a colony. In creating an agricultural system that depends so much on corn and soybeans, we have also displaced the crop diversity that provides the necessary habitat for bees to survive.

The loss of bees is not trivial because of their crucial role in producing food. Bees are said to be responsible for producing as much as one of every three bites of food that we eat. Corn and soybeans, the staples of American processed food, are self-pollinators. This means that they reproduce without depending on insects. Yet many of the fresh fruits, vegetables, and nuts that we eat—including apples, almonds, squash, and avocados—are largely dependent on bees.

An apple can only be produced, for instance, when pollen grains from the male part of the flower of an apple tree are transferred to the female part of the flower. The apple flower generally cannot do this on its own. A honeybee may visit as many as five thousand apple flowers a day, and bits of the female pollen get stuck to its body as it flies from flower to flower, creating the conditions in which an apple flower can pollinate and then fruit. Were bees to disappear, we would lose much of our ability to produce many of our healthiest foods.

After a year, Sarah began to help in the harvest of honey. We were able to get as much as one hundred pounds a year from each of our hives. We started selling bottles of "Urban Honey" alongside our worm castings. We were careful to leave enough for the bees to ensure the survival of their colony, and beekeeping became a part of our agricultural education program.

Between February and March 2003, Growing Power hosted four weekend workshops called "Grow Your Community Food System from the Ground Up!" Our breakout sessions included beekeeping, community-project design (taught by Erika, who came up from Chicago), vermiculture, aquaculture, composting, marketing, animal health, youth leadership, and the essentials of gardening.

Erika was assuming many of the responsibilities that Hope Finkelstein once managed, including grant writing. Although Hope flew from Anchorage to Milwaukee faithfully for every workshop and remained as invested in the future of the organization as when she began, by the summer of 2003, it had become clear to both of us that maintaining our working relationship at such a long distance was too difficult. Hope was still handling much of the financial paperwork for the organization, and it was challenging for us to coordinate payments. It was also hard to explain to funders why a Milwaukee-based organization had an address based in Anchorage.

Hope joined forces with me at a crucial time, and she played a large role in Growing Power's future. She gave me a name that precisely expressed our purpose. She helped me define my mission as a community food center. We parted on friendly but bittersweet terms. "It was hard for me to let go of Growing Power," Hope told me recently. She took comfort, she said, that the work of an organization she fostered would continue. By the time Hope left, we had grown to have a staff of seven people, with more than a hundred volunteers.

∾

Hope saw food as a tool to bring folks from different walks of life together to the same table. Across town, two other children of the

Great Migration were teaching me the power of gardens to rally a broken community.

In 2001, I met Sharon and Larry Adams. Sharon's father had fled Tennessee decades earlier after he was arrested for possession of a knife. He had been caught peeling an apple on a street. He had long been resented in a primarily white community for being a black landowner. After his arrest, he decided he was done with Tennessee. He moved to Milwaukee in the mid-1950s with a Mayflower truck and enough money to buy a house, but he couldn't find a white homeowner who would sell to him. He was a victim of the widespread practice of "redlining," when real-estate agents and homeowners denied African American migrants entry into white communities.

Sharon's father eventually settled his family on Walnut Street, in a neighborhood of sturdy single-family homes that was then becoming the center of the city's African American cultural life. Sharon remembers hearing her father speak fondly around the kitchen table of his land in Tennessee.

"They had horses, and all the food they could eat, and they could hunt on their land," Sharon said. "I had this experience hearing about this wonderful environment that I wasn't privilege to. But I lived it, because I heard their stories."

On Walnut Street, neighbors offered support and housing to newcomers from the Great Migration. "Segregation forced us to be self-sufficient and to rely on each other," Sharon said. By the late 1990s, however, Sharon's former neighborhood was rife with gang activity. Gunshots were frequently heard at night. Prostitutes walked the block. Many of the homes in the community had been demolished. This decline began in the wake of President Eisenhower's Federal-Aid Highway Act of 1956, which led to the demolition of homes and businesses across eighty-three acres of the community to make way for a proposed Park West Freeway. More than a dozen black-owned businesses were shuttered and destroyed, even though the freeway was ultimately never built. The neighborhood fell apart.

Returning to Milwaukee from New York in the 1990s, Sharon

hoped to play a part in repairing the broken fabric of her former community. The decaying Victorian house that she and her husband bought on 17th Street and North Avenue in 1997 was slated to be razed by the city—one of several abandoned homes marked for demolition in Lindsay Heights.

Soon after moving to the neighborhood, Sharon knocked on doors and gathered the remaining longtime residents for a planning and brainstorming session. She wanted to talk about how to rescue their community. She organized group walks as a show of force to signal that residents were taking their streets back. Larry and Sharon also started a nonprofit organization called Walnut Way Conservation Corporation, committed to the purpose of transforming the 110 blocks that made up Lindsay Heights. Sharon had heard of my work, and she asked me to visit the neighborhood.

Larry walked me through the community for the first time in 2001, and he spoke of his vision of restoring the homes and healing the land there. I respected Larry's optimism but most of the homes looked abandoned and in disrepair. A few young men with do-rags and tank tops walked the streets. They appeared to be up to no good. It felt unsafe even in daytime and more dangerous than my neighborhood along Silver Spring Drive.

"I'm not sure, man," Larry remembers me saying. "This is kind of crazy."

I still said that I was willing to help. Larry and Sharon and their neighbors soon planted tulips in raised flower beds in empty lots. I brought some of my compost and helped them plant a community vegetable garden in a lot outside of Sharon and Larry's home. In October of 2001, soon after the tragedy of September 11, Sharon and Larry hosted a harvest festival there—the first community block party in the neighborhood in twenty years.

By 2002, I was frequently hauling worms and compost to help Walnut Way. I assisted several residents as they built their own backyard vegetable gardens. Sharon and Larry helped set up rainwater collection systems that could irrigate them. Sharon worked independently of me to bring more trees and flowers to the community. One older resident told Sharon that as a child in the South she'd loved eating fresh peaches. Sharon thought peaches couldn't grow in a northern climate until she visited the backyard of another neighbor.

"I had never seen a peach tree, and she had a beautiful one," Sharon said. "She told me a story. Her grandmother had taught her to take a peach pit, put it in the freezer for a while, take it out, and to dig a small hole in the ground. She learned how to place the pit in the ground, and to put a small mason jar upside-down over top of it, to create a small hothouse. Then you left the pit alone. When the tree had taken firm root, you could remove the mason jar."

Larry tried this technique, and it worked. He soon had cultivated a Milwaukee peach orchard. In years to come, the community garden on 17th and North Avenue grew peaches, lettuces, collards, and kale. Some of it was sold at the Fondy Farmers Market, which was located on the northwest corner of the neighborhood. Walnut Way was also able to start its own urban agriculture intern program for young people in the community.

The greening of the Lindsay Heights neighborhood helped set the stage for other forms of reinvestment. Walnut Way secured forgivable loans to build and rehabilitate homes. More than sixty subsidized houses have since been built in the neighborhood, several existing homes have been restored, and crime has declined significantly. A number of small businesses have opened, including a new coffee shop called Coffee Makes You Black.

Sharon and Larry and members of Walnut Way also engaged in a fight in 2008 to prevent the opening of a fried chicken restaurant, Church's Chicken, in the neighborhood. If opened, the store would have been the third fried chicken restaurant in ten blocks along a stretch of North Avenue. Sharon spoke against the restaurant at zoning board meetings, organized a community vigil, and explained her reasoning to an often skeptical press.

"Any time you live in an area where you don't have healthy choices, you don't have a healthy community," Sharon told a local reporter.

Walnut Way's opposition drew sharp criticism. Patrick McIlheran, a columnist for the *Milwaukee Journal Sentinel*, called the organization's activities "anti-investment." He argued that Walnut Way's opposition could scare away investors from greater Milwaukee. One of his columns suggested that Sharon needed therapy. Sharon knew she was not anti-investment. She felt that if a neighborhood was a "fast-food alley," as she called it, it scared away other kinds of businesses. People found it harder to make good food choices even if they wanted to. Sharon wished to create a food environment where the healthy choice was the easy choice.

The debate over the proposed Church's Chicken spread through the neighborhood, including at a community center near the Fondy Farmers Market. Children in an after-school program at the center discussed whether they wanted to be part of Walnut Way's vigil to oppose the restaurant. Sixteen of the kids attended the vigil, holding signs with slogans such as NO MORE CHICKEN! WE WANT HEALTHY CHOICES. More than two-thirds of the children in the after-school program, however, chose not to attend. Many of them said they liked fried chicken, and that they thought the store would bring jobs.

Church's Chicken ultimately decided not to move into the neighborhood. Sharon and Larry want to bring healthier restaurants to the community, and they are expanding the offerings at the existing farmers markets there. Larry has become a beekeeper at the community garden adjacent to his house. The peach blossoms give his honey a memorable taste. Walnut Way's urban honey has become so popular that the Adamses must limit the number of bottles that each customer is allowed to order each year.

Sharon believes that the changes in Lindsay Heights began when the community started to heal the land. Large challenges remain: Four in ten of the residents in the neighborhood live in poverty, and nearly half do not have a high school diploma. There are still not enough grocers offering fresh food and no restaurants that serve healthy, affordable fare. Yet the trajectory of the community's future is different. Sharon is convinced that African Americans who have been divorced from their history can feel a little more whole when

Sharon Adams

they put their hands in the soil and grow food.

"By doing this work, we are giving respect to both the joys and struggles of our ancestors," Sharon says.

∾

For anyone who works to improve communities, the process of improving people's lives can be painfully slow, much like the processes of nature. Sharon and Larry have kept at their work for fifteen years now, and their impact is still unfolding. After a decade on Silver Spring Drive, I also felt that my own impact was hard to measure.

DeShawn began his senior year of high school in 2004. He had felt many pressures building inside of him. At his school, he had let some people know his sexual orientation. If there was a gay role in a play for acting class, DeShawn volunteered to take it. Several of the people whom he thought were friends suddenly didn't want anything to do with him anymore. Small things made him sad or angry.

"It got to the point where if I would see a couple holding hands, or if I saw a romantic movie, I would hurt," he said. "Because I knew that wasn't me. That wasn't what I could have."

"He kept things inside him for a very long time," says his sister, DeShell. "If you knew him, you knew how he was feeling based on his body. If he was slumped, if his shoulders were squared off, if he was trying to seek attention, you could tell by those things what was going on inside of him. But he wasn't able to express himself."

Soon after his senior year began, DeShawn was sitting in English class when suddenly, for reasons he didn't understand, the weight of what he had held within himself began to pour out of him. He began crying from the back of the classroom, and he couldn't stop. He felt

like a river that had tripped the dam. His classmates, who were usually a rowdy bunch, grew silent. His teacher did not know what to do.

DeShawn didn't have his phone on him, and he asked the person
sitting next to him if he could borrow hers. He got DeShell on the
line, and he said: "I can't do this. I don't want to do this." He meant
his life.

"I'm on my way right now," DeShell said.

DeShawn's English teacher escorted him to the office on the
lower level of the school. Within a few minutes, DeShell was there,
and she held her brother in her arms. She soon took him to the small
house where she was living while pursuing her master's degree in social work. DeShawn later reflected on the strength his sister gave
him that day by showing her own vulnerability.

"I always thought that my sister had her stuff together," De-
Shawn says. "She was always on the honor roll. She was always four
point. I was always two point. I was never up to her level. Yet that
day, she told me every negative thing that she had ever done. It
showed me that me and her were still the same. And I fell in love
with my sister even more."

During his senior year, DeShawn began to channel more of his
energy into the kitchen. For a long time, his mother, Karen, had been
in charge of cooking food for the lunches and dinners of our training
workshops. DeShawn always helped her. When our workshops began to grow larger and more frequent, Karen gave DeShawn more
responsibility. DeShawn asked to create his own items, including
Asian and Mexican dishes that he read about in cookbooks. He created delicious Italian dishes such as a lasagna with pesto, adding
herbs that he grew and picked in our back greenhouses. Though he
did not have full use of his hands since the fire, he was able to grip
enough of the utensils to do whatever he needed on his own.

I could sense the pride in him when people told him his food was
delicious, though he was often too shy to respond. DeShawn began
quietly to entertain the idea of becoming a chef.

In the spring of 2005, Lulu knew that DeShawn's prom was

DeShawn and Lulu at
DeShawn's senior
prom, 2005

coming up, and she started teasing him about it.

"Soooo . . . who are you taking?" she said.

DeShawn thought about it a little bit, and he decided to ask Lulu. She gratefully accepted. On the afternoon of the prom, Karen and DeShell paid for Lulu to go to a salon and get curls put in her hair. Earlier in the week, they also went shopping with Lulu to buy her prom dress. Karen hired a limousine to pick Lulu and DeShawn up from the house at Silver Spring Drive.

"I had never had anything like that," Lulu says. "That was special."

As Growing Power evolved, it had become a family. We quarreled sometimes, and things weren't perfect. But I took pride that the family on West Silver Spring Drive was one of many races and backgrounds. Milwaukee was recently ranked as the most segregated city in the country. But on our small piece of earth, we struggled and celebrated together—black and white, Hispanic and Hmong, young and old—as we worked to produce healthy food.

Will's Compost

Will Allen with his compost

As I travel the country to look at new urban agriculture projects, I can predict a group's future success by how much attention has been paid to creating fertile soil.

"It's all about the soil," I say.

It's very difficult to plant directly into city land and expect good results. In many industrial locations, the soil is not only infertile, but it is also contaminated with heavy metals and lead. One of the benefits of growing food in an urban setting, though, is that there is a vast amount of food and paper waste nearby that can be repurposed into growing soil and healthy food. It just needs to be redirected before it gets to the land-fill.

At my urban farm on Silver Spring Drive, we can grow so intensively because we plant directly in compost. A lot of our compost is created in "static" piles: We set up the compost bins and let nature do the work rather than turning it over from time to time. Static piles take longer to break down—as much as two years instead of three months—but they're also less labor-intensive. In an urban neighborhood, a static pile can reduce the release of smells that are unpleasant for your neighbors. We rely upon materials that are in broad supply in Milwaukee, such as "beer mash"—soggy grains that are left over from the brewing process. But for the most part, our raw materials are available in any community.

Here's how your community organization can create your own compost using my methods. I recommend building an entire compost bin all at once rather than incrementally. This will require collaboration with businesses in your community in order to obtain the large amount of raw materials you'll need. The process of obtaining sources of nitrogen and carbon can build relationships that will serve you well if you scale up your composting operation later.

SUPPLIES

1) A compost bin. You can build your own from discarded lumber, wooden shipping pallets, and wire mesh. Step-by-step building plans can be found online. Our bins are four feet high, four feet wide, and four feet long.

2) Roughly twenty wheelbarrows of organic material high in *nitrogen*. Examples include coffee grounds, fresh manure, food scraps, spoiled produce, young weeds, and beer mash. Sometimes we refer to our nitrogen sources as the "greens," though they are not always that color. Another way I like to think of nitrogen sources: They tend to be things that were recently fresh.

3) Roughly twenty wheelbarrows of organic material high in *carbon*. Examples include cardboard, hay, leaves, paper, napkins, sawdust, straw, and wood chips. We often call our carbon sources the "browns," because they often are brown.

4) Air and water.

HOW TO GATHER MATERIALS

It takes a lot of raw material to create even a little compost. A compost pile will shrink from when you first stack it. The nitrogen sources tend to be only about 20 percent solid, or less.

To access the organic materials listed earlier, you'll need to ask members of your community for donations of waste. These partners can include: coffee shops (for coffee grounds and filters, and chaff it they roast their own beans), local breweries (spent grain), food banks or food pantries (spoiled produce), grocery stores (produce scraps and cardboard, separated), restaurants (produce scraps), local farmers (manure, old hay, and straw) and city agencies (leaves, wood chips, and grass clippings).

Make it easier for businesses to collect this waste by offering twenty-five-gallon storage bins devoted to your project. Provide each business with a pickup time, make sure to be there, and give credit to those who donate at your event. Businesses are often looking for ways to improve their environmental profile, and you might be surprised by how eager people will be to participate.

BUILDING YOUR PILE

You'll want to build your pile by layering carbon and nitrogen in roughly equal amounts. I often say that a compost pile is about 75 percent carbon-heavy material and 25 percent nitrogen-heavy material. This is deceptive, though, because the nitrogen material is full of water and breaks down so much. So when you're building your compost pile, think of your carbon/nitrogen materials ratio as 1:1.

The bottom level of your pile should be about a foot thick and full of carbon material. This layer allows for proper aeration at the bottom. Air is important for the pile's proper decomposition. Without air, the pile will also be a lot smellier. Ideally, the bottom layer will have a lot of straw.

After this first layer of carbon is down, put in a layer of nitrogen-heavy material about a foot deep. Then put in a similar layer of carbon material. Then nitrogen. Then carbon. Then nitrogen. When you get to the top of the pile, make sure that your last layer is carbon. This will help contain the smells.

While you're stacking, invite young people to jump up and down on the pile periodically to tamp it down.

After you're done stacking, grab a hose and add water to the pile. The water helps support microbes that will digest it all. You'll want the compost material to be about as moist as a wrung-out sponge. If it is too wet, it can be hard for enough air to get in.

GO DO SOMETHING ELSE FOR NINE MONTHS

Keep yourself busy for nine months with other things. The pile may finish quicker in a warm climate and slower in a cold climate. You can check the pile periodically by digging your hands into it and feeling how hot it is. Ideally, the middle of your pile will get as warm as 150 to 160 degrees. If the pile is too dry and not breaking down fast enough, you can add some more water. You can tell when the pile is done when it cools down to about 80 to 90 degrees.

CONGRATULATIONS

When finished, I put handfuls of red wiggler worms in the compost pile to increase the soil's fertility. When your pile begins to cool down, worms will often find their way in on their own provided there are some nearby. In our greenhouses, we put our finished compost in pots that are twelve inches deep. We top off this compost with a three-quarter-inch layer of vermicompost—worm castings—for extra fertility.

Then we seed our pots with things like lettuces and mustard greens, arugula, and daikon radishes.

Some people sift their compost when it's done with a quarter-inch screen. I tend to like my compost chunky, with lots of wood chips. These chips are useful because during the process of composting, they become rich with fungi. Soil that is fungal has an easier time of transferring nutrients into the root systems of plants.

You'll get better at composting the more you do it. The naturalist John Muir once spoke of how meddling with the environment can have unintended consequences, and how the different parts of nature are "bound fast by a thousand invisible cords." When you compost, you are helping to strengthen the cords of nature.

PART 3

The Revolution

If we were to grow local food year-round in Milwaukee, we needed to find ways to grow food intensively indoors, even in the coldest months.

OVERNIGHT SUCCESS

In 1890, the U.S. Census Bureau ranked professions that had the highest rate of suicide. Tailors, accountants, bookkeepers, clerks, and copyists suffered the most. At the bottom of the list was a career least likely to lead to self-harm: farming. During the farm crisis of the 1980s, the suicide rate for American farmers rose in several states to double the national average. In an effort to combat mental health problems among farmers, Congress authorized the creation of a Farm and Ranch Stress Assistance Network in 2007.

Several recent studies have attempted to understand why many farmers are struggling emotionally. Some farmers who are asked about the high rates of suicide speak of a sense of loss: the loss of community, the loss of income, and not least, the loss of independence. Many rural farmers say that they are increasingly paid less for more work, and they owe more today for their seeds, fertilizers, equipment, and pesticides. They work one or two jobs outside of their farm in order to stay on their land. They feel ashamed that they cannot be self-sufficient in the way they believe their ancestors were. Instead of growing many crops, they plant hundreds of acres of corn or soybeans. They spray their fields with fertilizer and work off the farm while the corn grows. At the end of the season, the crop is harvested with a large combine.

This is an agriculture controlled by large machines. The land and the people on it are only units of production. The farmer may be compelled to grow on a scale that is uncomfortably large to him. He may borrow money for equipment he can't afford, and he may never meet the people (or the industrial animals) who eat what he produces.

The economist E. F. Schumacher wrote a book a quarter century ago called *Small Is Beautiful: Economics As If People Mattered*, in which he argued that the belief that "bigger is better" was not always true when you considered the emotional health of human beings. Schumacher argued that people need jobs where they "have a chance to enjoy themselves while working, instead of working solely for pay, and hoping, usually forlornly, for enjoyment solely during their leisure time." He argued for new agricultural methods that "build up soil fertility, and produce health, beauty, and permanence."

Instead of setting prices for their food in their own communities, farmers are now caught in a system where national or international markets set the prices. For every one hundred pounds of milk a farmer produces, it typically costs him around $18. Yet in the last decade, global competition has sometimes dropped the market price of milk to less than $12 per one hundred pounds. For the farmer already in debt—who rises early and works late—the mental weight of a drop in prices can be too much to bear.

In upstate New York in early 2010, one dairy farmer shot fifty-one of his cows before turning his gun on himself. When the farmer's friends buried the cows outside of his barn, none of the men agreed to speak to an Associated Press reporter about the reasons behind their friend's death. One man explained simply that "these are hard times to be a farmer." When the price of milk dropped precipitously in February of 2009, a string of suicides among dairy farmers in Vermont and Maine made local headlines. Male farmers take their own lives at several times the rate of female farmers, perhaps because they feel they must live up to an old American ideal of rugged independence and individualism. Farmers who take their own lives have also been found to be less likely to leave a suicide note than others. It is as if these men don't feel entitled to give voice to their feelings even in death.

If we are to make farming a profession that young people want to enter, we need to create new models for growing and distributing food that are emotionally satisfying. We have to be guided by the principle that small is beautiful. I feel fortunate that I have found a way to grow food on a human scale, and I have secured a certain kind of independence. I seed with my own hands. I participate in the harvest. I have always loved the process of trial and error in organic agriculture and the way the work engages both my body and mind.

At its best, farming can provide a lifelong education that engages you physically, intellectually, and spiritually. It takes intelligence, instinct, and lived experience to be able to predict when your crops are about to go south before they do, to know when they have been planted in the wrong spot or overwatered—and how to compensate for these problems before it is too late. I once spoke to an eighty-year-old farmer who told me: "I'm just learning how to grow food." I feel this way.

I think if we are going to foster a revolution in the methods of American agriculture, we must pioneer ways to make small-scale farming economically viable. We need to create farms that can grow multiple crops in an intensive way, even on small plots of land.

Nearly a decade ago, our work at Growing Power began to focus on ways to make this happen.

∾

During my early history at my roadside stand, my commercial vegetable production there had mostly been restricted to seed starts of lettuce and carrots and collards. Other gardeners could buy these seedlings and transplant them to their own gardens. Each spring, I also grew bedding plants in my greenhouses: perennials such as carnations, petunias, and marigolds. We raised a couple hundred tilapia in our "living system" fish barrels in our second greenhouse. We kept a demonstration garden for students. The produce that we sold in the store, though, had come almost entirely from my partners in the Rainbow Farmers Coop and from my acreage in Oak Creek.

Over a period of several years, this changed. My staff and I learned how to adapt the intensive organic growing practices from my own fields to our small urban plot on Silver Spring Drive. I became an urban farmer. Growing food on two acres appealed to me at first as a challenge: I wondered how much I could produce in five greenhouses and in my back lot.

In time, I came to see the potential benefits of agriculture in small urban spaces. The Milwaukee winters are bitter; the average low temperature in January is thirteen degrees. If people in the city were to have local food year-round, we needed to find ways to grow intensively even in the bitterest parts of winter. I also saw the opportunity that inner-city farms and high-yield backyard gardens had to remedy problems that are damaging our environment, morale, and health. In the last three decades, more than forty million acres of rural land in the United States have been developed—an area roughly the size of New Jersey and Illinois combined. This process of urbanization is likely only to increase in the future. Cities will continue to expand, and their populations will increase. I have spent enough time in the countryside and in cities to see that their fates are linked. When prices rise for wheat, corn, and oil, for instance, the urban poor are often unable to afford the higher food costs. A future urban population that depends entirely on distant rural farms will also place even greater demands on our infrastructure: roads, bridges, and airplanes.

We can't expect our food of the future to be produced only by traditional farming families in rural areas. These families have increasingly been pushed off their land, and the quality of the soil has been degraded. If we can figure out ways for more people to control the growth, marketing, and distribution of food on a local and regional level—and even to grow some food within cities—I believe we can play a part in remedying some of the problems that are troubling us as a country right now: the absence of jobs, the problems of waste, the crisis of rising energy costs, and the lack of access among low-income communities and people of color to healthy, affordable food. We need to create farmers who can produce $200,000 intensively on a single urban acre as well as those who can grow $500 on an acre in the countryside.

My composting operation demonstrated that an urban agriculture facility like ours could transform a city's waste stream—diverting discarded vegetables and paper and cardboard from landfills and turning it into healthy soil. From my early start with the Sendik's grocery store and Alterra Coffee, I developed more than a dozen other compost partners over time. I was picking up waste from a large Milwaukee wholesaler called Maglio's, Stone Creek Coffee, and a Piggly Wiggly grocery store. A large Milwaukee beer producer called Lakefront Brewery started giving me truckloads of the moist spent grains leftover from the brewing process. I was saving each of these businesses money that they had previously paid to hauling companies. I was making money from this waste by converting it into soil and fresh food.

A broad vision was taking shape in my head of a new urban ecology, where a city's waste could connect to its food-producing stream and where small facilities like my own could be not only food stands but also food producers. This dream was not fully formed. It appealed to me as a puzzle would. I set about trying to build it in my greenhouses and back lot, piece by piece.

ॐ

At my farm in Oak Creek, I had long ago adopted intensive growing techniques I learned from my father and from Belgian backyard
farmers. My level of productivity was possible only through the use
of compost and my seeding technique. For small farmers, the two
main ways to seed a field are precision seeding or broadcast seeding.
Precision seeding requires a machine that puts seeds one by one in
the ground. I always broadcast seeded by hand, scattering the seeds
onto the ground. Through years of experience, I had come to know
precisely how much seed I could use for each crop in the space I was
provided. I never let anyone else do the seeding for me, because I
didn't trust that they could do it right.

I could only seed my vegetables so closely together in Oak Creek
because of the quality of my compost. Almost all of the land in the
United States has been depleted of its natural health. Soil scientists
say that it can take as many as a thousand years to develop an inch
of nutrient-rich topsoil. Virgin topsoil provides an array of vitamins
and minerals that are necessary for both healthy plants and healthy
people: calcium, nitrogen, magnesium, and potassium. For short-
term gain over the last two centuries, we have stripped the land of
its ability to provide these nutrients. When we harm the soil, the soil
finds ways to harm us. The Dust Bowl of the 1930s was created in
part by farmers who had overplowed the topsoil of the Great Plains.
The land was tilled too deeply and abused for decades by planting
the same crop over and over again. The soil became vulnerable to
wind and dust storms.

In the last several decades, the industrial agriculture system has
depended heavily on chemical fertilizers that are high in nitrates,
which farmers feel are necessary to produce high yields year after
year. Plants use these fertilizers inefficiently, and when it rains, the
fertilizer ends up running off into our drinking water. More than a
quarter of wells in the United States now contain levels of nitrates
that are considered higher than the acceptable standard. Excess human consumption of nitrates has been linked to gastric and bladder

cancers. High levels in drinking water have also been connected to a condition called "blue baby syndrome." The nitrates begin a chain of biological reactions in infants that deprive the child's organs and tissues of oxygen. This syndrome is most common in rural agricultural areas where chemical fertilizers are widely used.

The gradual depletion of the land's natural health has also meant that most of our crops are now less nutritious than they were even fifty years ago. The amounts of protein, iron, calcium, phosphorus, iron, and vitamin C have all declined noticeably in all harvested fruits and vegetables in the United States from 1950 to 1999. Riboflavin, a B vitamin that helps the body convert food into energy—and that is necessary for healthy skin, eyes, hair, and liver—declined overall in fresh foods during that time period by nearly 40 percent.

I wanted to farm in a way that healed that damage. With my worm castings and compost at Silver Spring Drive, I believed that I could meet one of the biggest challenges of growing food in an urban environment: the problem of the land's fertility. I knew that healthy food starts with healthy soil.

As I began to think about bringing my organic techniques inside, I recognized that my greenhouses offered not just horizontal space but also *vertical* space. If you measured my growing capacity simply by the footprint on the ground, the greenhouses covered about half of an acre. Yet at their highest point, the greenhouses were as tall as fifteen feet. If I maximized the use of this space and the available light, I thought I could perhaps triple or quadruple the amount of food I could grow there.

In 2003, I invited a gentleman to my facility who had experience growing sunflower sprouts and pea shoots. At one of our workshops, he provided a lesson on his techniques. He planted seeds in bedding trays that were only a few inches deep, using a thin layer of potting soil and peat moss. (The peat moss increased the soil's capacity to hold water.) With this technique, he was able to go from seeding to harvest in little more than a week. He shaved the sprouts a couple of inches from the root when harvesting them, and the pea shoots would soon grow back again. He could harvest a tray two or three times before the soil was depleted.

I saw a future in sprouts. Sunflower sprouts are high in vitamin D, which helps with the absorption of calcium and is thought to help the immune system. People often obtain vitamin D through exposure to the sun. In the long Milwaukee winters, it can be hard for people to get the amount they need. Sunflower sprouts are also very high in protein, calcium, and not least chlorophyll—which some people have credited with everything from relieving inflammation to deodorizing the body.

The sprouts were also well suited as a cash crop for my greenhouses. They could be cultivated year-round, harvested frequently, and grown intensively. If we were to figure out how to grow food profitably in the city, we would need to maximize the amount of income generated per square foot. Growing in urban spaces often requires more money than growing on land in the countryside; there are higher energy costs, higher costs for land, and a farmer cannot take advantage of traditional economies of scale.

I began experimenting with my own method of growing sprouts. Instead of potting soil with peat moss, I helped create a special soil mix using our worm castings. It takes centuries to create peat moss, and many of the bogs where it has been mined commercially are now depleted. As a replacement, we bought blocks of coir—coconut fiber—which is a natural by-product of coconut farming. Our soil mix for sprouts was one part worm castings to one part coir.

With our fertile soil, I could broadcast our sunflower and pea seeds in ten- by twenty-inch trays. I was soon getting better results than the gentleman who introduced us to sprouts. The taste of the sprouts was full-bodied and vivid. With the idea of increasing the amount of sprouts we could grow in small spaces, my staff, volunteers, and I built shelves in the first greenhouse that allowed us to stack three rows of trays vertically. I quickly determined that if I had enough demand, I could make roughly $50 per square foot from my sprout trays every year, before expenses. If I could sell an acre of sprouts—nearly 44,000 square feet—that could potentially be a significant source of income. I began searching for markets, and I was able to entice several of the city's best restaurants to be our first customers.

One of my other interests was to see if I could get our food into Milwaukee's public schools. School district food managers in the United States have long faced difficult circumstances if they try to incorporate local food into school lunches. These managers are provided a limited budget at the beginning of a year, and they are often under pressure to cut costs. For several decades, they have generally depended on large regional wholesalers and on federal surplus programs for products like milk. Many schools also do not have in-house kitchens. The meals are prepared off-site, making it harder for schools to incorporate foods that are highly perishable.

In the mid-1990s, potatoes were the only vegetable in the top 10 food categories purchased by school food administrators. They were served mostly in the form of French fries. Milk, pizza, ground beef, cheese, chicken nuggets, and hot dog rolls all made the top 10 list. Advocates for children's health and for local farmers recognized that if there were ways to connect farmers to schools in the communities they served, it could potentially be a good thing for young people who were suffering the health effects of bad food—and a good thing for small farmers who were struggling for their livelihoods. Several "farm-to-school" initiatives began around the country, including in nearby Madison in 2002.

In 2005, the city of Milwaukee contracted with the large food distributor Sysco to provide most of the produce for its breakfast and lunch program. Soon afterward, I struck up conversations with several people in the Milwaukee public schools system to try to persuade them that purchasing our sprouts would be good for the health of the city's children. Sysco soon approached me, saying that the Milwaukee school system was interested in our products, and I negotiated a fair price with them. Within a year, our sprouts were in two dozen schools in the city of Milwaukee. I have been told the children eat them because they taste like real food. Most of their prior experiences with vegetables in school had been of the canned and soggy variety.

After we had refined our system for growing sprouts, I looked for other ways to use the vertical space in our greenhouses. We began planting salad greens in hanging pots that we filled with compost, topped with worm castings, and hung from long rods attached to the roofs of our front greenhouses. We were soon producing rainbow chard, beet greens, spinach, tat soi (a spicy Asian green with curled leaves), kale, dandelion greens, arugula, and several varieties of lettuces. As with the sprouts, we shaved the leaves when they were still tender, allowing for future harvests, and the taste was pungent and delicious. These greens were easy to market to upscale restaurants and cooperatives in the city, who could tout their relationship with an urban farm. We also sold the greens in our own retail store and distributed them as part of our market baskets.

I took pride as I walked through my greenhouses and saw a new "vertical farm" taking shape, with pots hanging on several levels.

I had been raising fish indoors in barrels since the late 1990s, and I began to wonder if it were possible to scale these systems up. Our

As we began to grow more food indoors, we improved our techniques of using vertical space.

dozen sets of three-barrel "living systems" allowed us only to raise a couple hundred tilapia at a time. Though the barrels always interested kids who visited my facility, we weren't growing enough fish to generate any kind of consistent revenue.

I saw a local market. Milwaukee was famous for its "Friday Night Fish Fry," a tradition that is said to have started decades ago among Catholics, who were supposed to refrain from eating meat on Fridays. Families turned to fish as an alternative to red meat. Today, nearly every self-respecting restaurant in the city offers fried fish on Fridays. I believed that I could do quite well by marketing tilapia locally, because I could save the buyer transportation costs. Most tilapia consumed in Milwaukee were being imported from China, or Central and South America.

At Growing Power, we undertook a few early experiments before we got the fish systems right. I was in Kmart one August day in 2003, for instance, and I saw that they had an end-of-summer sale on a five-thousand-gallon aboveground swimming pool. It cost $199. I decided to purchase the pool and create a pond in my fourth greenhouse. I adapted the basic principles that we had used in the barrel systems. I connected some PVC pipe to the pool, and we pumped the water out to a filtering tank before recirculating it back into the pool again.

I put several hundred tilapia in the pool, and within a few weeks, I saw that the new system worked. But I felt that the pump and tank were consuming too much energy. The thing I had admired the most about our old three-barrel "living systems" was how they replicated the processes of the natural world. Fish excrete ammonia after they eat, and in an enclosed space, this can soon become toxic to them. The fish can also starve for oxygen if the water is not aerated. Commercial fisheries often deal with these problems in a way that consumes lots of energy, employing mechanical aerators, filtration systems, and giant recirculating pumps. Our "living systems," on the other hand, used compost, snails, and vegetable matter to clean up the ammonia before the water returned to the fish tank. The only electrical part of the operation was a small $15 pump. Each system cost about $70 to build and about $50 a year to maintain.

I wanted to try to keep the spirit and the low costs of these natural systems while increasing their scale. I knew that the gentleman who had introduced our living systems to us, Jonathan Woods, had been experimenting for many years with a technique called "aquaponics." This was the practice of growing fish and fresh vegetables for market in the same linked system.

In the mid-1980s, horticulturalists at North Carolina State University had pioneered this technique by taking water from a tank containing tilapia and pumping it up into a large sand bed that was planted with bush beans, tomatoes, and cucumbers. The fish's wastewater was filtered by the sand and the plants' roots. Beneficial bacteria in the sand converted the ammonia into nitrogen, which the plants' root systems could use as a fertilizer. The planting bed was tilted very slightly, so that gravity drained the wastewater slowly from one end to the other until it spilled back into the fish tank again. The researchers were ultimately able to harvest more than five hundred pounds of fresh vegetables from their sand bed. The fish also did well. Of the 813 fish the researchers initially put in the system, about eight hundred survived and grew to market size.

I particularly liked the idea of an aquaponics system in an urban setting because of its efficient use of space. It provided several marketable products at once. The system also was consistent with the spirit of my compost operation: It was a "closed-loop," where the fish's waste was converted into life and energy and the water was recycled.

My staff and volunteers and I experimented with a few small-scale prototypes before I felt confident to build a larger aquaponics system. One of our first preliminary models used a 250-gallon tank. At one end of the tank we built two gutters that sloped gently down toward a separate holding tank of the same size. We placed pots of tomatoes and herbs in those gutters. When we turned the system on, overflowing water from the fish tank came slowly down the gutters and was absorbed into the plants' root systems. From the holding tank, the filtered water was then pumped back into the fish tank. The plants grew well, and the fish that we tested in the system did just fine.

On an early winter day in 2004, I was walking through the second greenhouse from the road when I allowed myself to dream bigger. At the time, I was still growing a large number of bedding plants there. Our greenhouses were one hundred feet long, and I thought about the potential of having a narrow tank that extended almost that entire length of one of them. I wanted to grow food in raised beds above the tank. Instead of raising a few hundred fish at a time, I thought we could raise several thousand. I also thought that digging down into the ground would be an effective use of available space. The earth would provide some insulation to keep the water warm. We would be growing vegetables in the air and fish in the ground.

A few months earlier, I had hired Rick Mueller, a soft-spoken and kind man who had recently lost his lease on his Waukesha aquarium shop in the wake of the recession in the early 2000s. Rick had been keeping aquariums since he was ten years old, and he had a special love for aquatic plants. I took Rick into our second greenhouse, and I stuck a spade in the ground there.

"What do you think about us digging out a raceway, three feet down, the entire length of this greenhouse, to grow tilapia?" I said.

Rick had questions about how we would filter all of the water. We soon came up with a design that adapted the techniques of the North Carolina State researchers. With the help of seventy-five volunteers, we dug a long trough without any power equipment. The soil was harder than we had thought, and this process took three months. We lined the walls of this giant raceway with wood and covered it with plastic pond liner.

Directly overtop of the raceway, on wooden platforms, we built two long planting beds. These beds were constructed to mimic the ecosystem of a small river or stream. Water from the fish system was pumped up to one end of the top bed, which we had also covered with pond liner, filled with tiny pebbles, and then topped with potted tomato and strawberry plants. The wastewater flowed gently down the first bed, which was slanted very slightly. The plants' root systems, which were exposed by holes in the bottom of their plastic pots, helped filter the ammonia. Then the water spilled onto the second bed, which was planted with watercress and slanted slightly in the other direction. By the time that the water spilled back into the fish tank, it had traveled nearly two hundred feet and passed through the roots and soil of several hundred plants.

When we got the pumps working and the plants in place, Rick ordered four thousand tilapia fingerlings. They arrived from New Mexico in four large trash bags that were filled with a little bit of water. Volunteers and staff stood around as we introduced the fish to the system. We lost only two dozen fish in the first couple of weeks, which was less than 1 percent of the total.

"After that, the fish were beautiful, and they did great," Rick remembers.

We were proud not only that our new aquaponics system worked, but about how inexpensive it was to build. We estimated that a commercial system to raise four thousand tilapia would cost $50,000 or more. We constructed our entire system—which consisted only of wood, pond liner, and a single pump—for $2,000. It had maintenance costs that were not insignificant: We had to feed the fish for nine months, and we had to pay the energy costs for the pump and

Our aquaponics system in our second greenhouse grew fish and vegetables in a closed-loop system that mimicked the processes of a natural stream.

for the system's use of an existing water heater (tilapia like water temperatures of about seventy-five degrees). Once the fish reached market size, though, we could sell them for $6 each. We could also harvest the plants continuously.

I knew it would likely take many years before I figured out how to make these tilapia systems work economically. I also knew I wanted to create urban agricultural systems that were inexpensive enough to build that they were doable for ordinary people. When my staff wanted a machine to sift our compost, for instance, I decided to retrofit an old clothes dryer that had its heating unit burned out. The spinning unit still worked, so I cut out the backside of the dryer and placed a quarter-inch screen behind the spinning drum. When we shoveled the soil into the drum, the largest wood chips remained there, and the soil passed through the holes and was sifted even more by the screen.

If we were going to create prototypes for growing food in inner-city neighborhoods, they had to be cost-effective. The 250-gallon tank for our first aquaculture system was donated to us from a paper mill. This tank had originally held ink, and we had given it a new life. In building our larger aquaponics system, we recycled a lot of secondhand lumber. Just as my grandmother Rosa Bell had done in different circumstances during the Great Depression, I was trying to make do.

I began looking for other ways to reduce my expenses. I knew that one of the biggest obstacles to growing food indoors in Wisconsin was the problem of energy. The ability to grow in greenhouses offered a chance to extend the growing season, but the costs of heating were prohibitive.

Farmers in Wisconsin were often at a distinct disadvantage because of our northern climate. Grocery wholesalers wanted a consistent product year-round, and this was an impossible obstacle for most farmers, given that our planting season for row crops extended only from April to late September. My earliest winter in the greenhouses at Silver Spring Drive had set me back $30,000 in heating bills. Even with a more efficient heating system, I was still spending too much money a decade later to keep the greenhouses warm. They were not insulated very well, and the heat generated by our Modine forced-air heaters was escaping out of the cracks in the glass on the roof.

One thing I noticed when we got our tilapia aquaculture system up and running was that it was much warmer in the second greenhouse than in the other four greenhouses. By heating the forty thousand gallons of water in the system, we were also heating the air. This humid heat was rising from ground level, so less of it escaped out of the greenhouses. Tilapia do well in water up to ninety degrees, so by turning up the heat slightly on the water heater we were soon able to turn off the Modine heaters entirely in the second greenhouse. As we built additional tilapia systems in other greenhouses over the next several years, we were slowly able to end our dependence on the forced-air heaters.

I was also looking for ways to decrease our dependence on fossil fuel. As I built my compost operation, I started receiving free wood chips from landscapers, the City of South Milwaukee, and the City of Oak Creek. Wood chips decompose slowly and give off radiant heat as they decay. By covering the floors of our greenhouses with them, I saw we could keep our greenhouses warmer in the winter. When the soil in the sprout trays was no longer fertile, we would also dump it into four- by four-foot bins in one of the greenhouses and let it compost for a while before we used it again. These bins would get as warm as 150 degrees and provide a constant heat source. Within a few years, our heating bill had declined by nearly 50 percent. Much of the warmth was being generated by biological activity.

If other people in inner-city communities were to adapt my models for year-round growing, few would have access to large greenhouses like my own. I wanted to see if the principles worked with even less investment. In 2005, my staff and I built our first "hoop house" in the back lot of my property. Hoop houses are simple, low-cost greenhouses that can be built in a single day for as little as

$1,000. They require little more than bent pipe, some lumber (to provide support for a door), and thin plastic sheets.

Once we had covered the entire frame of our first hoop house with plastic, we put piles of steaming compost in each corner inside. We also covered the floor with wood chips and piled warm compost on the exterior plastic sidewalls. After some adjustments, we soon saw that even on days when the temperature dipped well below freezing, we could keep the hoop house heated—with no electricity— to more than fifty degrees. This was warm enough to grow spinach and other greens. On the days when the temperature dipped below twenty degrees, we simply covered our beds of spinach with sheets of plastic to make sure that they did not freeze. Over the next several years, my staff and I built ten more hoop houses in our back lot, allowing us to grow intensively year-round.

As my staff and I worked to create a local food system, and to grow food indoors, a good food movement was taking root around us. Books like Eric Schlosser's *Fast Food Nation* (2001) and Michael Pollan's *The Omnivore's Dilemma* (2006) exposed some of the problems of our industrial food system. A new hunger for local food was being expressed throughout the country. In 1994, the year after I opened Will's Roadside, the U.S. Department of Agriculture began publishing a national directory of farmers markets. At that time, there were fewer than 1,800 markets listed in a nation of nearly three hundred million people. By 2006, there were almost 4,500.

Our organization was soon the beneficiary of these larger social changes. In October of 2005, I had received a $100,000 leadership grant from the Ford Foundation that I was able to channel into the work at my Silver Spring Drive facility. Around the same time, my daughter Erika had been able to work with Heifer to establish a nineteen-thousand-square-foot community garden in Chicago, with all of the produce going to soup kitchens and shelters in the city. Mayor Daley attended the opening ceremony.

Erika was also provided space by the city in Grant Park, often known as "Chicago's front yard," to build an edible "potager" garden there. The garden was ornamental, in a French style, and in it she grew 150 different varieties of herbs, edible flowers, and heirloom vegetables. Erika seeded her plants in beautiful spiral and checkerboard patterns, and they bloomed into a work of art. The project was a perfect combination of her interests in art and agriculture. She wanted to show everybody that growing food could not only have health benefits, but also add beauty to the land.

With these successes also came challenges. By 2006, we were generating nearly $375,000 in gross sales and more than twice that in grants, but our expenses still outweighed our income. I had hired several longtime volunteers like Sarah Christman, and our staff had grown to a dozen people. I wanted to pay a living wage to my full-time employees; these salaries alone cost more than $400,000. We also had our summer youth corps, who were compensated only a little for their work. By the time we added our truck and equipment rentals, payroll taxes, and other expenses, we were still running deficits.

Growing Power's board of directors put together a strategic plan in 2006. The board was headed by a new president, Jerry Kaufman, who had retired from the urban planning department at the University of Wisconsin. He began to invest more of his energies into helping me succeed. One of our goals in the strategic plan was to continue to diversify our sources of revenue and to reduce our costs. By 2007, with the growth of our aquaponics system and our vertical growing techniques—and by trimming some of our expenses, including electricity—we were bringing in $30,000 more in revenue and grants than we were paying out.

Yet this success was bittersweet, as it came in the same year we had two personal tragedies in the lives of our staff. Karen Parker's great nephew, eleven-year-old Purvis Parker, made the national news when he suddenly went missing on an icy day in March with his best friend, Quadrevion Henning. The police at first questioned Purvis's father, Purvis Sr., even though all of his family knew he had nothing to do with his son's disappearance.

Karen and my staff tied white ribbons on the trees along the front of our property. The community outpouring was tremendous, and it reinforced my sense of the inherent good in people. More than two hundred individuals—black, brown, and white, rich and poor, most of them volunteers—were combing our community every day looking for the boys. Twenty-seven days after they went missing, on a warm day in April, their bodies surfaced in a lagoon in McGovern Park, less than a mile from our facility. Investigators determined that it was a simple accident. The boys had fallen in and been trapped under the ice.

Only a month afterward came Lulu's family accident. Karen Parker cared deeply about Lulu, and she treated her as her own daughter. When Lulu was fifteen, Karen saw that she had fallen in with a bad crowd at a high school called South Division, and that she had too many obligations at home. Karen asked Lulu to move in rent-free to the yellow duplex across from my greenhouses, and encouraged her to transfer to a different high school. Lulu accepted the offer.

Lulu often wanted to do something to show Karen that she appreciated her kindness. Her parents received food stamps on Lulu's behalf, and whenever Lulu got her hands on them, she bought food for Karen as a gift. At Karen's house, Lulu and DeShawn stayed up late almost every night talking, and she fell in with a better friend group at her new school.

Lulu lived with Karen from the ages of fifteen to seventeen, but she felt an increasing obligation to help her parents and family. She was already giving her family half of her weekly check at Growing Power to help them with their rent. She moved back into their home during her senior year of high school.

On May 21, 2007, Lulu was at home on West Mineral Street in Milwaukee's Clarke Square neighborhood. The area houses one of Milwaukee's largest Latino populations. The average annual income in that neighborhood is less than $10,000. A week earlier, Lulu's family had their electricity shut off for nonpayment. Lulu's father was dependent on insulin, which needed to be refrigerated, so a friend of their family lent them a gasoline-powered generator. Lulu's parents decided to put it in the basement.

Lulu's uncle, Nolan Lopez, was also living at the house at the time. He was fifty-four years old and had part-time work at UPS, but the work wasn't regular. A few minutes after the family turned on the generator for the first time, Nolan went into the basement to watch a movie on a television there. Less than half an hour after her uncle went downstairs, Lulu and one of her sisters started feeling a little bit dizzy.

"It feels kind of weird in here," Lulu said.

Her dad noticed he was feeling strange, too. He decided to open up the basement door. As soon as he did, he began to feel even more dizzy. Lulu's father called out Nolan's name, but he did not respond. Her father could hear the engine of the generator. He decided to walk down the stairs to try to make sure Nolan was okay. Lulu and her sister followed him. When they reached the landing, they saw Nolan lying motionless on the floor.

Lulu's father tried to wake him up. When he was unsuccessful, Lulu and her sister and her father began to try to drag him up the stairs. At first, Lulu thought her uncle had just passed out, but it became clear to her as she tried to carry him that he might already be dead. The two girls then saw that their father was having trouble keeping consciousness. Lulu and her sister decided they needed to get help. Her family could not afford to keep a house phone, so the two young women ran up the stairs and out into their yard. They started yelling to their neighbors:

"Call the ambulance! Call the firefighter!"

❧

DeShawn rushed out the front door of his house that afternoon.

"I'm going to Lulu's," he told his mother. "I'm going to call you when I get there."

Karen asked him why, and DeShawn said that something was

wrong. About an hour later, Karen's phone rang. It was DeShawn, instructing his mother to turn on Channel 12. Karen did, and there was a story on the news about two Latino men being overcome by carbon monoxide, an odorless gas, because of a generator mistakenly placed inside of the house. The reporter said that one of the men was thought to be dead.

"That's Lulu's daddy and her uncle!" DeShawn said. "They think her uncle's dead."

DeShawn was with Lulu when he called. She had reached out to him on a friend's cell phone, and he was trying to provide her comfort. She had just been released from the hospital after getting checked for carbon monoxide in her blood. Her concentration levels were not as high as her father's; he was still undergoing treatment in a hyperbaric chamber to increase the level of oxygen in his blood. Nolan Lopez had died.

Lulu's parents felt guilty after the accident. They reflected that if they would have been able to pay for electricity, they would not have needed the generator. They didn't know that you weren't supposed to bring the generator in the house. They couldn't read the warnings in English.

The week after this accident, Lulu became the first of her ten siblings to graduate from high school. She credits Karen. "I consider her like a second mother to me," Lulu says. "She'll be there to give me advice like a mother would do. I feel that if it wasn't for me staying over there, and for her thinking I should change schools, I would not have graduated."

༄

The fates of human lives are often linked like the bonds that connect the different parts of nature. Karen's strength to stabilize her own life provided Lulu with enough stability to obtain a high school diploma.

On a day soon after Lulu's graduation, a group of nonviolent offenders were brought to my facility to fulfill their community-service hours. Karen was working in the front store when she heard a man call out her name. She turned around, but she did not recognize the man looking at her.

"How do you know me?" she said.

He explained. Karen had dated this man briefly, years ago, when her life was much different. She acknowledged the man, but soon retreated back into the kitchen. "I hid," she told me. "I didn't want anyone to know I knew him."

Karen avoided the group the entire morning and during the visits over the next two days. Before her former boyfriend left on his final day at Growing Power, though, Karen gathered the courage to approach him as he was leaving. As she walked toward the man, he nudged his friend and told him: "Yeah, that used to be my girl."

Karen felt sympathy for him. He was missing many of his front teeth. His eyes were sunk deeper, and he looked so much older than she remembered him. They had a brief conversation, and before leaving, he told her something quite unexpected.

"I'm proud of you," he said. "I'm proud of seeing where you are today."

Karen felt her own pride. She saw in this man's situation how her life could have turned out quite differently. As Growing Power gained more attention in Milwaukee, Karen had taken on new responsibilities. She often appeared on local television, describing our market basket program and our outreach projects. She could tell any customer what vegetables grew in what season and the name of every fresh thing we sold, and she had an encyclopedic memory for

Karen Parker at her front door, with her dog, Mr. Bigg

prices. She managed the entire Youth Corps program. She oversaw our staff, which had grown by early 2008 to a dozen people.

"So many people come through here from my past," Karen said. "And they are just overwhelmed to see what I'm doing. If they glance at me on TV, or they see me here, they can't believe it. They say: 'That's Karen Parker.'"

❦

On an August morning in 2008, I was preparing to harvest lettuce on my own farm in Oak Creek when my phone rang. A man's voice I didn't recognize came on the line. He asked if I was Will Allen. I said I was.

"What are you doing?" he asked.

"I have my knife and I'm getting ready to cut some salad mix," I said.

"Why don't you put down that knife," he said. "I have some good news for you."

I wondered at first if this was someone I knew who was playing a joke on me. The voice seemed slightly familiar.

"Have you ever heard of the MacArthur Foundation?" he said.

I told him I had heard of it, but I didn't know what they did. That's when the gentleman introduced himself, and he told me that I had been named a MacArthur Fellow. It was an award for creative people who had shown originality, dedication, and self-direction. The foundation sought to make the world more "peaceful and verdant." He soon explained to me the financial piece of the award, and that it offered $500,000 over a period of five years, and that the money was unrestricted. He asked that I tell no one but my wife until it was announced a couple of weeks later.

On the day of the MacArthur announcement, in early September of 2008, I was at Kalamazoo College in western Michigan. I had been invited to give a talk to incoming freshmen and sophomores. I was getting ready to go on stage when the person introducing me let the crowd know that I had been chosen a MacArthur "genius." As I

walked onto the stage, the students rose and gave me a standing ovation. This was before I had said a word.

I was surprised. I had been doing the same work for many years.
It is very humbling work. The physical nature of it keeps you
grounded, as well as the fact that at any point you could lose your
crop. As a former athlete, I also knew that one day you could be at
the very top, and on the next day the very bottom.

I had not changed, but I saw that the MacArthur award changed
how people saw me. It gave me a stamp of approval, and it validated
that what I was doing was meaningful. I also could sense the pride
that other African Americans felt in me as a person of color who was
working in this arena. Few black people who were struggling to
change the food system had received this type of validation, though
poor food affects people of color more than other communities.

I realized that by bringing farming and fresh food to the city, I
could play a part in healing a painful rift in African American history between its agricultural past and its urban present. I could help
to rebrand farming as something that could be entrepreneurial and
black-owned rather than something associated with sharecropping
and slavery. I felt a deeper sense of obligation to forward the revolution in the food system in which I had now invested my life.

Grit

Worms don't have teeth to digest their food, so they have to swallow soil or sand to have the right amount of grit in their gizzards. This grit grinds the sweet fruits and vegetables that they eat and helps worms break their food down. A worm cannot thrive only on sweet, soft things.

Human beings need the right amount of grit: not too much, but not too little, either. As parents, we often want to protect our children from challenges. Yet it can be precisely in those moments when a child faces and overcomes difficulties—when he tries and fails, but survives and tries again—that character is formed. Growing food reinforces those lessons. Farming is difficult work, and there are often setbacks: crop losses, spoilage, insect infestations. If you persevere through these setbacks, there is still a harvest. The lessons conveyed in farming are applicable to all other areas of life. All the good things that have come in my life were only because of grit, and my willingness to forge ahead even in the face of uncertainty and mistakes.

Because of the rising costs of production, the economic pressures on many small farmers have become too much to bear. If we can make small farming economically viable again, and if we can involve young people in this work, we can go a long way in teaching lessons of character that will produce more resilient and capable citizens.

Giving a lesson at my compost workshop

NEW FRONTIERS

As I refined my urban farming techniques, I wanted to share our hard-earned knowledge with other small farmers. Over a period of several years, we had trained several thousand people at our workshops in Milwaukee. By 2008, we were often attracting nearly two hundred people a month to our weekend training sessions. Visitors could learn composting, worm breeding, sprout production, marketing, beekeeping, and other elements of urban food production. I knew that our approach to education had limitations, though, that were primarily geographical. Most people who could benefit from learning these intensive agricultural techniques did not have the luxury to fly to Milwaukee, spend several nights in a hotel, and fly home.

On Wednesday, November 5, 2008, the day after Barack Obama

was elected President of the United States, I set off in a green van with some of my staff for a trip through the Deep South. We would later call it "the freedom ride," after the famous 1960s interstate bus trips where whites and blacks tested the limits of racism and Jim Crow. There were six of us in the van: three black men and three white men, including our board president, Jerry Kaufman. We were leaving under happy circumstances, feeling pride in our first African American president-elect. We were traveling to share our aquaponics and intensive growing techniques in Mississippi, Arkansas, and Louisiana.

We headed first to New Orleans, where we helped an urban farming project strengthen their hoop house. In the evening after we had finished our work, we held a potluck dinner on the site, where both black and white people ate together. Two of the folks were musicians—an African American singer and young white man who played the banjo—and they played for us during the sunset, as we ate okra and salad. Toward the end of the evening, the singer paused and told us: "Look, I rarely sing this song."

He began to sing the national anthem. We all stood up, and many of us put our hands on our hearts. I looked over at Jerry Kaufman, whose brother had fought for civil rights, and I saw tears in his eyes. "We all started singing," Jerry remembered, "minorities and whites together. There was this glorious sense of communal victory." I hope President Obama knows how good this was for us.

The next day reminded us of a different reality. We were driving up Louisiana's Interstate 55 toward our second stop in Forrest City, Arkansas, when our driver, Martin Bailkey—a lecturer at the University of Wisconsin-Madison who was helping us evaluate our programs—noticed flashing lights out of the rear window. I was asleep until the van pulled over.

"I was not speeding," Martin recalls. "We were just in this green van with tinted windows and Wisconsin plates on a drug route, with a white guy driving, and a big black guy sitting next to the driver."

The officers asked Martin to step out of the van. He gave them his driver's license, and he saw that they were drug enforcement agents. They asked Martin what we were doing and where we were going. Martin said we were an organization based in Milwaukee that trained people to create sustainable urban agriculture and community food projects.

"I realized as I was talking," Martin told me later, "that this wasn't making any sense to them."

The two DEA agents proceeded to inspect our van. In New Orleans, I had been given a huge piece of sugarcane as a gift. We had placed it on top of the seats from front to back. The agents peered inside the hollow cane but didn't know what to make of it. After thoroughly scouring the trunk of the van and most of our bags, they let us on our way to our workshops in Arkansas.

I was not the first African American farmer and teacher to make trips through the South to teach people how to farm. The educator and agriculturalist George Washington Carver has long served as an inspiration to me. Much of Carver's life was devoted to the cause of increasing the self-sufficiency of black farmers.

"My idea is to help the 'man farthest down,'" Carver said.

Carver's work took many forms. He published bulletins in clear, simple language that told farmers how to use acorns for livestock feed or how to grow sweet potatoes. At the end of the nineteenth century, Carver also began hosting monthly agricultural seminars for African American farmers at Tuskegee Institute, the black college in Alabama originally founded by the educator Booker T. Washington.

My workshops at Growing Power were in the spirit of Carver's own. Carver had used the occasions to demonstrate the natural fertilizers he used—including "muck" out of a bog on the Tuskegee campus—and teach his innovative organic growing techniques, including crop rotation.

Booker T. Washington realized that most small farmers who could benefit from Carver's work could also not afford to pack up and visit Tuskegee. Washington came up with the idea of retrofitting a wagon to serve as a traveling agricultural school. Carver embraced the idea, and a New York banker named Morris Jessup underwrote the project.

The Jessup Agricultural Wagon first set out in 1906, and one of Carver's African American students operated it. During the first summer, two thousand farmers in Alabama were instructed through the traveling program. The same spirit that had guided the creation of the Jessup Agricultural Wagon prompted me in 2004 to imagine outreach training centers for Growing Power. I wanted to create partnerships with regional organizations where we could train more people in our techniques.

"The Jessup Agricultural Wagon," and a successor, The Booker T. Washington Agricultural School on Wheels, were models for my regional training outreach.

The idea first took root when I met Dorothy Grady Scarbrough, an African American nurse in her fifties who was trying to grow community gardens in Bolivar County, Mississippi. I met her at a conference where she was trying to build relationships to strengthen her organization, Mississippians Engaged in Greener Agriculture, or MEGA. Her goal was to improve the capacity of Mississippi farmers with limited resources to provide more food for their communities.

"I was working in the hospital and seeing the illnesses that were coming through," Dorothy said. "My concern was, 'What's different now than when I was growing up? Why are these people all so sick?' One of the things that came to me was that it was based on our food, and how it was grown. Back then, we had a local food system. If you had a house, you had your own produce, and you had your own livestock."

The lower Mississippi River delta is home to some of the most severe health problems in the entire United States. For the six million African Americans who left for Northern cities during the Great Migration, there were also many who stayed behind in the South. The people who live in the 240 counties that surround the Mississippi River from Southern Illinois to the Gulf of Mexico are among the poorest and the least healthy of all Americans. A person in the Delta is nearly 25 percent more likely to die each year than the typical U.S. citizen. The prevalence of obesity and diabetes is staggeringly high.

I gained a greater understanding for the reasons during my visit to Mound Bayou, Mississippi, Dorothy's hometown. We had come to help Dorothy and her volunteers do some strategic planning for her organization as it moved forward.

Mound Bayou holds an important place in African American history as one of the prominent "black towns." A dozen black men founded Mound Bayou in 1887 to better themselves and their families in an area of toxic racism. The town thrived for several decades. By 1915, the population had grown to eight thousand, and Mound Bayou had six churches, its own post office, and several schools, both public and private. The local government was entirely controlled by black residents. Crime was almost nonexistent. Booker T. Washington wrote about the community as an example of how black people could lift themselves up.

When cotton prices plunged in the early 1930s, though, much of the town departed during the Great Migration. When we visited in 2008, fewer than two thousand people were living in Mound Bayou. The average resident made less than $9,000 a year. The food environment was also very, very poor. The only grocery stores nearby were ten miles away, in Cleveland, Mississippi. The one food store in town did not have fresh fruits or vegetables. Instead, there were cans of pork rinds and cooking oil and soup, and loaves of white bread. The gentleman behind the counter told me that the store was soon expanding to have a meat counter, but not a produce section.

The Southern food tradition in the United States has many healthy aspects. This diet has traditionally contained a lot of dark green leafy vegetables like collard greens, yellow vegetables like squash, as well as lentils, peas, and peanuts. But much of the healthy food is fried in things like pork fat.

I have seen in my trips through the South that there is a deep reliance on meat, which can often lead to colon cancer and heart disease if consumed continuously and in large portions. Meat was likely a treasure to Southern black farmers in the past, when pork and beef could only be obtained in small portions. Today, industrial beef and chicken are much less expensive, widely available, and overused. Nearly thirty chickens are killed on average each year for every man, woman, and child in the United States. The typical American consumes more than two hundred pounds of meat in that same period. Fresh fruits and vegetables, on the other hand, have become scarce in some areas.

Dorothy is part of a growing movement of Southerners who are trying to adjust that balance, and to improve people's access to healthy food. My brother Ray is another soldier in this movement. Ray took the train with my mother from Ridge Spring to Washington, D.C., more than half a century ago. After my mother and Major Kenner split, Ray returned to South Carolina, where he has mostly lived since. In his fifties, Ray was diagnosed with asbestos-related lung cancer from his civil engineering work. Instead of chemotherapy, Ray decided to combat his illness by going completely vegetarian and eating only organic foods.

Ray is now eighty years old. He is the only person he knows with his form of cancer who is still alive. He has started an heirloom seed business with twelve hundred varieties that he offers through the mail. His business card reads: "Raze Organic Grown Products: Consulting and Specializing in Heirloom, Rare and Traditional Plants & Seeds, Victory Garden Since 1941, Division of Ray Kenner Company . . . Never go hungry—Plant a Garden!"

The victory garden that Ray refers to is a tiny plot he planted as a boy, after he heard Franklin Delano Roosevelt on the radio. The president had encouraged his listeners during one of his "fireside

My eighty-year-old brother, Ray Kenner, with one of his kenaf hibiscus plants in South Carolina

chats" to plant a garden to improve food security during the rationing of provisions that was necessary during World War II. Ray has since become a student of soils and of the healing power of fresh vegetables and seeds. He cultivates kenaf hibiscus seeds for their oil, which are rich in omega polyunsaturated fatty acids. These fatty acids can reduce cholesterol and the risk of heart disease. He eats mustard greens three times a day.

"I try to eat only what I grow," Ray told me recently. At eighty, he is writing a book in longhand about natural amendments for the soil, to show others how to increase the soil's fertility without chemical fertilizers. He has accumulated more than a hundred pages.

Both Dorothy and Ray know trade secrets that their grandparents knew. They know how flour and a bit of cayenne pepper can keep bugs away from watermelons. They know that putting a clove of garlic in the watering can help plants ward off soft-bodied insects. They are reclaiming the soil's fertility and growing food on a human scale. They possess the kind of skills that George Washington Carver taught generations ago. Their efforts also offer a protest against the destructive agriculture that treats the land as a conquest, that batters the earth with pesticides and artificial fertilizers, and that degrades not only the health of the land but also of people.

❧

By the end of 2008, Growing Power had developed regional outreach training centers in more than half a dozen locations, from

Mound Bayou to Louisville, Kentucky, to Lynchburg, Virginia. My staff and I tried to visit each training center at least once a year and conduct weekend workshops. I realized, though, that this limited training was not enough to ensure that people knew even the basics of farming, such as how to compost and seed correctly. If Growing Power were to play a part in building the good food movement, I thought we needed to provide better training to the leaders of our regional centers.

In the winter of 2008, we inaugurated a "commercial urban agriculture" program. We asked people to come to Milwaukee over a three-day weekend for five consecutive months. My goal was for the graduates of the program to know how to do everything that we did in our greenhouses and hoop houses, and to offer lessons that we had learned from nearly two decades of experience.

A few of the early members of our commercial urban agriculture classes were from an organization called the Detroit Black Community Food Security Network. One of the group's founding members was Malik Yakini, a community activist from Detroit. Speaking to Malik allowed me to recognize that the challenges and possibilities of the local food movement are nowhere more evident than in the Motor City.

Detroit was one of the great repositories of African American hopes during the Great Migration. In 1910, fewer than six thousand African Americans lived there, comprising only 1 percent of its total population. By the early 1970s, black people accounted for nearly half of the city's one and a half million people. Many of the initial settlers came from farms as far as Alabama when they heard of Henry Ford's 1914 promise of $5 a day—an unprecedented salary for blue-collar workers at the time.

Some arrived at the Detroit train station "not knowing where they would sleep, who they were going to see, or who would be interested in them," wrote John C. Dancy, who headed the Detroit Urban League, a black-led social service organization. "When the train reached Detroit, they would just go into the station and sit down."

While many Southern blacks looked to Detroit as a "new

Canaan," the reality they confronted was most often different. Restrictive housing covenants—"redlining"—forbade homeowners from selling to blacks in large swaths of the city. Few white-collar jobs were available. Even though Henry Ford was among the most progressive of industrialists, and a friend to George Washington Carver, only a small fraction of the jobs in his plants were offered to African Americans. The black immigrants who came to the city were mostly forced to live in communities on the Near East Side, one of which was called "Black Bottom." When they tried to move out into other neighborhoods, they were often greeted with violence. In the two decades after the Second World War, more than two hundred black family homes were attacked by whites. These homes usually belonged to "the first or second [families] to move into all-white neighborhoods," writes the civil rights historian Thomas Sugrue.

Detroit's racial divisions were only made worse with the decline of the city's industrial economy and the suffering of the automotive industry. The home of the Model T and the Temptations is often considered "the poster child of urban decay," says Yakini. Its population has declined by more than half in the last four decades. White families fled to the suburbs on the city's outer ring while most black families in the city were hemmed in on the southern side of 8 Mile Road. Houses fell into disrepair, and the city began demolishing many of them as a way of trying to improve blight. Today, the amount of vacant land inside of Detroit—more than twenty square miles—is roughly equal to the size of the island of Manhattan.

In the absence of other good options, some have wondered whether Detroit's vacant lots could be repurposed for growing fresh food. The racial and economic divisions in Detroit have created two food systems: one for the haves and another for the have-nots. More than 90 percent of food stamps in Detroit are spent at what the food-system researcher Mari Gallagher calls "fringe retailers": liquor stores, party stores, gas stations, dollar stores, and the like. More than 500,000 people in the city have to travel twice as far to reach a grocery store than a fringe store. More potato chips are consumed in Detroit per capita than in any other city in the country.

These changes have had effects not only on the health of people in Detroit, but also on the city's culture. The merchants in many of Detroit's African American neighborhoods come from an Iraqi community in the suburb of Dearborn. Both the Iraqi and the black communities inside Detroit often look upon each other with distrust.

"There is a phenomenon in Detroit that I call 'wordless transactions,'" Malik says. "All of the convenience stores in Detroit have Plexiglas to protect the merchants. The merchant sits behind Plexiglas, and he might be on his telephone. You put your goods into a turnstile, and he rings them up. You see the price on a machine. You stick your money in a slot that's just big enough to put your money into. He gives you change, and not one word is exchanged."

Early in 2006, Malik made a purchase at a gas station and convenience store four blocks from his house. He handed over his money, but from the merchant there was "no acknowledgment of my humanity," he said.

"You don't say thank you to your customers?" Malik asked the merchant.

The merchant cursed at him, and the two men got into a heated argument. The next day, Malik brought in a contract that he had titled "The No Disrespect Pledge." Malik took it to the owner and told him: "You need to read this and sign it." The letter told of Malik's experience and demanded that the merchants at the gas station treat their customers with dignity. At the bottom of the contract, Malik explained that if the owner did not sign it, Malik would share his experience with the local media. The owner cooperated.

The same year of this encounter, Malik helped launch the Detroit Black Community Food Security Network. He wanted to improve access to healthy food for the African American community and to do his part in developing a better food environment in the city for people of color. In 2008, the network obtained two acres as a growing site in Detroit's Rouge Park, not far from Ford's giant River Rouge car factory.

Malik and a dozen volunteers from the community started D-Town Farm, growing food to sell at farmers markets and for their own

Malik Yakini of the Detroit Black Community Food Security Network, at D-Town Farm

consumption. I started visiting this project whenever I was in Detroit. Visitors who come to D-Town often have impromptu conversations about food and race. At a workshop I attended at the D-Town farm in the fall of 2010, some of the participants kept warm during breaks in a finished hoop house at the north end of the farm. The group included Lila Cabbil, who had been close to the civil rights icon Rosa Parks, and who is president emeritus of the Rosa Parks Institute. The conversation turned to the future of Detroit. Lila spoke about white flight from the city.

"Some people feel if they come back to Detroit, it's not safe for them," Lila said. "What's wrong with that picture? There's no concern for the other people. So there's damage to everybody, because that's not a natural human reaction: to care about yourself, your children, and not care about other children."

"That's why I talk about everybody's responsibility in the plight that we're in," I said. "That's why we have to do this work in a multicultural way. No single group is going to solve all the problems of Detroit, Milwaukee, Flint, Buffalo, or New York City. All of these cities are suffering from the same issues. The most progress we've made in Milwaukee is by bringing people together and having them work together, and by having events like today's."

A young man who was still in college followed my comment by speaking about the evils of capitalism and the U.S. government. He had theories that U.S. intelligence agencies were helping to pump drugs into inner-city communities in order to keep African American communities poor and suffering.

There was a trace of condescension in the young man's comments. Lila has edited a book called *Accountability and White Anti-Racist Organizing*, and one of its frequent arguments is that people who do social work often consider themselves saviors of the black communities they have purportedly come to serve. She and the black elders in the community listened to the young man patiently until he said, "Detroit gets worse and worse."

"We don't speak that to claim it," Lila interrupted. "You say that like it's going to happen. We want to be talking about our future in terms of what we can do about it. Just think about how we spend money on food . . ."

"We continue to shop at corporate businesses, and the money quietly leaves the community," the young man said.

"Yes," Lila said. "We want to get people growing their own food, so that they have more power. With Obama, people voted for change, but they're sitting back waiting for him to do it. It ain't going to happen. But I can say: I can change me. If I can change me, and I am part of a collective, I can be a part of creating a different outcome. But I've got to start with me."

Lila paused for a moment.

"The reason we're drugged the way we are is because of what we eat," Lila said. "If we were eating the right food, we wouldn't need the drugs."

∾

As Growing Power contributed our knowledge to efforts like D-Town in Detroit, we were also adding new pieces to our growing urban farm on Silver Spring Drive. My goal was to make my facility into a laboratory of intensive growing techniques that other organizations and commercial urban farmers could transplant into their own communities.

One desire I had was to show that livestock larger than worms could peacefully inhabit an urban area. Our first animal was Oakley, a billy goat with a musky odor whom we used to mow some of the tall grasses behind our greenhouses. We soon brought Oakley a she-goat for companionship, and he sired a number of young Alpine goats that we began to keep in an enclosure in the back lot. I hoped eventually to be able to create goat's milk, but in the meantime, the animals always attracted the interest of young people who visited our facility.

Once, a young boy from the neighborhood stole one of our smallest baby goats. The boy's teenage friend persuaded him that a goat would be hard to keep as a pet, paid him $5 for it, and then returned it to us safely only a few hours after it disappeared. I took it as a sign that we had developed good relationships in the community that the young man would want to help us retrieve the goat.

We also built a chicken coop in a hoop house on our back lot to raise fresh eggs. More than 90 percent of the eggs that we eat in this country come from birds confined in "battery cages"—a cruel system that provides hens little more space than the size of a piece of paper to move the entire two years of their lives. Our coops were without cages. I explained to our customers that happy hens made for delicious eggs. We sold the eggs in our store and at farmers markets, and we provided some in our market baskets.

Whenever I went into the hoop house with the chickens, it was always very warm. My staff and I did a little research, and we found that a single chicken produces about ten watts just with its body heat. In the summer, the chicken house got so hot that we had to vent it well to make the sure the birds could breathe. In the winter, though, I realized that the extra heat from the chickens could potentially help us grow food. My staff and I set up a hoop house that was partly devoted to chickens and partly to spinach. We put down fresh straw every day to absorb the ammonia from the chicken waste. The idea worked even better than we'd intended: We were soon growing winter spinach with chicken heat.

We explored other novel ways to create energy. In 2006, we began a partnership with a compost machine manufacturer called CBT Wear Parts to build an "anaerobic digester." If the digester worked properly, it would transform organic food waste into gas that could be used to create electricity. An anaerobic digester has some similarities to the digestion process of a cow. The rumen, one of the four compartments of a cow's stomach, is full of microbes that allow the animal to digest food. There are more bacteria in a single cow's rumen than there are people who inhabit the entire earth. These billions of microbes quickly consume the small amount of oxygen in the rumen, so the food that enters is ultimately broken down "anaerobically"—without oxygen. When organic waste is digested without oxygen, it produces methane gas.

In the atmosphere, methane turns into carbon dioxide and contributes to global warming. In an anaerobic digester, you put organic waste in a sealed environment, add some acetic acid to digest the waste, and capture the methane that is released. The methane can then be cleaned and used as a heating gas, or diverted into an engine that can convert the gas to electricity. The gas also can be stored until you need it: a clear advantage over solar or wind power. The sludge that is left over is often rich in nutrients like phosphorus and potassium and can be used as a fertilizer for plants.

There is potential with organic waste for energy production. At least one-quarter to a half of the fresh food that we create in this country is thrown out before it is eaten—enough food waste, as the author Jonathan Bloom has pointed out, to fill the Rose Bowl in Pasadena every day. The U.S. Environmental Protection Agency says that wasted food is one of the largest producers of methane in the United States. According to one estimate, if we were somehow able to gather all of this wasted food, trap its released methane, and convert the methane into energy, we could power nearly one out of every twenty homes in this country.

With the help of a grant from the State of Wisconsin and funds from the U.S. Department of Energy, CBT Wear Parts built a digester in our back greenhouse. The main piece was a ten-thousand-gallon cylindrical tank. In 2008, during our first successful test of the system, we shoveled food waste into the tank, sealed it, and then heated the tank to nearly one hundred degrees to aid in the digestion. The machine worked as intended, and we were able to capture dozens of cubic yards of gas, which we stored. We hope in the coming years to develop enough relationships to process more organic waste, convert the gas to electricity, and have the machine running full-time.

If we are going to be able to make urban farms economically viable in the future, we are going to have to figure out how to create inexpensive renewable energy. We need energy sources that don't place insupportable burdens on the environment and people, as fossil fuels do. The troubling reality is that our current models for alternative energy—solar and wind power, in particular—are not powerful or efficient enough to replace coal and oil altogether. Bill Gates has said that if he had one wish to improve the fate of human beings over the next half century, it would be for an "energy miracle": He wants something that could produce the same energy as coal without carbon emissions, and at half the price.

Anaerobic digesters are not that miracle, but I see them as one of many stopgaps until we figure out Gates's dream. With the help of Wisconsin Energy Corporation, the local utility in Milwaukee, I have also been able to install solar panels at Growing Power to help heat our water systems. In addition, we have partnered with the Milwaukee Metropolitan Sewerage District, who provided a grant of $35,000 to create a rainwater catchment system. It now captures most of the rainfall on our greenhouse rooftops and redirects it into our fish systems.

My intention in time is to build a facility that is entirely off the grid and that uses only the power of the sun, the earth, and decaying waste to grow food. I'm not there yet, but I believe I can make it happen.

❧

All of these innovations at Growing Power came from relationships. I could not grow my compost without companies that were willing to provide their organic waste to me. The work of creating renewable energy required me to develop lasting partnerships with utilities and machine companies. I did not have a market for my products without building a reliable customer base at restaurants, cooperatives, and farmers markets throughout the city. Industrial farming has disrupted these kinds of relationships, and it has torn at the fabric of communities.

We now had the hopes of Milwaukee invested in Growing Power. Milwaukee's progressive mayor, Tom Barrett, asked our staff in 2009 to plant a garden at city hall, and we were glad to do it. Mayor Barrett's initiative came in the wake of the good work of Michelle Obama, whose demonstration garden at the White House has, I believe, inspired many more Americans to plant gardens at their own homes.

As our capacity to do work throughout Milwaukee became greater, I also began to form relationships with several corporations in the city. One of Wisconsin's best-known homegrown businesses is Kohl's, which runs one thousand department stores throughout the country. Their corporate office, just a few miles north of my facility, was a gleaming building of black glass and white marble that was home to more than three thousand employees.

Kohl's had a volunteer program, and they began to partner with us by sending five employees a week to work for several hours alongside our inner-city youth, hauling worms and compost. The corporation also sent us $100 each time one of their employees volunteered. This seemed unfair: We were getting free labor *and* money.

I spoke to John Fojut, the vice president for corporate sustainability at Kohl's, and said I wanted to form a closer relationship. I didn't want Kohl's just to throw money at us and then move on. I asked him how we could do more work together. John mentioned that Kohl's had green space adjacent to its large parking lot, and I went out to visit.

My staff and I soon created a small garden in a median of the parking lot. We built a separate garden next to the day-care center that Kohl's provided for its employees. The children of Kohl's employees soon were learning to harvest and plant food. We opened a small farmers market on Friday in the corporate cafeteria so that employees could buy fresh food before they went home for the weekend. The cafeteria staff at Kohl's began setting aside all of its food waste (except the meat), and we started composting it. This was a productive partnership in all aspects.

In 2010, regional executives at Walmart toured my facility, and they began to have similar conversations with me about how we might work together. They said that Walmart was launching a new initiative intended to increase the amount of local food it bought by 2015 to 9 percent. This is not insignificant, especially for a company with Walmart's buying power. The average American eats less than 1 percent of his or her food from local sources. Representatives of the company also said it was investing $1 billion in its supply chain to better accommodate perishable and local food, and that it would commit $1 billion in its new markets to buy from farmers who grew on fewer than fifty acres.

I was not unaware of the reputation that Walmart had in the progressive community. For years, Walmart has been viewed as undercutting small businesses with its pricing, making it difficult for family businesses to survive. The addition of supermarkets to Walmart megastores in the mid-1990s has made the corporation the largest food retailer in the United States, and the company has undoubtedly contributed to a decades-long trend that has made it difficult for smaller grocers and a regional food system to thrive.

In essence, Walmart seemed to be for everything that I was against. Yet I have always been a pragmatist. Jerry Kaufman, my board president, once framed a question to a group of planners that also informs my own thinking about Walmart or its competitors.

"How do we deal with the industrial agricultural system?" Jerry asked. "Are we going to take the position that we want it to go away? Or do we recognize that it's still a nine-hundred-pound gorilla in the living room, and that it won't go away, but that maybe we can change its ways?"

Simply wishing Walmart gone is not going to make it go away. Many low-income people shop there because the prices are what they can afford, and these people don't have the luxury to consider the social implications of a big box store economy. If Walmart was trying to buy more local food, I was willing to partner with them to try to make that happen. The whole work of my life has been trying to leverage people's strengths. This view has informed not only how I deal with people but also how I work with corporations, who are made up of people.

My relationship with Walmart began when they agreed to give me seventy thousand pounds of organic waste a week from ten local stores. I did not have enough space to compost so much waste on Silver Spring Drive. One of my staff members was able to appeal to a Milwaukee Metropolitan Sewerage District plant that had a vacant field, and we began each week to ship the thirty-five tons of Walmart food waste there, where we mix it with wood chips from the city of Milwaukee and other paper waste. I set up nine new hoop houses within a mile of this composting facility, and we are now growing fresh greens year-round primarily from Walmart waste. When you fly out of Milwaukee's Mitchell Airport, our composting operation is visible from the air.

In 2011, executives at Walmart told me that they wanted to give Growing Power $1 million to help strengthen our dozen existing regional training centers as well as to build three more, where others could learn our sustainable growing techniques. I gratefully accepted this grant without hesitation. I knew the money would permit more local food to get to more people. It would permit Dorothy Grady Scarbrough in Mississippi, for instance, to close a deal on a two-acre farm and have a commercial kitchen for her organization for the first time.

I held a press conference in September of 2011 at Growing Power's headquarters to announce the grant. The news prompted the largest wave of criticism I have ever experienced in any of my careers. On the Web site Civil Eats, Andy Fisher, who served for many years as the director of the national Community Food Security Coalition, denounced our willingness to take Walmart's money by saying that "we in the movement don't have to define our game as including those entities whose practices undermine our long-term goals."

Many of my supporters wrote me to say that they understood why I took the grant, but they felt my choice was not in the spirit of our organization or my values. Some progressive writers who did not know me were less diplomatic. "The Allen example already looks like yet another in the long, dreary menagerie of sellouts," said one. Others accused the Walmart corporation of buying my silence and said that the grant was simply corporate "green washing"—an attempt to make the corporation look like an environmental steward by throwing money at a good cause, while their real intentions were to carry on business as usual.

I think progressive critics of corporate business practices play a vital and important part in creating social change. In the absence of effective government, activist citizens and journalists need to take matters into their own hands. They need to point out injustice where they see it. The criticisms of Walmart have often been just, and it is also fair to criticize me.

When Martin Luther King, Jr., spoke of the arc of history being long, though, he was right. The current food distribution system is so entrenched that it is going to take decades to modify it. In the short term, we need to work with the institutions that we have. If Walmart wants to buy more local food and to invest in local farmers, I am going to meet that gesture in good faith.

∾

To some, the more troubling question that the Walmart donation to Growing Power raised was whether the urban agriculture movement could be economically sustainable without outside funding. This is an important question to confront directly.

"To motivate young people to be farmers now," says Dorothy Grady Scarbrough in Mississippi, "they are going to have to see the money first. We have to be able to lay this out and say that with this amount of acreage, you can make this certain amount of money, if you follow these guidelines."

The honest truth is that with urban agriculture, we are not there yet. We have not yet made it reliably profitable. I think we can, though. I see my own work as part of a long continuum. Every industry needs investment in basic research. The industrial agricultural system in this country has been sustained only through billions of annual subsidies and the government's historical investment in irrigation systems and technology suited to large-scale farming. All of the experiments that we have tried at Growing Power—and most recently our work with solar and geothermal heat—have been an attempt to drive down the costs of production for small-scale farming and to make the work sustainable both environmentally and economically. We have done this work with relatively little investment.

I am trying now to quantify the expenses and income generated by the urban growing systems we have created. I am working with the Great Lakes Water Institute at the University of Wisconsin-Milwaukee to study the economics of our indoor fishing systems. With our intensive indoor sprouts and greens production, I believe I could sustain at least a half a dozen jobs on the proceeds alone, but not the larger staff that is partially funded through grants. I think if we can create low-cost forms of renewable energy, it will go a long way to making small-scale agriculture more possible for more people.

The creation of a new food system that is economically viable is going to need people like Jeremy Brosowsky, a graduate of an Ivy League university and the London School of Economics. His first job was as a research analyst for Goldman Sachs on Wall Street covering beverages and tobacco. He was making good money, but he wanted to believe in the social value of what he was doing.

"I remember rationalizing to myself: 'Well, we're adding liquidity to the marketplace, which is good for the economy, because we're making information readily available,'" he said. "You can justify almost anything."

He left that job by the time he was twenty-five to start a local business magazine called *Washington Business Forward*. He was soon able to open up a similar magazine in Boston, but was forced to close it in the deteriorating business climate following the attacks of September 11. His next venture was an online business that failed during the 2008 financial crisis.

By this time Jeremy was in his mid-thirties and had four children. He and his wife had a mortgage on a home in Washington, D.C. He wanted to make money, but having kids had also shifted his priorities.

"You look at your work differently if you filter things through the lens of 'Is this something my children would be proud of? Or care about?'" he said.

In 2009, Jeremy came across an article about my work in *The New York Times Magazine*. He kept talking about the piece to his wife, Beth. She told him: "You need to meet this guy." Jeremy began to research other urban agriculture projects. He read about an operation in Brooklyn called the Eagle Street Rooftop Farm, and he became fascinated by the idea of rooftop agriculture. He soon had dreams of fostering rooftop gardens throughout the metropolitan Washington, D.C., area. There was one big problem: He had lived in cities his whole life, and he had never grown anything more than a tomato in his backyard. He heard about my commercial urban agriculture program, and he signed up.

I met Jeremy in January of 2010 on his first day at our facility. Despite our differences, I saw myself in him. He had a scientific curiosity and a head for business. I was impressed that this young man who had spent much of his life in offices was soon enthusiastically dumping boxes of rotten egg shells and rotting cabbages into our compost bins and asking so many questions about our worms systems.

"I was learning a ton," he said.

By the time he arrived for the third month of the program, though, he was struggling with how to create an agricultural-based business that could survive financially. The winter of 2010 was one of the worst on record in the Northeast, and most of Washington, D.C.'s rooftops were clogged with ice and snow. It was a hard climate to sell the idea of rooftop gardens.

Jeremy was watching me conduct my composting lesson on a Saturday in late March of 2010 when his thoughts drifted back to the previous day. He had made a compost run with one of my drivers in a large truck that we lease. They picked up raw materials from

a bakery, a cafeteria, and several other locations. The drive time between pickups was sometimes longer than half an hour. He thought
of the time and resources wasted in this process, and he was considering ways to make the trip more efficient. He suddenly remembered a business he respected in his home city of Washington, D.C.
It was called Propane Taxi.

If you had a gas grill in your backyard, Propane Taxi offered to
come to your house and exchange your old tank instantly for a full
one. The service cost about $4 more than what it cost if you discon-
nected the tank from the gas grill, put it in the car, drove it to Home
Depot, filled it up, and returned it. The business made propane replacement effortless.

"Once I heard of this business," Jeremy said, "I would never buy
propane any other way."

Jeremy started wondering whether the Propane Taxi model
could be altered to fit the business of composting. He wanted to
make it very easy to pick up compost from the people who were producing it—consumers and businesses—and very easy for urban
farms that needed it for food production to receive it. A name came
into his mind: Compost Cab.

Jeremy suddenly excused himself from my workshop. He needed
to write this down. He found a small, empty table at the back of my
front greenhouse. There, over the next two hours, he typed into his
laptop a model for the whole business. The main premise was simple.
Customers would pay to have their compost picked up, and Jeremy
would deliver it for free to urban farmers. After he typed out the
plan, he walked into my front store, where he could access our spotty
wireless Internet service, and he bought the domain compostcab.com.

When Jeremy returned home to Washington, D.C., he sat his
children down and explained the new business he was creating. "I
asked them, 'What if we could take our garbage and grow food in
it?' Any six-year-old will tell you that is awesome. Because it *is* awesome. So now when you ask my kids, 'What does your dad do?'
They say 'My dad grows food out of garbage.'"

By September of 2010, when he launched his business, Jeremy

had signed up thirty-seven residential customers in Washington. He had done no advertising other than putting up his Web site. He bought an inexpensive dump truck off of eBay. He painted it yellow, and he decorated it with a COMPOST CAB sign and checkered stickers purchased from a New York taxi-supply company.

Whenever a customer joined, Jeremy sent her an e-mail welcoming her and explaining the system. (He noticed that his early residential customers were "overwhelmingly female.") A subscription costs $32 a month. Each customer is given an airtight bucket bearing the Compost Cab logo, and a compostable bag. The organic waste is collected once a week, the buckets are cleaned on the spot, and the customer is provided with a new compostable bag. He delivers the compostables to ECO City Farms, on the edge of the city, in Edmonston, Maryland, as well as to a small farm adjacent to a D.C. public school. He helps create the compost, too, using Growing Power's techniques. He tweets pictures of the piles—and updates on their progress—to followers of Compost Cab on the social network Twitter.

"Our residential customers are paying us to pick up their garbage in a town where garbage pickup is part of your tax base," Jeremy says. "You've got to really want to do this. And our customers do." Jeremy also set up a dump site at the popular Dupont Circle Farmers Market in Washington, where people could pay him $2 to dump their organic waste. Roughly three dozen people take him up on the offer each week.

By late summer of 2011, Compost Cab had grown to have more than 160 residential customers as well as a number of businesses, including offices of the Peace Corps, Bloomberg, the financial news company, and the kitchen of the Hyatt Regency. The only residential customers who had ended their subscriptions were people who have moved elsewhere. With the larger subscriber base, Jeremy has been able to hire a young man in his twenties, Alec Brown, to do most of the pickups. He offers him a salary of $30,000 a year. By creating one job in the middle of the economic downturn, Jeremy has done more than many of the politicians in Washington.

On a balmy August day, Alec steered the yellow Compost Cab dump truck with broken air-conditioning down small Washington alleyways. The fermented smell of decaying fruits and vegetables in the back—"it has a *tang* to it," Alec said—blew in his open windows. Alec had worked on Capitol Hill but lost his job when a Tea Party candidate defeated his Boca Raton representative in the fall 2010 elections. He began to rethink what he wanted to do with his life. Alec met Jeremy when he was volunteering at an Earth Day event.

"When I was on the Hill, we did amazing things," Alec said. "We passed the health care bill. We reformed Wall Street. Yet we never *saw* the effects of those things. Whereas *this* . . . this is different. This compost pile is turning into dirt. On some level, I think I was tired of the macro. I wanted to do the micro."

Alec hopped out of the dump truck and soon emerged from underneath the staircase of a Washington town home with a Compost Cab bucket in hand. He unloaded the compostables in the back, cleaned the lid and the bottom of the bucket with a washcloth, and hopped back in the truck. He scribbled the weight of the compost next to a name on his list—one of fifty customers that day—and the time of the pickup. He quickly glanced at his next destination.

Alec was sweating. As he drove, he was listening to National Public Radio, where two pundits were discussing the debt limit crisis on Capitol Hill. The announcer asked: "Has this impacted the U.S. standing in the world?" Alec often sees the capitol dome on his Compost Cab route, but his former life there feels a million miles away.

∽

Jeremy often rises at 5:30 A.M. on weekday mornings to prepare the compost pickup map for Alec. He's not taking any salary himself at this point. His wife's job provides enough at the moment that he's able to get by. He recognizes this is a luxury that many do not have, and his idealism is tempered by economic challenges. He wants to be able to franchise the model he has developed to other cities by

*Jeremy Brosowsky
and the
Compost Cab*

2012, and to take a percentage. He is committed to a for-profit model because he thinks it is the only way that the good food movement is going to succeed in the long term.

"This is not Google we're building. But the waste industry in this country is a 100 billion-dollar-a-year business," Jeremy said. "Half of that belongs to thirty companies. The other half—fifty billion—belongs to thirty thousand little companies across the country: haulers, recyclers. Fifty billion is a big business. If you can capture some piece of that, in a way that's beneficial to everyone, that's a huge victory. Thirty years ago the recycling industry was the domain of hippies and freaks. Composting is basically where recycling was thirty years ago. It is a fringe movement that is about to become mainstream. And the reason is because there is money in it. It's only going to scale because there's a nickel in it for somebody."

In the future, I think there should be room in the world for both for-profit and nonprofit community food projects. Many urban agriculture initiatives like Walnut Way's efforts in Milwaukee have social and economic benefits that extend beyond the organization's own balance sheets. These efforts survive through the generosity of local businesses and governments who want to help the communities these projects serve. They impact people's lives and health in a positive way, and they are not reliant on federal subsidies, as many farms growing commodity crops are.

Dereck Cunningham is proof of why nonprofit farms can matter. He first came to one of my workshops in Milwaukee in the spring of 2004. On a recent December day, Dereck told his story as he wended his way with his two crutches through the rows of lettuce and spinach in a greenhouse in Lynchburg, Virginia. He was born with spina bifida, a birth defect that created a hole in his spine and left him partially paralyzed from the waist down. His parents were told when he was born in 1971 that he would likely not live past twelve years old. Dereck stubbornly defied expectation.

Dereck and a young attorney, Michael Van Ness, had a vision. In 2003, they started a nonprofit called Lynchburg Grows with the hopes of creating gardening programs for low-income individuals and people with disabilities. Michael and Dereck's inspiration came when they helped an elderly man in the nearby town of Bedford, Paul Lam, replant his vegetable garden. Lam had a severe speech impediment. The garden he had carefully tended for years outside his group home had been accidentally razed.

In 2004, Lynchburg Grows found a home from a local family who owned nine large 1920s-era greenhouses in an industrial corner of Lynchburg. At one time, the family of Herman Schenkel, Jr., produced a quarter of Virginia's cut flowers there. A growing international flower market undercut the family's prices, though, forcing the Schenkels to sell their roses at 25 cents a stem rather than a dollar, and ultimately pushing the family out of a business they had kept up for fifty years. The family hoped to see the agricultural legacy of their greenhouses preserved, and they decided to sell their property to Dereck, Michael, and Lynchburg Grows for well below the market rate.

Volunteers from Lynchburg College helped clear the greenhouses of old rosebushes, and Dereck soon started offering workshops in the greenhouses for children with special needs, including autism. He taught them how to plant and harvest kale, spinach, onions, and beets. He also began to grow food commercially and started cold-calling several chefs at restaurants in the area to ask them to take his produce. In late 2006, Dereck became president of Lynchburg Grows and got off Social Security.

"I was receiving disability checks at the time," Dereck said. "I could have stayed on disability. I didn't have to be working. But I felt like I had so much talent and motivation, and I got tired of sitting at home. I didn't want just barely to live."

Dereck has since helped build a formidable composting operation. It saves the city over $50,000 each year in landfill fees by taking half of the leaves the city collects. Lynchburg Grows also sells its lettuce to four local school systems, and Dereck has formed business relationships with more than a dozen local restaurants in the city. The organization runs a farmers market that is manned by community members with both mental and physical disabilities. This work indicates how the local food movement has the potential to provide meaningful employment for people who have been shut out of the traditional workforce. Recently, I partnered with the Badger Association for the Blind, a Wisconsin organization, to teach a client of theirs how to seed sprouts in my greenhouses. The lady who visited learned the entire process within an hour, and the trays she seeded were better than many created by my experienced staff.

Dereck is working hard to make his organization less dependent than grant money. "We're up to at least three days of sustainability out of a week," Dereck says, meaning that at least three of every seven days are financed internally from selling food or services. Lynchburg Grows has been creative in trying to cover four more days. The organization recently rented one of their greenhouses to a local congregation. The church grows two tons of fresh food there annually for its soup kitchens, which feed fresh greens to a clientele who have often come to expect donated canned food and stale bread. Lynchburg Grows has also converted one of their extra greenhouses into an event hall for weddings.

I hope Dereck can make Lynchburg Grows sustainable seven

Dereck Cunningham walks over raised beds in the former rose greenhouses owned by his organization, Lynchburg Grows.

days out of seven, but I don't see the harm if he doesn't. His non-profit can coexist with for-profit ventures like Jeremy's Compost Cab. His organization is supported by the donations and volunteer hours of people who want to better their community and who know that there are values more important than money.

I recently gave a workshop on composting at Dereck's facility in March of 2010. More than fifty people learned from me about carbon and nitrogen ratios and how to grow fresh soil. Dereck watched the whole time, his frail legs held up in the air by his strong upper body and his crutches. The crowd that he and his colleagues had assembled was diverse in every sense. Some of them sat in motorized wheelchairs and some had Down syndrome. Some were black and some were white. Some were old, and some were young. After I took my last questions about composting, I surveyed this crowd. They looked like what I wanted the good food movement to look like. I asked them the question I always ask when I finish my compost lesson.

"Can you do this?" I said.

"Yes," they said back quietly.

"I can't hear you," I said. "Can you do this?"

"Yes!" they yelled back in unison, with fists pumped into the air.

World Without Fences

I have worked with community gardening projects that don't do a good enough job of involving the garden's neighbors. "We've got to put up a fence to protect our garden," people will say. I tell them no, you don't. You have to do the harder work of engaging the community. You've got to make sure the neighbors know that the garden is their own, not yours.

Kids in the neighborhood threw rocks at my greenhouses when I first opened in 1993, but they stopped several months after my arrival. I had not retaliated or chased them away. Instead, I invited the young people to come see what we were doing. I gave them summer jobs. Neighbors started respecting the fact that I was bringing good food into the community. They started being eyes and ears for me. The community felt ownership in our shared success.

In order to build a new food system, we're going to need a world without fences. We all have a responsibility to work together. We need everyone at the table. We're going to need black and white, young and old, rich and poor. We're going to need university folks who can study and foster new organic techniques. We're going to need politicians who can help create an easier political environment and public space for a local food system. We need entrepreneurs who can create niche food products and graphic designers who can create packaging. We're going to need planners who design inner-city neighborhoods with the idea of food security in mind. We're going to need educators and nutritionists who teach people the benefits of healthy food. We're going to need architects who can retrofit old warehouses and greenhouses to the new purpose of growing food. We need contractors. Composters. Plumbers. Not least, we're going to need a new generation of farmers.

Growing Power's community food center, 2011

THE DREAM

> *I have the audacity to believe that people everywhere can have three meals a day for their bodies, education and culture for their minds, and dignity, equality, and freedom for their spirits.*
>
> MARTIN LUTHER KING, JR.

Damien Coleman arrived at my facility for the first time on the last Saturday of July in 2009. He was a thin young African American man, twenty-one years old, wearing a pitch-black Milwaukee Brewers baseball cap that he liked to pull down to his eyebrows. He lived with his parents and his brothers in a crowded apartment on Sixty-fifth and Carmen streets, ten blocks from Growing Power. He had cobbled together whatever work he could find since he was eighteen.

He had worked as a caddy at a country club, where he carried sixty-pound bags for an exclusively white clientele. He had held down two fast-food jobs. Yet he was having difficulty finding full-time employment. He had applied for entry-level jobs wherever he could: Sears. General Mills. He never got an offer.

"The stress was getting to me," he says. "People weren't hiring me. First of all, I'm an African American human being. And a male at that. Two, the economy was so bad. I didn't have a criminal record. My plate was clean. And I didn't want to do no more fast-food restaurants. I like to cook, but that wasn't me."

Damien had seen my roadside stand whenever he went to play basketball at a nearby park. When a friend who worked there told him about it, he decided to come by. He walked up to a compost pile and asked Sarah Christman, who was now our facilities manager as well as beekeeper, "Can I have a job?" Sarah said that there weren't any jobs at that time, but that he could come and volunteer.

"Cool," Damien said.

He began showing up four hours every day. He dressed like a gangster, but it soon became evident to everyone that there was nothing hard about him. He baked apple pie for the farm's interns. He liked to make Italian food; his mother teased him about being part Italian. His hope was that we would see he was a hard worker and offer him a position. He did whatever was asked of him: shoveling compost, sifting worm castings, hauling boxes of food waste. I did not find out until later that to try to earn a little extra money at that time, Damien was donating his blood plasma two times a week. He got $40 each time he donated. This allowed him to buy food and not to feel like a drain on his parents. He kept applying for full-time jobs while he volunteered, but no one seemed interested. After two months, Karen called Damien into her office.

"I heard you want a job here, Damien," Karen said. "And I heard a lot about you. I heard you've been working hard, and that you've shown consistency. How many hours are you volunteering a day?"

"Four," he said.

"We want to give you an internship," Karen said. "You know you would have to work from eight to five. It's hard work. Can you do this?"

"I can do this," Damien said. "I need a job real bad. Anything I can do, I will do it."

The internship only paid $100 a week at first, though we soon made him an apprentice and paid double that. We wanted to see how he would do. Damien had told us that he was claustrophobic. He never went to parties because he feared being around a lot of people. At Growing Power, though, he was often working in tight quarters with many others, and he had learned to overcome it. He soon felt at home here. He was especially interested in soil production, and he spent most of his time working with the compost.

"I was liking the job," he said. "The environment was good. I loved the hard work. I was on my feet every day. And it's a different thing every day. You're not sitting at a desk all day or standing there taking customer orders."

Several months later, I called Damien into my office along with Karen and Sarah Christman. Damien had looked nervous after I asked him for this meeting. He wasn't sure if he was going to be reprimanded or if something good was going to happen. We started the meeting by telling him that we liked what he was doing, but that there were some areas where we felt he needed to improve. He took in what we were saying, and he said he agreed, and he would work on his problem spots. Then I told him that since he had been here, we had never had better compost or soil production. I said that I appreciated his work.

"Are you willing to join us as full-time staff?" I said.

"Yes!" Damien said. "Of course I will. Thank you. I won't let you down. You'll never regret it. I promise you won't."

He shook our hands as he left. His smile was as wide as Kansas.

"With the economy the way it is, I realized I needed to show consistency," Damien told me later. "I needed to show that this is what I wanted to do."

In the summer of 2010, I was giving a tour of our greenhouses with Damien's help. I had leaned a fishing rod against one of our fish systems, and I decided to teach him how to catch a tilapia in front of the dozen or so people who were following me. I helped him thread a worm onto the hook and showed him how to cast the line gently. Damien soon had a large tilapia tugging passionately on the hook, and he reeled it in.

When I was helping him remove the fish from the hook, a tear rolled down Damien's cheek. He began wiping his eyes with his arm, embarrassed at himself.

"Me and my dad don't see eye to eye," he explained later. "He left when I was five. That was actually the happiest day of my life. I always wanted to fish with my dad, and I never got the chance."

When you work in agriculture and with young people, it makes you think quite a bit about the future. You have to imagine the world you want to create before there is any evidence you can bring it into being.

I think about driving my pickup truck through Milwaukee a hundred years from now, long after I have passed away. I see changes. In the city's low-income neighborhoods, like Arlington Heights and Havenwoods, I see people who are growing fresh vegetables intensively in their backyards. I drive past waste trucks that are in the business of composting, a practice that has become mandatory for urban residents along with recycling. These companies collect organics and paper, and they sell the soil they create to farmers. I see fifteen-acre for-profit farms that are zoned into cities. They are considered as necessary a part of urban infrastructure as the sewer and water systems. These farms have cafes and cooperative grocery stores where people can buy locally grown food at affordable prices.

At farmers markets, I see that the future equivalent of the food stamps program offers people three times more buying power there than at corner stores. I see fast-food restaurants that find it necessary to ensure that the animals used in their products are treated humanely, that their food is sourced locally, and that they do not create products that harm the health of the people who are their patrons. Urban hospitals have greenhouses to raise fresh vegetables. The fresh food is harvested and served the same day on patients' dinner plates, fulfilling the Greek physician Hippocrates's wish that "food be thy medicine, and medicine be thy food."

I drive by post-secondary schools that teach young people the science of intensive agriculture. When the students graduate, they are called agriculturalists. This has become a respected profession, and the work pays well enough to afford a decent middle-class existence. I see former industrial buildings that have been turned into fish and vegetable factories, and that are powering themselves by solar panels, food-waste biodigesters, and clean forms of energy not yet invented. Many of these businesses are owned and operated by people of color. As I drive out of Milwaukee, I see small farmers with multiple crops that exist on the perimeter of the city. With the help of high-quality compost, they are growing sprouts and microgreens in hoop houses, providing their families year-round food and a modest income. In the summer, they are able to grow row crops. They sell to community food centers and high-end restaurants within a twenty-five-mile drive of their home.

Finally, I drive past Fifty-fifth and Silver Spring Drive, where my dream began in 1993.

I see our original farm stand, much as it stood a century before. Directly next to it, though, is a gleaming five-story structure. It is known as the first vertical farm of its kind in the world. It has tiered greenhouses that absorb natural light and capture rainfall, recirculating the water inside the farm to irrigate the plants and to replenish the fish systems. The building is not connected to the energy grid; it is run by the power of the sun and by food waste and other biological forms of energy.

Inside, young farmers from around the country are learning the latest intensive urban agriculture techniques in our growing spaces and classrooms. Planners come to learn how to build food-secure

communities. Academics and agriculturalists share their latest research. Local mothers and young African American men and
women take free classes in our commercial kitchen, and they come
away knowing how to cook simple, healthy meals at home with real
ingredients. They shop in our retail store on the lower level, where
we offer affordable fresh greens picked that same day from only a
few feet away.

Recently, I began a capital campaign to try to raise the money to
build this vertical farm. An award-winning local design firm,
Kubala Washatko Architects, has finished preliminary drawings
that express our vision. The City of Milwaukee's planning commission passed an order, with an unanimous vote, to change the area's
zoning to allow for a structure of this size in our residential neighborhood. Our first donations for the vertical farm have come in
small increments—$25 or $50—from people in our community
who hope to see us succeed. I hope this building will provide a legacy that will ensure the survival of my organization and its mission
when I am gone.

When I think of this hopeful future, I see a world that has regained a proper balance between manual and intellectual work. For
decades, we have taught our young people to pursue jobs that use
the mind but not the body. We have segregated our exercise to the
sterile environment of the gym. We have made people spend entire

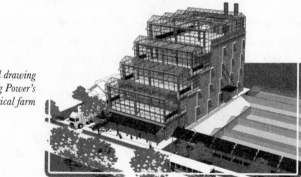

*A conceptual drawing
of Growing Power's
vertical farm*

years at work moving nothing but their steering wheel, their mouse, or a cursor. We no longer teach many manual trades in high schools. We encourage many of our best and our brightest young people to go into think tanks or into law.

We were not made to sit in cubicles or stare at screens or papers all day. My most intimate and lasting learning experiences have come not through books or computers but through my patient inter-action with the land. The work of creating a new food system will of-fer work that engages both the spirit and the body. It will allow people the satisfaction of seeing and tasting the results of their labor. It will require the cultivation of human relationships that are off the grid, as well as an attitude of respect toward the natural world. This movement—this "good food revolution," as I like to call it—will de-mand the best efforts of our hearts, bodies, and minds.

∾

The revolution has already begun. A few years ago, I told my staff that I wanted to host a gathering in Milwaukee that would help build the local food movement. I decided to call the gathering the "National-International Urban and Small Farm Conference."

I hoped such an impressive name would draw an impressive crowd. In reality, I wasn't sure who would come. My idea was to bring together people from across the country who were working to build a new food system, and to allow them to share ideas and to build re-lationships. When we opened our conference at the Wisconsin State Fair Grounds on September 10, 2010, I looked out on a crowd of a thousand people who had come from across the United States and from more than a dozen countries. The state fair sits near an ancient Indian burial site, and I felt there was something sacred about the space.

"I'm really happy today as I look out at this mass of humanity," I said in my opening remarks. "Many of you I know and have been friends with in this good food revolution. But as I look out, I also see a lot of new faces. What especially encourages me is that I see a lot of young folks. I see a multicultural group that really reflects what our country is all about."

The conference offered more than thirty different breakaway sessions, where visitors could learn about water chemistry for indoor fish production, wind energy, and organic pest control. They could learn to make biodiesel from restaurant grease or to farm safely on former industrial sites. They could hear from Malik Yakini about the future of urban agriculture in Detroit or learn from the experiences of Richard Cates, who started the Wisconsin School for Beginning Dairy and Livestock Farmers. Richard's school has graduated more than four hundred new farmers since it was founded in 1996. DeShawn Parker was the chef for the conference, and he stage-managed a staff of more than twenty people.

On September 11, an afternoon breakaway session brought together young people who had worked for Growing Power's Youth Corps. One by one, the young people spoke of their experiences at Growing Power and the lessons they took from their time there. Unexpectedly, Karen's daughter, DeShell, asked to speak at the end of the session. When she first took the microphone, she spoke quietly, but her voice gained strength as she continued.

"My name is DeShell Parker," she began. "I am Karen Parker's daughter. I am also the sister of DeShawn Parker, and he's responsible for all the food you're eating. He is in school now for the culinary arts.

"When I was fourteen, my mom said that Will was going to open up a store," DeShell continued. "She said that she was going to help run it with him. She said she was going to be working hard for a long time, and that she was going to move us into the house next door so she could keep an eye on us. That essentially meant to me at fourteen that I wasn't going to be able to do nothing.

"Then on top of that, I was expected to work harder than others," she continued. "Work was right next door. I've got to get up and work every day, after school, and on weekends. I'm bookkeeping, I'm customer servicing, I'm fronting the shelves, I'm stocking, I'm unloading trucks, and I'm loading trucks. And I think my momma done lost her mind. And I think that Will is the most unreasonable man in the world. I can't wait to get grown and go to college.

"I didn't like farming," DeShell said. "But if you look at the youth who came through here, you see what we're doing now in the community. One of us is a supervisor on the Milwaukee County Board. Another is on the board of Growing Power. We have a youth corps member who works for the U.S. Department of Agriculture. And you have me. I built a career in social work, giving back to children in foster care. I help provide market baskets to foster parents, pulling in my past with Growing Power. And I stand before you today not only certified in social work in the state of Wisconsin, but with two master's degrees.

"You ask me, what does Growing Power mean to me now? At thirty-one? It means integrity. It means strong thinking. It means willpower. It means confidence. It means assertiveness. It's so far beyond dirt and worms."

DeShell asked her eight-year-old daughter, Helea, to come up beside her. DeShell said that she had been bringing Helea with her to Growing Power since she was an infant. The young girl, who refers to me as Big Poppa Will, recently told DeShell that she wanted to be a farmer and a chef when she grows up. I was one of her two role models. The other was her uncle DeShawn.

The graduation for our 2010 commercial urban agriculture students was held the same summer that DeShell gave this speech. We conducted the ceremony in a tent pitched in the parking lot between Growing Power's greenhouses and Karen Parker's house. Two hundred other people were in attendance as part of our weekend workshop program.

One of the most dedicated students of the commercial urban agriculture class was Greg Thompson, an Atlanta-based chef for *The Steve Harvey Project*, a show on Black Entertainment Television. Greg had noticed how hard DeShawn worked in the kitchen. He also noticed that DeShawn didn't wear a chef coat when he cooked, only his Growing Power T-shirt.

Greg reached out to Michelle Thomas, a Washington-based physician who was also in the class, and they hatched a plan together. They had two chef coats embroidered for DeShawn. One had DeShawn's name and the Growing Power logo, and the other had just DeShawn's name, in case he could use it for private catering work. Karen and I knew that Greg and Michelle planned to honor DeShawn, but we pledged to keep the news a secret.

Soon before we sent our graduates home, I called all of my staff members to the front of our tent to recognize them. I briefly thanked them all. Finally, I asked DeShawn to come forward. Karen nudged her son toward me. He looked at me with shy and confused eyes.

"All morning, everybody kept telling me to be on my best behavior," DeShawn said later. "You told me that. My mom's telling me that. I'm like, 'What's going on? Have I not been good?'"

Though his face was still scarred from the fire, it was remarkable to me how handsome DeShawn had become. He was twenty-four now. In the last two years, I'd felt that he held himself with greater confidence, and he was polite and attentive to strangers. I told the audience that there would now be a special presentation. Greg Thompson came to the front and stood beside DeShawn and me. I handed Greg the microphone.

"The definition of a chef is someone who is skilled in the art of preparing food," Greg said. "DeShawn, you've shown great skill in cooking for us. We recognize that you are still in culinary school, but in the eyes of everyone in our class, you are already a chef. We're presenting these to you as a small token of our appreciation."

Greg extended the two folded chef's coats. DeShawn looked at Greg with confusion, and then with surprised gratitude. DeShawn fought tears and lost. He hugged Greg. As DeShawn unfolded one of the coats, everyone assembled in the tent rose and gave him a standing ovation. He looked out at the crowd and absorbed the attention, accepting it.

"It was a wonderful moment in my life," DeShawn explained

later. "I felt so special. I had never won anything. I have never tried to be competitive. I'd rather give than receive. After I got home, I tried to stop crying, but I kept going for like the next five hours."

DeShawn graduated with a culinary degree from Milwaukee Area Technical College in 2010, and he began work at Meritage, one of Milwaukee's best restaurants. By the time you read these words, he will be the lead chef at a new cafe that Growing Power is opening on Milwaukee's Martin Luther King Boulevard. The cafe will bring fresh food to a neighborhood that has struggled with crime and that has long been a food desert. DeShawn only wears his chef's coat on special occasions, because he is afraid to get it dirty.

"I'm okay," DeShawn told me recently. "I got some bumps and hills here and there, but nothing I can't manage."

DeShawn today

In the last decade, my body has begun to betray me: the endgame of years of the pounding my body took on basketball courts. I have had surgery recently to replace one of my knees, and in November of 2011, I had another surgery to resurface my left hip. Before my hip surgery, I could often walk only in halting steps. When I got into my pickup truck, I had to grab my left leg with my left arm in order to haul it in. I started taking pain relievers several times a day, as well as large supplements of vitamin D, which a friend recommended to me to help my immune system. I have been in the unusual position with my staff of giving orders but no longer being able to work too long side by side with them. I have increasingly spent my time traveling the country and trying to do my part to build the local food movement. I feel urgency to do this work.

I know myself to be lucky. I have had the advantage of a good family and people who have believed in me. If you start in the middle of a rough neighborhood and with a broken family, it is difficult just to be a functioning person. It is tough to get up in the morning. It is hard not to be overwhelmed and not to be disillusioned about the gap between the person you are and the person you hope to be. It is hard to be scared you're not going to have enough to pay your rent or put food on your table. It is hard to have a family that leans too hard, or to be in a joyless or abusive relationship, or to have a criminal record because of something you did when you were too young to know better, or to have chosen the wrong path because a straighter path seemed to offer no opportunity. It is hard to have people look at your skin and make assumptions about you before you have a chance to prove them wrong. It is difficult to suffer the health consequences of a diet you didn't know could damage you so much until it was too late.

A better food system will not fix all these problems. It won't heal everyone. But if we can take control of the food environment in our inner-city communities—and if we can knit together the broken fabric between local farmers and our cities, and repair the damaged urban land and grow fresh soil and food there—it can provide a chance for people to have lives with greater dignity.

Access to reasonably priced, healthy, fresh food provides a defense against the dehumanizing and debilitating effects of diabetes and other food-related illness. A better diet will allow our young people to find more joy in their own bodies and in their minds. Growing food intensively in cities and on the edge of cities will offer the chance for new kinds of work. Creating opportunities for local farmers to connect to urban communities can help heal an emotional rift between the countryside and the ghetto. Not least, planting a small garden in your yard can provide the self-respect of being a little more self-sufficient in a world where we often are made to feel the powerless victims of the Dow Jones Industrial average, or the rise and fall of oil prices, or the employment market, or the fates of large corporations.

My model for the food system can't feed the world right now. Yet it is helping to feed neighborhoods, one at a time. It is nurturing communities. Together with others who share my hopes, we are changing the food system block by block, hoop house by hoop house.

Join us. Pick up a shovel, get your hands dirty, and let's begin.

ACKNOWLEDGMENTS
OF WILL ALLEN AND
CHARLES WILSON

This book became a reality only through the generosity of others.

We want to thank our agent, Betsy Amster, who is a rare find. She has a sharp editorial eye that strengthened the manuscript in countless ways. She also has a great business sense, and she guided us to the right publisher.

Lauren Marino at Gotham showed enthusiasm for this project from the first day. She offered valuable guidance that made this a better book. She also demonstrated great patience. At Gotham, it was a delight to interact with Cara Bedick, who was diligent and hardworking. Rick Willett provided a careful copyedit of the manuscript, Sabrina Bowers crafted its design, and Andrea Santoro shepherded the project through production. Susan Barnes guided us into paperback. We are grateful to Beth Parker, Lisa Johnson, Laura Gianino, and Jessica Chun at Penguin, for their commitment to this book and its message. We appreciate the faith that Bill Shinker invested in us.

We want to thank Joan Fischer, a graceful writer who helped get this project off the ground. Joel McNally, Jim Price, and Elizabeth

Royte have also written eloquently about Growing Power's work and Will's personal history.

We want to thank the staff at the Jane C. Sween Library in Montgomery County, Maryland, and particularly Patricia Abelard Andersen, for their research assistance. Ray Kenner was a delightful host in South Carolina and a living repository of family history. His wife, Joy, lives up to the full meaning of her name. Mary Buckingham, Karen Jackson, Mary Knight, and Marshall Stewart were important in helping our understanding of the history of Ken Gar. Kay Frank provided hours of help in telling the story of her family. Sharon Griggs spent hours compiling family trees, answering fact-checking queries, and connecting us to other family members. Joe and Joyce Allen provided helpful insight on Willie Mae's life and on growing up in Rockville. Abby Bussler McGurty's knowledge of the Bussler family history was essential. Martin Bailkey strengthened the book by sharing ideas and resources.

This book would not have been written but for the help of Dan and Jerry Kaufman. The authors also are grateful for the assistance of Sharon Adams, Larry Adams, Alma Allen, Tom Allen, Dena Aronson, Fred Binkowski, Bradley Blaeser, Pamela Broom, Jeremy Brosowsky, Alec Brown, Sophie Brown, Dick Cates, Marcia Caton Campbell, Sarah Christman, Lauralyn Clawson, Alison Meares Cohen, Damien Coleman, Barry Colley, Dereck Cunningham, Nick DeMarsh, Anne Eaton, Lindsey Day Farnsworth, Hope Finkelstein, Tom Fox, Eric Frank, Mari Gallagher, Andrea Godshalk, Billy Gordon, Gary Griggs, Bob Guy, Kate Hanford, Peter Helf, David Hester, Lyn Hildenbrand, Willie Hines, Beckett Horowitz, Matthew Howard, Mike Hutslar, Ming Hwong, Kim Iczkowski, Joan Jacobs, Maureen Landy Kelly, Tom Kubala, Peter Leeds, Rocky Marcoux, Loretta Mays, Tammy McIntyre, Tracie McMillan, Linda McNease Younger, Rick Mueller, Abdul Alim Muhammad, Leana Nakielski, Annie Novak, Cynthia Parker, DeShawn Parker, DeShell Parker, Karen Parker, Tony Perez, Pauline Peyer, Jennifer Baynes Picciolo, Robert Pierce, Michael Pollan, Claude Prather, Rodney Raiford, Janice Raiford, Lessie Raiford, Don Richards, Allen Riddick, Joel

Rissman, Lulu Rodriguez, Jennifer Ruetten, Joel Salatin, Welford Sanders, Laurell Sims, Brendan Sinclair, Mitchell Smith, Greg Thompson, Kimberly Trent, Nat Turner, Lydia Villanueva, Ron Welch, Earl Walthall, Alice Waters, Joe Watson, Ron Welch, Gladys William, Sarah Wisniewski, and Malik Yakini.

Any errors in the manuscript are entirely our own.

Will Allen

My work in Milwaukee has been aided by too many people to properly credit. My debts run deep. I want to thank my family most of all, as well as the board of Growing Power. I appreciate the assistance of Mayor Tom Barrett, Commissioner Rocky Marcoux, and Alderman Willie Hines, who are helping to make Milwaukee the urban farming capital of the world. I will always be grateful for the help of the John D. & Catherine T. MacArthur Foundation in bringing attention to our efforts. Michael Pollan has been an eloquent advocate for the good food movement, and I have benefitted from his support. It was one of the great honors of my life to be invited by the First Lady, Michelle Obama, to kick off her "Let's Move!" campaign. Mrs. Obama is creating a better world through her example. I appreciate more than I can say President Clinton's voice of support for my work and the passion he has brought to issues of global health in his post-presidential career.

Jerry Kaufman has played a pivotal role in my life and the life of my organization. His generosity and quiet strength are my inspiration.

∞

Charles Wilson

I would like to thank Eric Schlosser, who has been my mentor and friend for more than a decade. Eric sets a model of professional integrity, intellectual rigor, and compassion that inspires me. He made it possible for me to have a career I love, and he graciously agreed to write our foreword.

Shauna, Mica, and Conor: you have made my life significantly happier. George and Shay Hirsch, I value your support and friendship, and you have provided me a model of kindness and determination.

Ashley Catalano was an unwavering support during this process. I have been the lucky beneficiary of her intelligent feedback and tender heart. I send love to my parents, Charles L. and Miriam J. Wilson, who gave me the freedom to make my own road. I am very lucky to have Becky Winnette as my sister, and Rod Llewellyn as my brother-in-law. I will always be grateful to Will and Cyndy and Erika and Jason and Adrianna for providing me this opportunity and to the Parkers for their generosity and trust in me. Jerry Kaufman and Judith Zukerman provided detailed feedback that encouraged me when I needed it most. Amanda Chen, Hayley Kallenberg, and Amy Kuhn offered invaluable and timely help. Loretta Mays coordinated my time with Mr. Allen and gracefully managed his busy calendar.

My life has been made better by the support and friendship of Tanya Baibabaeva, Richard Bernstein, Mark Bittman, David and Zivit Cohen, John de Csepel, Leila Gazale, Yuki Kaneshige, Belinda Lanks, Thomas and Genie Lin, Elizabeth O'Donoghue, Jay Pingree, Angela and Rob Riordan, Abby Rogosheske, Karen Shelby, Rebecca Skloot, Tyson Strang, Lesley Sykes, and Tompaul and Lisa Wheeler.

CREDITS

Cover quote by Bill Clinton © William Jefferson Clinton

Image Credits:

1, 43: © Sharon Griggs

5: © Darren Hauck

10, 19, 52, 57: © Will Allen

18: © Michael Sears/*The Milwaukee Journal Sentinel*

29, 174: © Karen Parker

51: © Tuskegee University Archives

67: © Kathleen Frank

74, 78, 88: © Abby Bussler

81: © University of Miami

63, 91: Courtesy of Will Allen

99: Courtesy of Library of Congress, Broadside Collection

111, 148, 192, 205, 208, 237, 247: © Jennifer Picciolo

130, 153: © Hope Finkelstein

152, 175, 183, 196: © Growing Power

163: © Jaclyn Sarah Nussbaum

172: © Sharon Adams, Walnut Way

211: Courtesy of the National Archives, from the Office of the Secre-

NOTES

**To get involved in the Good Food Revolution—
and to learn about opportunities for a hands-
on education in intensive agriculture—visit
GrowingPower.org.**

These endnotes seek to provide acknowledgment to the many people whose hard work is appropriated in these pages. We hope these
citations and Web links provide an easy reference for those who seek
to do further research.

More than seventy-five people were interviewed for this book.
Many of the conversations and anecdotes in *The Good Food Revolution*
have been reconstructed to the best of our ability from these inter-
views and Mr. Allen's own memories. Any errors are our own.

The author and farmer Wendell Berry has written eloquently—in
books such as *The Unsettling of America* and *What Are People For?*—
about the social, emotional, and ecological effects of industrial

agriculture. His ideas about farming and community underlie *The Good Food Revolution*, though he is nowhere mentioned in it.

xii **A recent study in Southern California:** Sarah Burd-Sharps and Kristen Lewis, "A Portrait of California: California Human Development Report 2011," American Human Development Project of the Social Science Research Council (2011), 33, table 3. http://www.measureofamerica.org/docs/APortraitOfCA.pdf (accessed November 28, 2012). The life expectancy in Beverly Hills is listed as 82.1, while it is 72.8 in Watts.

xii **"Clearly the sole reason for B&W's interest in the black and Hispanic communities":** Brown and Williamson Tobacco Corp., "Discussion Paper: Total Minority Marketing Plan Limited," Tobacco Documents Online (1984). http://tobaccodocuments.org/youth/AmToBWC19840907.Rg.html#images (accessed November 28, 2012).

xiii **Between 1995 and 2011, American farmers received about $277 billion in federal subsidies:** Environmental Working Group, "Farm Subsidy Database," EWG Farm Subsidies (2012). http://farm.ewg.org/region.php?fips=00000xiv (accessed September 30, 2012).

xiv **Last year the revenues of the fast food industry were about $168 billion:** "Restaurant Industry 2011," National Restaurant Association, http://www.restaurant.org/pdfs/education/study-groups/finance/20110622_hudson_riehle_industry.pdf (accessed September 30, 2012). This figure is a projection for 2011 provided by Hudson Riehle, senior vice president of the Research and Knowledge Group of the National Restaurant Association.

xiv **Those two costs alone add up to about $320 billion:** Robert L. Scharff, "Health-Related Costs from Foodborne Illness in the United States," The Produce Safety Project at Georgetown University (March 3, 2010). http://www.pewtrusts.org/uploadedFiles/www.pewtrustsorg/Reports/Produce_Safety_Project/PSP

-Scharff%20v9.pdf?n=1136 (accessed November 28, 2012). Robert L. Scharff of the Food Safety Project at Georgetown University estimated the annual cost of foodborne illness in the United States to be $152 billion.

John Cawley of Cornell University led a study with Lehigh University's Chad Meyerhoefer that estimated the annual cost of treating obesity at $168.4 billion. John Cawley and Chad Meyerhoefer, "The Medical Care Costs of Obesity: An Instrumental Variables Approach," NBER Working Paper, no. 16467 (October 2010). http:// www.nber.org/papers/w16467 (accessed September 30, 2012).

5–6   **In 1920, there were more than 900,000 farms operated by African Americans in the United States. Today, there are only 18,000 black people who name farming as their primary occupation:** The 1920 figure (925,710) was drawn from Spencer D. Wood and Jess Gilbert, "Returning African American Farmers to the Land: Recent Trends and a Policy Rationale," *The Review of Black Political Economy* (2000), table 1, which relied on figures from the United States Commission on Civil Rights.

The 2007 USDA Census of Agriculture—which offers the most recent statistics available—indicated there were 41,024 "black farm operators," but only 44 percent of those (roughly 18,050) name farming as their primary occupation. US Department of Agriculture, "2007 Census of Agriculture: Black Farmers," National Agriculture Statistics Service, USDA Census of Agriculture. http://www.agcensus.usda.gov/Publications/2007/Online_ Highlights/Fact_Sheets/Demographics/black.pdf (accessed September 30, 2012).

6   **"The Negro race is going to be saved by its exceptional men":** Booker T. Washington, *The Negro Problem: A Series of Articles by Representative American Negroes* (New York: James Pott & Company, 1903), 33. The quote in full reads: "The Negro race, like all races, is going to be saved by its exceptional men." *The Negro Problem* is available for free here: http://books.google.com/books?id=A8RtAAAA MAAJ&ots=y0wr6A0yyj&dq=DuBois%20%22The%20 Negro%20Problem%22 (accessed November 28, 2012).

6 **"Agriculture is, or has been, the basic industry of nearly every race or nation that has succeeded":** Booker T. Washington, "The Case of the Negro," *The Atlantic Monthly* 84, no. 5 (November 1889): 577–87. http://www.theatlantic.com/past/docs/unbound/flashbks/black/washbh.htm (accessed November 28, 2012).

For a good discussion of the competing views of DuBois and Washington, see Clayborne Carson, *DuBois and the Great Depression* (lecture, Stanford University; Palo Alto, CA, September 27, 2007). http://www.urbanministry.org/african-american-history-modern-freedom-struggle-lecture-2-17 (accessed December 16, 2012).

7 **Nearly half of African Americans born in the year 2000 are expected to develop type II diabetes:** K. M. Venkat Narayan, et al., "Lifetime Risk for Diabetes Mellitus in the United States," *Journal of the American Medical Association* 290 (October 8, 2003): 1886. http://helios.hampshire.edu/~cjgNS/sputtbug/416K/Endo/DiabetesRisk.pdf (accessed September 30, 2012). The authors suggest that 40.2 percent of black men born in 2000 have a lifetime risk of a diabetes diagnosis; 49.0 percent of black women do.

7 **Four out of every ten African American men and women over the age of twenty have high blood pressure:** Centers for Disease Control and Prevention, "High Blood Pressure Facts," http://www.cdc.gov/bloodpressure/facts.htm (accessed November 28, 2012). These figures indicate that 43.0 percent of African American men over twenty have high blood pressure—and 45.7 percent of African American women.

7 **Blacks are 30 percent more likely to die young from heart disease than whites:** Kenneth D. Kochanek, et al, "Deaths: Final Data for 2009," *National Vital Statistics Reports* 60, no. 3 (December 29, 2011): 65, table B. http://www.cdc.gov/nchs/data/nvsr/nvsr60/nvsr60_03.pdf (accessed September 30, 2012).

7 **Almost one out of every six households in the United Sates will find themselves fearful sometime this year of not having enough food to eat:** Alisha Coleman-Jensen, et al., "Household

Food Security in the United States in 2011," Economic Research Service Report Summary (September 2012). http://www.ers.usda.gov/media/884529/err-141-summary.pdf (accessed September 30, 2012). In 2011, 14.9 percent of households were deemed "food insecure."

8   **In 1974, farmers took home 36 cents of every dollar spent on food in the United States. Today, they get only 14 cents:** For the 1974 figure, see United States Department of Agriculture, Economic Research Service, "Food Cost Review, 1984," Agricultural Economic Report, no. 537 (July 1985): table 13. http://naldc.nal.usda.gov/download/CAT87214690/PDF (accessed November 28, 2012). (We divided the 1974 farm value of food, $56.4 billion, by the consumer expenditures on food, $154.6 billion.)

For the current figure, see the United States Department of Agriculture, Economic Research, "Food Dollar Series." http://www.ers.usda.gov/data-products/food-dollar-series/food-dollar-application.aspx (accessed October 1, 2012). The farm share for the 2010 food dollar was 14.1 cents.

20   **Wisconsin would lose 200,000 acres of farmland in 1993. . . . Each year from 1978 to 1992, the state lost 1,000 to 1,500 individual farms. . . . The average farm in Wisconsin grew by seventy acres from the late 1950s to the early 1990s:** The 200,000-acre figure came from National Agricultural Statistics Service, "Land in Farms: From States and the United States, 1993–97," *Farms and Land in Farms Final Estimates 1993–1997*, bulletin 955 (January 1999). http://usda01.library.cornell.edu/usda/nass/SB991/sb955.pdf (accessed November 28, 2012).

The remaining figures come from Doris P. Slesinger and Julie Whitzker, "A Portrait of Family Farmers in Wisconsin," Center for Demography and Ecology, University of Wisconsin-Madison, CDE Working Paper 98-30: chart 1, "Number of Farms and Average Farm Size, Wisconsin, 1959–1992." http://www.ssc.wisc.edu/cde/cdewp/98-30.pdf (accessed November 28, 2012).

20   **From 1978 to 1984 alone, Safeway closed more than six hundred stores located in inner cities:** Elizabeth Eisenhauer,

"In Poor Health: Supermarket Redlining and Urban Nutrition,"
GeoJournal 53 (2001): 128.

35   **"We learned how to plant right, how to put down fertilizer"**: Georgia Pabst, "Teens enter the world of farming and self-
sufficiency," *Milwaukee Journal Sentinel*, August 6, 1995.

43–4   **My story begins before I was born, in the fields of western South Carolina**: The authors wish to thank the many people who helped reconstruct Mr. Allen's family history, especially
Ray Kenner, Sharon Griggs, Janice Raiford, and Linda Mc-
Nease Younger.

51   **"I went to the trash pile"**: Gary R. Kremer, *George Washington Carver: A Biography* (Westport, Connecticut: Greenwood, 2011),
62. Kremer's biography, which offers a nuanced portrait of
Carver, was our principle source for information about the scientist.

51   **"How to Grow the Peanut and 105 Ways of Preparing It
for Human Consumption"**: Ibid., 107. The full bulletin is
available here, as slightly revised by Mr. Carver in later years:
http://aggie-horticulture.tamu.edu/fruit-nut/carver-peanut/ (accessed October 1, 2012). Peanut butter is item #51. Other recipes—
such as liver with peanuts (#37)—have proven less enduring.

53   **There were fifty-seven schools and nearly 3,000 black
students in Montgomery County**: Nina H. Clarke and
Lillian B. Brown, *History of the Black Public Schools of Montgomery
County, Maryland, 1872–1961* (New York: Vantage Press, 1978), 125
and 127.

54   **In the early twentieth century, more than 90 percent of
the people living in Montgomery County made their
living from agriculture**: Montgomery County Historical Society, "Agriculture." http://www.montgomeryhistory.org/node/
108 (accessed October 1, 2012).

54 **Frozen food output grew fivefold in the decade from 1945 to 1955**: United States Department of Agriculture, "Catalog of Selected Charts Available from U.S.D.A.," Miscellaneous Publication 799 (June 1959): 49, Production of Principal Frozen Foods.

55 **Ken Gar, an African American community consisting of six dirt roads sandwiched between Kensington and Garrett Park**: Munro P. Meyersburg, "A History of Ken-Gar," Ken-Gar Civic Association (1987). http://www.ken-gar.org/history.html (accessed December 4, 2012). The authors gratefully acknowledge the help of Mary Buckingham, Mary Knight, and Marshall Stewart for providing a greater understanding of Ken-Gar's history.

63 **"At the heart of the deterioration of Negro society"**: United States Department of Labor, Office of Policy Planning and Research, "The Negro Family: The Case for National Action" (March 1965): chapters 2 and 3. http://www.dol.gov/oasam/programs/history/moynchapter2.htm.
    See also http://www.dol.gov/oasam/programs/history/moynchapter3.htm (accessed November 29, 2012).

68 **"We shall have to begin to count the many hidden costs of what we are doing"**: United States Congress Senate Committee on Government Operations, "Hearings, Reports, and Prints of the Senate Committee on Government Operations, Part 1," Records of the United States Senate (Washington, DC: United States Government Printing Office, 1964): 206 and 209.

72 **Miami University Signs Willie Allen, Negro Cager**: "Miami University Signs Willie Allen, Negro Cager," *Jet*, July 20, 1967.

74 **"black favoritism"**: A good discussion of black favoritism, Ray Bellamy, and black history at the University of Miami can be found in J. D. Simon, "Celebrate Black History at the U," Hurricanewarriors.com. http://hurricanewarriors.com/joomla/index2.php?option=com_content&do_pdf=1&id=225 (accessed October 1, 2012).

75 **"four years in hell"**: Ibid.

76 **"two wonderful people who happened to fall in love"**: *Guess Who's Coming to Dinner,* directed by Stanley Kramer (1967). http://www.youtube.com/watch?v=9Yt0wxoFl4o (accessed October 1, 2012). Spencer Tracy died before the movie premiered. This scene is available to watch online.

78 **"The Hurricanes' problem last night"**: Jim Huber, "Stetson's Mad Hatters Just Kill(um) U-M," *Miami News,* February 5, 1969. All mentions of Will Allen in the University of Miami student newspaper, *The Hurricane,* were researched through the university's digital collections: http://merrick.library.miami.edu/digitalprojects/archives .php (accessed October 1, 2012).

81 **"Willie Allen is UM's 6'6" center who has been plagued by inconsistency"**: Scott Bressler, "Winning Hurricanes Face Loyola," *The Hurricane,* February 14, 1969.

82 **"He's a big man"**: Barbara Wooden, "All American Gilmore Made Presence Felt All Over Dinner Key," *The Hurricane,* March 6, 1970.

84 **"To put it mildly, the crowd went berserk"**: Tony Musto, "Great Expectations Bear Little Fruit," *The Hurricane,* August 4, 1972. Musto said about the Allen dunk over Gilmore: "Easily the top moment of the past four years came in what turned out to be the last Hurricanes basketball game."

84 **"temporarily until such time as a permanent field house"**: University of Miami, "2006 University of Miami Basketball Guide": 125. http://graphics.fansonly.com/photos/schools/mifl/ sports/m-baskbl/auto_pdf/0607_mg_history.pdf (accessed November 28, 2012).

94 **One study showed that a young person was four times more likely to develop cancer**: I. Ross McDougall, *Thyroid Cancer in Clinical Practice* (New York: Springer, 2007), 7.

100 **"The Decline of Black Farming in America"**: US Commission on Civil Rights, "The Decline of Back Farming in America: A Report of the United States Commission on Civil Rights" (February 1982). http://www.law.umaryland.edu/marshall/usccr/documents/cr11b562z.pdf (accessed October 1, 2012).

101 **By the late 1970s, payments for participating small farmers were as low as $365**: Ibid., 60.

102 **a fourth-generation farmer named George Norman**: For the story of George Norman, we drew heavily on David C. Ruffin, "America's Vanishing Black Farmer," *Black Enterprise* (January 1985): 33.

103 **In 1984 and 1985, the agency lent $1.3 billion dollars to farmers in order to buy land. Sixteen thousand farmers received these loans. Only 209 of them were black**: Cited in Osha Gray Davidson, *Broken Heartland: The Rise of America's Rural Ghetto* (Iowa City: University of Iowa Press, 1996), 37.

103 **about 115,000 black farmers left the profession**: Spencer D. Wood and Jess Gilbert, "Returning African-American Farmers to the Land: Recent Trends and a Policy Rationale," *The Review of the Black Political Economy* (Spring 2000): 45, table 1. http://www.landloss.org/Wood%20--%20Returning.pdf (accessed October 2, 2012). This figure compares the number of black farmers in 1969 and 1993.

103 **fewer than five hundred African American farmers under the age of twenty-five in the entire United States**: Cited in "Tenure and Characteristics of Operator and Type of Organization for All Farms and Farms Operated by Black and Other Races: 1987, 1982, 1978," Census of Agriculture (1987), Geographic Area Series, (Washington, DC: US Government Printing Office, 1989): 20, table 16. http://usda.mannlib.cornell.edu/usda/AgCensusImages/1987/01/51/28/Table-16.pdf (accessed December 3, 2012). The 1987 Census of Agriculture estimated that there were only 428 farms operated by African Americans under the age of twenty-five.

107 **It was costing the city $73,000 a year**: Leonard Sykes, Jr., "3 Markets are Likely to Survive: Growers Want to Take Up Where City Left Off at Produce Stalls," *Milwaukee Journal Sentinel*, March 15, 1993.

112 **The percentage of farmers who work somewhere outside of their farms has tripled since 1959**: Brian C. Briggeman, "The Importance of Off-Farm Income to Servicing Farm Debt," Federal Reserve Bank of Kansas City: 64. http://www.kansascityfed.org/publicat/econrev/pdf/11q1 Briggeman.pdf (accessed October 2, 2012).

112–13 **In 2008, 90 percent of total income for all farm households in the United States came from work outside of the farm**: Ibid., 63.

113 **For farmers whose annual sales are $100,000 or less—and who often operate at a loss—off-farm income often accounts for 100 percent of their yearly income**: Farm Bill Forums, "Farm Family Income," United States Department of Agriculture, Farm Bill Forum Comment Summary & Background: 1. http://www.usda.gov/documents/ FARM_FAMILY_INCOME.pdf (accessed October 2, 2012).

113 **At larger farms, with $250,000 or more in annual sales, off-farm income is less than a quarter of annual pay on average**: Ibid., 1.

113 **"get big or get out"**: The "get big or get out" phrase was initially voiced by Ezra Taft Benson, Secretary of Agriculture for Dwight Eisenhower, though Butz repeated it.

114 **From 1970 to 1980, the total farm population in the United States declined by almost 30 percent**: US Department of the Commerce, Bureau of the Census, "Farm Population of the United States: 1980," Current Population Reports, series P-27, no. 54 (August 1981). In the 1970s, the number of

people living on farms declined by an average of 2.9 percent per year.

114   **The average size of a single farm grew, however, to nearly 430 acres**: "The Decline of Black Farming," 50.

114   **"American farmers will always be grateful to you"**: Butz's resignation letter appears in Gerald R. Ford, *Public Papers of the Presidents of the United States: Gerald R. Ford, 1976*, (Washington, DC: US Government Printing Office, 1977), 849.

A fuller accounting of the joke that led to Butz's resignation can be found in "Exit Earl, Not Laughing," *Time*, October 18, 1976. http://www.time.com/time/magazine/article/0,9171,946703,00.html (accessed October 2, 2012).

114   **In 2000, nearly half of the net income for corn farmers in the United States was paid for by subsidies**: The National Family Farm Coalition, "The Facts Behind King Corn," The National Family Farm Coalition. http://www.nffc.net/Learn/Fact%20Sheets/King%20Corn%20Fact%20Sheet.pdf (accessed October 2, 2012).

114   **In 1972, by contrast, the average annual federal subsidy to a corn producer was less than $100**: Figure cited in William Winders, *The Politics of Food Supply: U.S. Agricultural Policy in the World Economy* (New Haven: Yale University Press, 2009), 100. Corn producers received an average subsidy of $94 in 1972.

114   **By 2011, three-quarters of government commodity payments were given to the same top 10 percent of recipients**: The Environmental Working Group's Farm Subsidies Database, "The United States Summary Information." http://farm.ewg.org/region.php?fips=00000 (accessed September 30, 2012).

118   **"If you love it enough"**: The quote in this form has long been attributed to Carver, though no books we found cited its

source. This popular version of the quote may be a slight amendment of a comment in Glenn Clark's biography, *The Man Who Talks With The Flowers*, when Carver is quoted as saying that "anything will give up its secrets if you love it enough."

122 **The lawyers from Bic argued that no green lighter was found at the scene**: *DeShawn Parker, by his Guardian ad Litem, Joseph Doherty, and Karen Parker v. Bic Corporation*, no. 95-2958, (Wisc. Ct. App., District 1, October 1, 1996). Details about the green and red lighter controversy are explained in the Appeals court decision ruling on DeShawn's case.

124 **FoodShare's facility sat in the Port Lands district:** The description of FoodShare was drawn from several sources. Michael Spillane, "Higher Ground: Three Farmers Organically Grow Hydroponic Crops in the City," *The Best of the Growing Edge*, (Corvallis, OR: New Moon Publishing, 2000): 250–52.

See also Lauren Baker, "Warehouse rooftop supports urban agriculture," *In Business* 22, no. 2 (March/April 2000).

Jonathan Woods's Urban Aquaculture Manual is available here: http://www.webofcreation.org/BuildingGrounds/aqua/TOC.html (accessed December 17, 2012).

129 **"face is marred by dust and sweat and blood"**: Theodore Roosevelt, "The Man in the Arena: Citizenship in a Republic" (speech, Sorbonne, Paris, France, April 23, 1910). The full transcript of Roosevelt's famous (and frequently quoted) "Citizenship in the Republic" speech is available here: http://www.theodoreroosevelt.org/research/speech%20arena.htm (accessed December 17, 2012).

131 **2,500 murals, 100,000 paintings, and 17,000 sculptures:** David E. Kyvig, *Daily Life in the United States, 1920–1939: Decades of Promise and Pain*, (Westport, CT: Greenwood Publishing Group, 2002), 213.

142   **"a vista of the finest farmlands in America"**: Marc Linder
      and Lawrence S. Zacharias, *Of Cabbages and King County: Agriculture
      and the Formation of Modern Brooklyn*, (Iowa City: University of Iowa
      Press, 1999), 1.

142   **"last farmer"**: Ibid., 4.

143   **The average item of food consumed in the United States**:
      Martin C. Heller and Gregory A. Keoleian, "Life Cycle-Based
      Sustainability Indicators for Assessment of the U.S. Food System,"
      Center for Sustainable Systems: University of Michigan, report no.
      CSS00-04 (December 6, 2000). http://css.snre.umich.edu/css_
      doc/CSS00-04.pdf (accessed October 8).

143   **To feed just one American, the industrial agricultural
      system requires on average the equivalent of 530 gallons
      of oil a year**: David Pimentel, "Reducing Energy Inputs in the
      U.S. Food System," *Human Ecology* 36 (2008): 459. Pimentel says,
      "In total, each American requires approximately 2,000 l/year in oil
      equivalents to supply their food, which accounts for about 19 per-
      cent of total energy use in the USA." We converted liters to gallons.
      (Food transportation and preparation account for 5 percent of US
      energy use.)

143   **Fresh green beans . . . have been shown to lose nearly
      80 percent of their Vitamin C**: L. A. Howard, et. al., "Beta-
      Carotene and Ascorbic Acid Retention in Fresh and Processed
      Vegetables," *Journal of Food Science* 64 (1999): 933, figure 5. http://
      www.tweiss.net/freshfrozen/pdf/beta.pdf (accessed October 8,
      2012).

143   **Less than half of one percent of the food they eat
      comes directly from farmers**: Sarah A. Low and Stephen Vo-
      gel, "Direct and Intermediated Marketing of Local Foods in the
      United States," United States Department of Agriculture Eco-
      nomic Research Report, no. 128 (November 2011): 19. http://

www.ers.usda.gov/media/138324/err128_2_.pdf (accessed December 4, 2012). This is a modest estimate. According to the 2008 Agriculture Resource Management Survey, farm direct-to-consumer sales accounted for only 0.4 percent of all farm sales nationwide. The percentage of direct-to-consumer sales in many urban inner-city communities is likely to be substantially smaller.

143 **One recent study has shown that a two-thousand-calorie diet can cost as little as $3.50 a day**: Pablo Monslavis and Adam Drewnowski, "The Rising Costs of Low-Energy-Density Foods," *Journal of American Dietetic Association* 107 (2007): 2071–76.

A good summary of the research is found in Stacy Kish, "Healthy, Low Calorie Foods Cost More on Average," United States Department of Agriculture Cooperative State Research, Education, and Extension Service. http://naldc.nal.usda.gov/download/15381/PDF (accessed October 8, 2012).

143 **"If you have $3 to feed yourself"**: This is Adam Drewnowski of the University of Washington, quoted in Tara Parker-Pope, "A High Price for Healthy Food," *The New York Times*, December 5, 2007. http://well.blogs.nytimes.com/2007/12/05/a-high-price-for-healthy-food/ (accessed October 8, 2012).

144 **The health costs associated with obesity have been estimated at nearly $170 billion annually:** John Cawley and Chad Meyerhoefer, "The Medical Care Costs of Obesity: An Instrumental Variables Approach," NBER Working Paper no. 16467 (October 2010). http://www.nber.org/papers/w16467 (accessed September 30, 2012).

144 **"anti–free market do-goodnicks"**: "A Red Tape Wonderland," The Center for Consumer Freedom, January 5, 2005. http://www.consumerfreedom.com/2005/01/2718-a-red-tape-wonderland/ (accessed October 8, 2012).

144 **A 2006 analysis compared eleven hundred ads**: Corliss Wilson Outley, "A Content Analysis of Healthy and Physical

Activity Messages Marketed to African American Children During After-school Television Programming," *Pediatric &Adolescent Medicine* 160 (April 2006), table 1. http://archpedi.jamanetwork. com/article.aspx?articleid=204838 (accessed October 8, 2012). 65.6 percent of the fast-food ads among the three channels ran on BET.

144 **A 2011 study by researchers at Yale:** Jennifer L. Harris, et al., "Evaluating FastFood Nutrition and Marketing to Youth," Food Advertising to Children and Teens Score, Yale Rudd Center for Food Policy & Obesity (November 2011): 63. http://www.fastfood marketing.org/media/FastFoodFACTS_Report.pdf (accessed October 8, 2012).

146 **"Instead of regarding man's relation to air, waiter, soil":** Lewis Mumford, *The City in History: Its Origins, Its Transformations, and Its Prospects,* (New York: Harcourt, 1961), 527.

146 **"equal opportunity to develop his potentialities":** Kevin Mattson, "Re-Reading The Radical Liberal: Revisiting Arnold Kaufman," *Dissent* (Summer 2000). http://dissentmagazine.org/ article/?article=1472 (accessed October 8, 2012).

147 **"The Food System: A Stranger to the Planning Field":** Kameshwari Pothukuchi and Jerome L. Kaufman, "The Food System: A Stranger to the Planning Field," *Journal of the American Planning Association* 66 (Spring 2000): 113–24. http://www.clas.wayne .edu/multimedia/usercontent/File/Geography%20and%20 Urban%20Planning/K.Pothukuchi/thefoodsystem_japa.pdf (accessed October 8, 2012).

155 **According to the National Agricultural Statistics Service, the average age of all farm operators:** United States Department of Agriculture, "2007 Census of Agriculture: Farmers by Age," National Agricultural Statistics Service. http://www.ag census.usda.gov/Publications/2007/Online_Highlights/Fact_ Sheets/Demographics/farmer_age.pdf (accessed October 8, 2012).

155 **The average price of an acre of American farmland is now more than \$2,300**: USDA figures cited in "U.S. Farmland price boom to slow but not plateau," Reuters, April 11, 2012. The average figure for 2012 was \$2,350/acre.

156 **"warehouses for the poor"**: Vincent Lane quoted in William E. Schmidt, "Public Housing: For Workers or the Needy?" *The New York Times,* April 17, 1990.

166: **there are forty percent fewer honey-producing hives in the United States**: United States Department of Agriculture, "Honey: Preliminary 1981," Crop Reporting Board, Statistical Reporting Service (January 15, 1982). http://usda01.library.cornell.edu/usda/nass/Hone//1980s/1982/Hone-01-15-1982.pdf.

See also United States Department of Agriculture, "Honey: United States Honey Production Down 16 Percent," National Agricultural Statistics Service (March 30, 2012). http://usda01.library.cornell.edu/usda/current/Hone/Hone-03-30-2012.pdf (accessed October 8, 2012). There were 4.14 million bee colonies in 1980 and 2.49 million colonies in 2011.

170 **"Any time you live in an area where you don't have healthy choices"**: Patrick McIlheran, "Diet Control on the Agenda Tonight," *Milwaukee Journal Sentinel,* July 31, 2008.

171 **"anti-investment"**: Patrick McIlheran, "Snobbery, Neighbors and Food," *Milwaukee Journal Sentinel,* December 13, 2008.

183 **In 1890, researchers for the U.S. Census Bureau ranked professions that had the highest rate of suicide**: US Department of the Commerce, Bureau of the Census, "Report on Vital and Social Statistics in the United States at the Eleventh Census: 1890," Prepared by the Department of the Interior, (Washington, DC: US Government Printing Office, 1896): 472.

183 **the suicide rate for American farmers rose in several states to double the national average**: P. Gunderson, et al.,

"The Epidemiology of Suicide Among Farm Residents or Workers in Five North-Central States, 1980–1988," *American Journal of Preventive Medicine* 9 (1993): 26–32.

183 **Several recent studies**: Michael R. Rossmann, PhD, provides a good summary of research on the mental health of farmers/rural populations in "Behavioral Health Issues of the Aging Agricultural Population," Agricultural Safety & Health Network. www.agsafe tyandhealthnet.org (accessed October 9, 2012).

184 **"have a chance to enjoy themselves while they are working, instead of working solely for pay"**: E. F. Schumacher, *Small is Beautiful: Economics as if People Mattered,* (Reprint, New York: HarperCollins, 2010), 22.

184 **market price of milk to less than $12 per one hundred pounds**: Len Richardson, "Diary Margins Stay in Red," *California Farmer* (November 2009). http://magissues.farmprogress.com/ CLF/CF11Nov09/clf025.pdf (accessed December 4, 2012).

184 **In upstate New York in early 2010, one dairy farmer shot fifty-one of his cows**: "N.Y. dairy farmer kills 51 cows, commits suicide," Associated Press, January 23, 2010.

185 **"these are hard times to be a farmer"**: Ibid.

186 **In the last three decades, more than forty million acres of rural land in the United States have been developed**: United States Department of Agriculture, "Summary Report: 2007 National Resources Inventory," Natural Resources Conservation Service (December 2009): 7. http://www.nrcs.usda.gov/Internet/ FSE_DOCUMENTS/stelprdb1041379.pdf (accessed December 4, 2012).

189 **The amounts of protein, iron, calcium, phosphorous, iron, and vitamin C have all declined noticeably in all harvested fruits and vegetables in the United States**

from 1950 to 1999: Donald R. Davis, et al., "Changes in USDA Food Composition Data for 43 Garden Crops, 1950 to 1999," *Journal of the American College of Nutrition* 23 (2004): 669–82. http://www.jacn.org/content/23/6/669.long (accessed October 8, 2012).

189   **Riboflavin ... declined overall in fresh foods ... by nearly 40 percent**: Ibid.

191   **In the mid-1990s potatoes were the only vegetable in the top 10 food categories**: "School Food Purchase Study: Final Report," United States Department of Agriculture Food and Nutrition Service (October 1998). http://www.fns.usda.gov/Ora/menu/Published/CNP/FILES/SFPS-Execsum.pdf (accessed October 8, 2012).

194   **horticulturalists at North Carolina State University had pioneered this technique**: http://www.ces.ncsu.edu/nreos/wild/aquaculture/ (accessed December 4, 2012). North Carolina State now has an Aquaculture Extension.

199   **fewer than 1,800 markets listed in a nation of nearly three hundred million people. By 2006, there were almost 4,500**: United States Department of Agriculture, "Farmers Market Search," Agricultural Marketing Service. http://search.ams.usda.gov/farmersmarkets/ (accessed October 8, 2012). The most recent list includes more than 7,800 markets.

210   **"My idea is to help the 'man farthest down'"**: Kremer, *George Washington Carver*, 77.

211   **The Jessup Agricultural Wagon first set out in 1906**: "Movable School," National Park Service. http://www.nps.gov/museum/exhibits/tuskegee/gwcwagon.htm (accessed October 8, 2012).

212   **A person in the Delta is nearly 25 percent more likely to die each year:** David M. Mirvis, et al., "Health Improvement in the Lower Mississippi River Delta: Opportunities and Challenges,"

Mississippi State Department of Health. http://msdh.ms.gov/msdhsite/_static/resources/3114.pdf (accessed October 8, 2012).

212 **A dozen black men founded Mound Bayou in 1887**: Herbert G. Ruffin, "Mound Bayou (1887–)," Blackpast.org. http://www.blackpast.org/?q=aah/mound-bayou-1887 (accessed November 15, 2012).

212 **The average resident made less than $9,000 a year**: US Department of the Commerce, Bureau of the Census, "2005–2009 American Community Survey." http://factfinder2.census.gov/faces/tableservices/jsf/pages/productview.xhtml?pid=ACS_09_5YR_B19301&prodType=table (accessed December 4, 2012).

213 **Nearly thirty chickens are killed on average each year for every man, woman, and child**: United States Department of Agriculture, "Poultry Slaughter: 2011 Summary," National Agricultural Statistics Service (February 2012). http://usda01.library.cornell.edu/usda/current/PoulSlauSu/PoulSlauSu-02-24-2012.pdf (accessed November 15, 2012). In 2011, the USDA estimated that 8.68 billion chickens were slaughtered in the US. The US population was roughly 311 million that same year, so that works out to about 27.9 chickens per person.

213 **The typical American consumes more than two hundred pounds of meat in that same period:** "Average Annual Per Capita Consumption of Meat (Retail Weight)," National Cattlemen's Beef Association. http://www.beefusa.org/CMDocs/BeefUSA/Resources/Statistics/annualpercapitaconsumption-meat-retail.pdf (accessed November 15, 2012).

215 **"not knowing where they would sleep"**: Elizabeth Anne Martin, "Detroit and the Great Migration, 1916–1929," Bentley Historical Library at the University of Michigan. http://bentley.umich.edu/research/publications/migration/ch1.php (accessed November 15, 2012).

216   **"the first or second [families] to move into all-white neigh-
      borhoods"**: Thomas J. Sugrue, "A Dream Still Deferred," *The New
      York Times*, March 26, 2011. http://www.nytimes.com/2011/03/27/
      opinion/27Sugrue.html?_r=0 (accessed November 15, 2012).

216   **the amount of vacant land inside of Detroit—more than
      twenty square miles:** "NYC Statistics," nycgo.com. http://
      www.nycgo.com/articles/nyc-statistics-page (accessed December
      4, 2012). Rob Linn of Data-Driven Detroit provides an estimate of
      21.39 square miles of vacant land in Detroit. The total area of
      Manhattan is 23.7 square miles.

      See also Kate Davidson, "Detroit has tons of vacant land. But
      forty square miles?" Michigan Radio. http://www.michiganradio.
      org/post/detroit-has-tons-vacant-land-forty-square-miles (accessed
      December 4, 2012).

216   **More than 90 percent of food stamps in Detroit are spent
      at what the food-system researcher Mari Gallagher
      calls "fringe retailers"**: "Examining the Impact of Food Des-
      erts on Public Health in Detroit," Mari Gallagher Research &
      Consulting Group (2007). http://www.marigallagher.com/proj-
      ects/2/ (accessed November 15, 2012).

220   **More than 90 percent of the eggs that we eat in this coun-
      try come from birds confined in "battery cages"**: The Hu-
      mane Society of the United States, "Barren, Cramped Cages,"
      April 19, 2013. http://www.humanesociety.org/issues/confinement_
      farm/facts/battery_cages.html (accessed November 15, 2012).

220   **More potato chips are consumed in Detroit per capita**:
      "Facts About Wayne County & Michigan," County of Wayne,
      Michigan, USA. http://www.co.wayne.mi.us/3986.htm (accessed
      December 4, 2012).

221   **At least one-quarter to a half of the fresh food that we
      create in this country is thrown out before it is eaten—
      enough food waste, as the author Jonathan Bloom has**

pointed out, to fill the Rose Bowl in Pasadena every day: Jonathan Bloom, *American Wasteland: How America Throws Away Nearly Half of Its Food (And What We Can Do About It)*, (Cambridge, MA.: De Capo Press, 2011), 313.

221   **we could power nearly one out of every twenty homes in this country**: The EPA suggests that "if 50 percent of the food waste generated each year in the US was anaerobically digested, enough electricity would be generated to power over 2.5 million homes each year"—or 5 million homes if we could (improbably) recover 100 percent. There are roughly 112 million occupied homes in the United States. For housing inventory statistics, US Department of the Commerce, Bureau of the Censu s, "Total Housing Inventory for the United States: 1990 to 2010," Statistical Abstract of the United States: 2012: 615, table 982. http://www.census.gov/compendia/statab/2012/tables/12s0982.pdf.

For the EPA estimate, see also U.S. Environmental Protection Agency, "Turning Food Waste into Energy at the East Bay Municipal Utility District," EPA.gov. http://www.epa.gov/region9/waste/features/foodtoenergy/ (accessed December 4, 2012).

224   **Walmart was launching a new initiative intended to increase the amount of local food it bought by 2015 to 9 percent**: "Walmart: 2012 Global Responsibility Report," Walmart Corporation: 91. http://www.walmartstores.com/sites/responsibility-report/2012/pdf/WMT_2012_GRR.pdf (accessed November 15, 2012).

225   **"we in the movement don't have to define our game"**: Andy Fisher, "Growing Power Takes Massive Contribution from Wal-Mart: A Perspective on Money and the Movement," Civil Eats (blog), September 16, 2011. http://civileats.com/2011/09/16/growing-power-takes-massive-contribution-from-wal-mart-a-perspective-on-money-and-the-movement / (accessed November 15, 2012).

226   **"The Allen example already looks like yet another in the long, dreary"**: "Who's the Rope For? (Walmart and Growing

Power)," Volatility (blog), http://attempter.wordpress.com/2011/09/ 18/whos-the-rope-for-walmart-and-growing-power/ (accessed No- vember 15, 2012).

233 **At one time, the family of Herman Schenkel, Jr., pro- duced a quarter of Virginia's cut flowers there**: Interview with Michael Van Ness, Lynchburg Grows.

BOOK CLUB / STUDY GUIDE FOR *THE GOOD FOOD REVOLUTION*

The Good Food Revolution *is much more than a book about food.*

It is also a book about African American history, American agriculture, resilience, and the challenges facing inner-city communities. The book is filled with engaging human stories, and it can provoke useful discussions about race, class, opportunity, health, and the future of our food system. Below are questions for discussion as well as key terms and characters.

Questions for Your Book Club / Classroom Discussion

1) *The Good Food Revolution* traces Will Allen's personal history, the history of his family, the history of African Americans in agriculture, and the stories of several lives that intersected with Mr. Allen's in Milwaukee. Why do you think the authors chose to commit to several narrative strands? Would you have wanted the story told differently?

2) Mr. Allen devotes several chapters to his backstory—as a professional basketball player, corporate salesman, and discotheque and fast-food manager. Mr. Allen also is open about his own failures and setbacks, including his financial struggles and his battles with cancer. One review of the hardcover edition suggests that "Will Allen's life proves that success often grows from failure." Do you feel that this is true? Do you feel that detours and failures you have experienced personally have been beneficial or destructive to you?

3) "The fate of a seed can be predicted by the health of the soil where it takes root," the authors write. "This is true of summer crops. It can be true, in another sense, of people." In what ways does *The Good Food Revolution* try to draw a connection between ecology and human development?

4) Why do you feel that the authors devote so much time to telling the stories of Karen, DeShell, and DeShawn Parker? Do you feel that the challenges Mr. Allen faced in entering an interracial marriage are comparable to DeShawn's challenges in accepting his sexual identity? Why do you feel that the authors wait to tell details about Karen Parker's past until later in the book?

5) The development of Growing Power depended on a number of committed individuals—from Alison Meares Cohen of Heifer International, who funded Mr. Allen's first work with worms, to Hope Finkelstein, who provided the organization its name and shaped its mission as a "community food center." What does the book seem to say about the roles of chance encounters in our lives? How much does it suggest that we are self-determined and how much the product of other people?

6) Early in the book (page 32), the authors tell the parable of a sparrow. What significance does this parable have in relation to Mr. Allen's life and work? Does the book convey the spirit of this parable? In what ways? Do you feel that the lesson the bird imparts is true?

7) Mr. Allen has described his urban farm as a "work in progress," and the book reveals how his urban farm has developed incrementally over two decades. He says that "all big things are created by a slow and steady accumulation of small, stumbling steps." Are there cases in your life where you have not pursued a passion because the road ahead seemed too long or where your idealism has led to inaction?

8) What attitude does Mr. Allen take to his critics who accuse him of working with Walmart? Do you feel that he should have accepted their grant and worked with them to compost their waste—or refused on principle?

9) After reading the book, how do you feel about Mr. Allen's vision for the food system? Are you more or less skeptical about the future of food? Did the book change you in any way or inspire you to do things differently?

Key Terms to Explore in *The Good Food Revolution*

anaerobic digester, aquaponics, bee colony collapse, black favoritism, black gold, black towns, *Brown v. Board of Education*, civil rights movement, closed-loop, composting, CSA, disinvestment, farm subsidies, Federal-Aid Highway Act of 1956, fencerow to fencerow, food desert, forty acres and a mule, Freedmen's Bureau Act of 1866, fringe retailers, The Great Migration, Jim Crow, megalopolis, planogram, reconstruction, redlining, Rust Belt, segregation,

sharecropping, slavery, suburbanization, the Talented Tenth, Tuskegee Institute, urban renewal, USDA, vermicomposting, vertical
farm, waggle dance, worm castings, worm tea

Key Characters in
The Good Food Revolution

Erika Allen: Will Allen's daughter, who works hard as a young
woman to escape farming, only later to expand Growing Power's
work to Chicago.

O. W. Allen: Will Allen's father, an illiterate sharecropper who moved
north and married Will's mother in the mid-1940s. "Everybody wants
to go to heaven, but no one wants to die," he tells young Will.

Will Allen: An urban farmer and coauthor with Charles Wilson of
The Good Food Revolution. "I believe that equal access to healthy, affordable food should be a civil right—every bit as important as access to clean water or the right to vote," Allen writes.

Cyndy Bussler: Will Allen's wife. She meets Will when she is a senior at the University of Miami, and her parents initially disapproved of the wedding. Her mother later provides Will with a place
to grow food.

Major Kenner: The first husband of Will Allen's mother—a
sharecropper who leaves the South and moves to Maryland during
the Great Migration with the hope of a better life.

Ray Kenner: Will Allen's eighty-year-old half brother, who runs
an heirloom seed business in South Carolina. He believes he has

survived cancer because of his diet of natural foods. "I try to eat only what I grow," he says.

Willie Mae Kenner: Will Allen's mother, who fled her sharecropping past by train in 1934 to a new life in Maryland. "She rarely spoke of her Southern past, as if it were a secret that was best not talked about in polite company," Allen and Wilson write.

DeShawn Parker: The son of Karen Parker and younger brother of DeShell. He is disfigured by a house fire at age three, and he struggles with his identity before finding his calling as a chef.

DeShell Parker: The daughter of Karen Parker, she initially resents her life at Growing Power. In a speech she gives at a farm conference near the end of the book, at age thirty-one, DeShell says she recognizes now that the lessons she learned go "far beyond dirt and worms."

Karen Parker: Will Allen's longest-standing employee. She moves her family to an aging yellow duplex next to Will's Roadside Farm Market in 1993. After leaving a series of dead-end jobs and broken relationships, she becomes director of Growing Power.